The Columbia Guide to American Indians of the Great Plains

———❦———

The Columbia Guides to American Indian History and Culture

THE COLUMBIA GUIDE TO
AMERICAN INDIANS
OF THE GREAT PLAINS

Loretta Fowler

COLUMBIA UNIVERSITY PRESS

NEW YORK

Columbia University Press
Publishers Since 1893
New York   Chichester, West Sussex

Copyright © 2003 Columbia University Press
All rights reserved

Library of Congress Cataloging-in-Publication Data
Fowler, Loretta, 1944–
The Columbia guide to American Indians of the Great Plains / Loretta Fowler.
p.   cm. — (The Columbia guides to American Indian history and culture)
Includes bibliographical references and index.
ISBN 0–231–11700–0
1. Indians of North America—Great Plains.   I. Title.   II. Series.
E78.G73 F69 2003
978.004'97—dc21
2002073708

CONTENTS

LIST OF MAPS

The Columbia Guide to
American Indians of the Great Plains

Part I

History and Culture

CHAPTER 1

Introduction

The Great Plains is a land of sun, wind, and grass stretching 1,500 miles north to south from the Prairie Provinces of Canada to west central Texas and about 1,000 miles east from the base of the Rocky Mountains. Regions within the Plains vary in environmental conditions to the extent that five areas can be identified: the Southern Plains (today, roughly far eastern New Mexico, north central Texas, and west central Oklahoma); the Central Plains (roughly eastern Colorado, Kansas, far western Missouri, Nebraska, and far western Iowa); the Middle Missouri (roughly west central North and South Dakota); the Northeastern Periphery (the boundary of which has fluctuated over time with changing environmental conditions, but which is roughly eastern North and South Dakota, southwestern Minnesota, southern Manitoba, and southeastern Saskatchewan); and the Northwestern Periphery (the boundary of which has also fluctuated, but which is roughly northern and eastern Wyoming, most of eastern Montana, southeastern Alberta, and southwestern Saskatchewan). This is a vast, semi-arid, and generally treeless grassland, the elevation of which gradually decreases from west to east. The lack of trees gives high-velocity winds a free sweep, which has a drying effect. This upland steppe region is covered with shallow-rooted short grasses that provide good winter forage and a variety of flowering plants that survive with little rain. The short grass in the uplands gives way to mixed and deeply rooted tall grasses in the lower prairie elevations. On the northern edge of the Plains, the tall grass grades into a forested parkland; to the east of the Plains are woodlands. Along the watercourses, such as the Missouri River, which begins in the Rocky Mountains and flows into the Mississippi River, belts of forest two to ten miles wide once provided a home for woodland animals, as well as a wide variety of plants.[1]

The formation of the Great Plains began ten million years ago when there was an uplift of the Rocky Mountain region and drier conditions caused a replacement of forest by grassland. Large grazing animals, now extinct, thrived under these conditions in the late **Pleistocene era**, when the Great Plains began to be occupied by big game hunters. Unlike anyplace else on the continent, here one species or another of **bison** flourished in abundance throughout the period of human occupancy of North America. Once anthropologists thought that the Great Plains was a desolate place visited only periodically by hunting groups from the west and east and that native people could not have lived there permanently before they adopted horses and guns from Europeans. In fact, for thousands of years this region has been continuously occupied by people who relied on herds of grazing animals, particularly the bison. The life they made for themselves involved increasing technological sophistication and cultural diversity as they adapted to a series of environmental challenges.[2]

The first occupants of the Great Plains came in many small bands during the last glaciation. Scholars disagree on the timing of the migration. Some argue for 28,000 years ago, others for a more conservative estimate of 12,000 to 16,000 B.P. (before the present), and others for prior to 28,000 years ago, during an earlier glaciation. The migrants mostly came across a land bridge between Asia and Alaska and moved south along the base of the Rockies, although other routes could have been used. Referred to as Paleo-Indians by archaeologists, these people hunted the large grazing animals that lived on the grasslands. Traces of hunts that occurred approximately 11,500–11,000 years ago have been uncovered on the southern and western Plains in sites where Clovis spear points are found in association with various species of mammoth (members of the elephant family) remains. Other large animals, extinct before Europeans came, also were hunted: mastodons, horses, camels, ground sloths the size of elephants. The hunters' spears had a distinctive fluted stone point. The Clovis spear point had one or more long flakes removed from its base to its center, which created a channel in which a preshaft fitted; this in turn was inserted into or tied to a spear shaft. Spears manufactured in this way were strong and effective. Other stone tools were made to be used as scrapers, drills, and knives. Flint, a stone widely available throughout the Plains, often was the material of choice for these points. Hunters apparently selected their prey carefully, for most of the mammoth remains are those of females and immature animals, ambushed in places where they could be routinely found, for example, at water holes.[3]

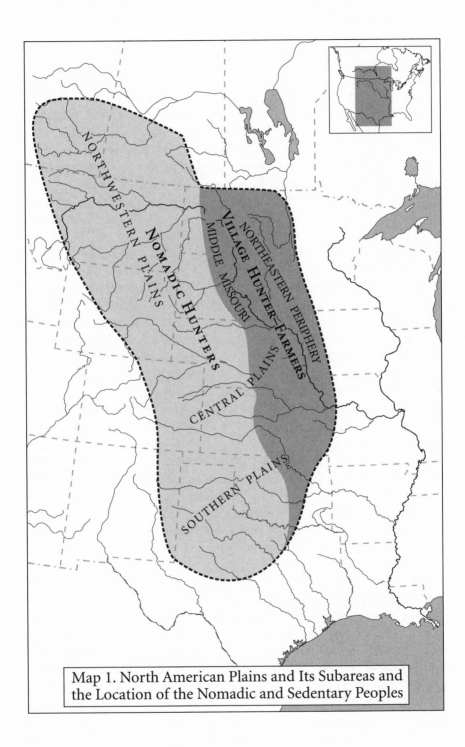

NORTHWESTERN PLAINS

NOMADIC HUNTERS

NORTHEASTERN PERIPHERY

VILLAGE HUNTER–FARMERS

MIDDLE MISSOURI

CENTRAL PLAINS

SOUTHERN PLAINS

Map 1. North American Plains and Its Subareas and the Location of the Nomadic and Sedentary Peoples

About the time these large game animals became extinct (approximately 11,000 years ago, when the climate became hotter and drier), humans developed a new technology (the Folsom point and a wide array of other tools) and made adjustments to their hunting methods for other kinds of game. Archaeologists have studied the lifeways of these hunters and the earlier Clovis peoples by locating sites where game was killed and processed. They look for the remains of tools, animals, and plants in association with each other; study the environment in which the remains are located; and try to date these remains. Organic material can be dated by chemical calculations. By comparing hundreds of such camp or kill sites, archaeologists try to establish relationships among the peoples who occupied them. Did they have similar lifeways? Were they in contact with one another? How did their technology and other conditions change over time? Change over time can be demonstrated by excavating layers of occupancy at a particular site (the oldest remains are found at the deepest level) as well as by absolute dating. Folsom hunters left remains at many sites throughout the Plains during this period of grassland expansion. These Paleo-Indians relied on a smaller species of bison that was better adapted to the drier conditions. Small groups of hunters were widely dispersed in small family groups that returned to the same springs and camp locations each season. They were astute observers of the bison, a skittish animal that stampedes easily, and took advantage of that knowledge to organize communal drives of dozens or hundreds of bison into natural corrals or over cliffs. At other times they stalked game individually. They subsisted on other animals (for example, antelope) and vegetal foods and made use of the bison hides, probably for clothing and shelter. Probably meat was preserved through drying, as well as being eaten at the time of a hunt. Although the Folsom people continued to hunt with spears, they used a smaller stone point. The Folsom point was fluted like the Clovis point but an improvement because it was lighter to carry and more easily made, and its edges were painstakingly reworked to make them sharper. Other groups of hunters used other kinds of points, which were not fluted.[4]

After about 7,600 years ago, as the climate became warmer and drier, the large species of bison hunted by peoples on the Plains became extinct. A species of bison evolved between 6,500 and 4,500 years ago that was smaller and better adapted to the drier conditions, and it survived into modern times. During the drought conditions, bison herds began moving to the less arid north and east regions of the Plains, and some human populations followed. Other groups, especially in the Northwestern Periphery region, relied on a more diversified economy wherein bison was one of several forms of game, including pronghorn antelope and mule deer, and plants such as roots, nuts, berries, and seeds became important to survival. Grinding basins used to process vegetal foods have been found at some of their sites. There also is evidence of fishing and hunting of waterfowl by local populations in river valleys. These "foraging" people occupied sites for longer periods of time than the big game hunters, who had generally exploited sites seasonally. Some foragers lived in rock shelters. Archaeologists studying these sites refer to them as Archaic (roughly corresponding to 7,600 years ago to 2,000 years ago in some regions) and their work shows that throughout the Plains local communities developed specialized subsistence strategies and new tools in order to adapt to local conditions. In the early Archaic period, some populations developed a new kind of stone point with a side notch. This innovation allowed stronger and tighter binding of the point to the spear handle. There is evidence that by 5,000 to 3,000 years ago humans made more improvements in tool kits and hunting methods as they adapted to the drier conditions on the Plains. Better meat preservation techniques likely developed, and in some less dry regions communal hunting of bison continued and became more efficient. By about 3,000 years ago, more innovations appear in the archaeological record. The bison population was on the rise and communal hunts increased in importance in many areas toward the end of the Archaic period. Hunters deliberately built corrals for communal bison drives, and there is evidence of ritual activity in the hunt (although this occurred prior to the Archaic era as well). The invention of the bow and arrow assisted hunters in obtaining game more efficiently, as it allowed for longer range and was lighter and more easy to carry.[5]

From about 2,250 years ago to 1,000 years ago (950 A.D.), ideas and technology from the Eastern Woodlands entered the Great Plains. The most significant innovations were pottery and burial mounds. **Eastern Woodland** peoples settled on the eastern margins of the Central Plains, some at the junction of the Missouri and the Kansas rivers during 100–300 A.D., where evidence of **Hopewell** traditions is present, including some maize horticulture. Woodland influences are evident at many sites that show long occupancy; in small unfortified villages, early horticultural activity was present, including the cultivation of some indigenous plants such as squash, beans, pigroot, goosefoot, and sunflowers. Hunting and gathering of wild plant foods continued as well. Plains Woodland sites are found in eastern Nebraska and southern Iowa along the Missouri River and in other parts of Nebraska, South Dakota, and Kansas, and in eastern Colorado and south central Oklahoma. On late sites there is evidence for corn horticulture, although it is of minor importance. No one knows if the people in the small villages occupied for short periods of time in the Central and Southern Plains were immigrants from the Eastern Woodlands or descendants of Archaic hunters and gatherers who adopted new ideas through trade or intermarriage. Possibly both processes were at work. In the upland Plains, hunting and gathering of plants continued and bison hunting gained importance in some areas as far north as southern Manitoba. But Woodland influences can be seen also in the introduction of pottery and mounds in shapes both conical and linear (effigy mounds in geographical, animal, and human form). The atlatl (dart or spear thrower) was developed and efficiently used along with the bow and arrow by many groups who hunted bison communally, especially in the Northwest region. Hides were tanned and decorated with porcupine quills, and dogs were used to pull **travois** loaded with meat or household goods.[6]

While in the upland short-grass Plains, a way of life oriented toward bison hunting continued to the time of the coming of Europeans, shortly before 900 A.D. the Plains Woodland complex began to give way or develop into a more sedentary way of life along the streams of the mixed- and tall-grass prairie from the Dakotas to Texas. During four centuries of warmer, moister conditions the tall prairie expanded west even to the foothills of the Rockies along the Arkansas River and into Texas. These conditions allowed for a mixed economy based on farming, supplemented with hunting and gathering. Buffalo hunting remained a part of the villagers' subsistence. Corn was first domesticated in Mexico, then introduced into the Southwest and Eastern Woodlands about 200 A.D. It was introduced into the Great Plains probably by peoples from the Eastern Woodlands, and corn and beans became important staples after 950 A.D. Regional experimentation produced varieties in different areas. These communities farmed in the stream bottoms and hunted bison on the nearby grasslands. They traded corn and other crops with the nomadic bison-hunting groups in the short-grass upland area. The Plains Village communities, as archaeologists refer to these farming people, lived in multifamily houses more substantially built than those of the Woodlands people. They had permanent villages, many of which were fortified by ditches and stockades. They had underground storage pits for their crops and made a type of pottery different from the Woodland style. Other innovations include a hoe made with a wooden handle, a blade from the shoulder blade of the bison, and triangular stone arrowheads smaller than in prior eras. Archaeologists have been able to learn much about the Plains Village peoples because they have excavated sites that have been occupied for long periods of time. Traces of houses and fragments of pottery help archaeologists describe the lifeways of these people. Wood used in the building of homes is dated by comparing tree-ring patterns in house posts to known patterns of tree rings in the region over time. Styles of pottery are compared to show trade relations and to develop a chronology of relative dating. Plant and animal remains are compared to indicate the relative importance of farming to hunting. These Plains Village traditions existed in three regions, referred to by archaeologists as Middle Missouri, Central Plains, and Southern Plains.[7]

The first wave of Middle Missouri people came about 950 A.D. by way of southwestern Minnesota and northwestern Iowa. They settled in South Dakota along the James and Big Sioux rivers. About two centuries later, another wave of migrants came from the same area and settled in North Dakota along the Missouri River, near the Knife River. These immigrants were probably associated in some way with **Cahokia**, which was an urban center near modern-day St. Louis. The two peoples expanded toward each other, eventually meeting in the region of the Bad and Cheyenne rivers in South Dakota, where they came into conflict. In fact, the sites of their villages show evidence of fortification. In the mid-fifteenth century, people from the Central Plains tradition entered the Middle Missouri region to escape a drought in their homeland. They introduced new elements, including the four-post round earth lodge, and adopted local styles of fortification. The blend of these two traditions has been referred to by archaeologists as a coalescence of the two ways of life, beginning in approximately 1450.

The Middle Missouri villages had a fairly reliable food supply and stored surpluses for the winter. In addition to farming, they hunted bison and other game and collected wild plants, including chokecherries and other berries and wild tubers. They also fished in the Missouri River. Their social organization was likely somewhat less egalitarian than that of the nomadic hunting and gathering peoples. They lived in multifamily households in long rectangular houses, each built over a shallow pit. The entrance to the house was a sloping passage. Timber that grew in the river valley provided fuel, house posts, and cover for game animals. The hearth and storage pits were inside the house. A village had up to 300 people, with probably six to 20 houses, and was compact and fortified. Farming traditions built on indigenous roots as well as influences from the Northeastern Periphery. Middle Missouri people were good farmers, despite uncertain rainfall, a short growing season, and early frost. They continued to genetically alter corn, a warm-weather plant, into a tough, compact, fast-maturing plant resistant to drought, wind, cold, and frost. American seed distributors relied on this Indian corn to develop modern varieties of corn grown today on the Northern Plains. Beans also developed from seeds from the Middle Missouri tradition. Squash and sunflowers, along with corn and beans, were important staples. Trade with the Eastern Woodlands area was well developed, as was trade with nomadic people to the west. Burials likely were of the scaffold type, for cemeteries are not found in the villages. Clothing was made from hide, as were containers, and tools were manufactured from stone and bone. Clothing was adorned with clamshell beads. The villagers made a very durable grit-tempered pottery.[8]

The early village traditions in the Central Plains are located on rivers in Kansas, Nebraska, eastern Colorado, and western Iowa from about 1000 A.D.

This was a region of fertile, well-watered alluvial bottom and terrace-lined valleys. In about 1200 A.D. the more westerly sites began to be abandoned due to drought conditions, and the people there moved, probably northeast to the Middle Missouri area and perhaps to the Texas-Oklahoma region. There was another exodus in the fifteenth century, although the lower Loup River area was never entirely abandoned. The houses of Central Plains villagers were made differently than those of the Middle Missouri peoples. Houses were square or rectangular earth lodges (earth-covered dwellings) with rounded corners and long, covered entrance passages. The villages were not fortified and the houses were smaller, the settlements less compact. Central Plains houses were widely spaced and strung along terraces above a waterway for some distance. Settlements were dispersed. Each house had a central hearth, four main posts, and subfloor storage pits. Hamlets of up to 100 people probably had 50–75 houses. These villages generally buried their dead in communal pits. They grew corn, beans, squash, sunflowers, and other crops but also hunted bison extensively, fished, and gathered wild plants. They produced hardy varieties of corn through selective breeding. Their sand-tempered pottery was better made than Plains Woodland pottery and differed in style from Middle Missouri pottery. There also are differences between regional pottery styles. The domesticated dog was present in these villages. Trade relations were maintained with peoples to the east, including the Cahokia sphere, and with the nomadic hunters to the west.[9]

The Southern Plains Village tradition, with roots in the Plains Woodland tradition, is represented by sites along the Canadian, Washita, and Red rivers in western Oklahoma. Until about 1000 A.D., this country was largely mixed-grass and tall-grass prairie. Bison, antelope, elk, and deer were plentiful. Referred to by archaeologists as the Custer focus, the village sites are dated between 800–950 A.D. and are antecedent to the Washita River focus (1100 to 1375 A.D.) in west central Oklahoma. Drought conditions and possible incursions by raiders from the Southwest (Apache and/or Kiowa) resulted in the abandonment of the Washita villages and the relocation of their populations. In 1120 to 1450 in the Oklahoma and Texas panhandle, farming villages took advantage of a wetter climate than in the Washita area. The panhandle houses had an architectural style with **Pueblo** Indian influences, including stone-slab wall foundations and adobe walls. In the Custer and Washita traditions, the villagers lived in square or rectangular houses of wattle-and-daub construction and thatched roofs. Their small villages were often built near the junction of two water sources and in associated farmsteads. In late fall and early winter they went on hunting expeditions where they occupied hunting camps in more upland areas near streams. They also occupied small winter camps in protected locales. They used cache pits to store food. They hunted bison and grew corn, beans, and squash, adjusting their subsistence activity to environmental conditions. Among the plants collected were hackberries, plums, persimmons, walnuts, and hickory nuts. Hide clothing was manufactured, and there is evidence that fabric was made from plant fibers. Southern Plains villagers had close ties with Pueblo peoples and with the large administrative and trade centers on the eastern margin of the plains, known as **Spiro** and Cahokia.[10]

By the sixteenth century, there were farming villages on the Great Plains occupied by peoples who are identified in the accounts of European travelers during the early phase of colonization. Archaeologists can match the sites they excavate with the sites recorded in journals and maps. Linguists, able to study vocabularies of languages recorded in the villages visited by Europeans and the speech of descendants of people who lived in these villages, can establish relationships between languages. Similarities are used to determine genealogical relationships. On the Plains are speakers of many languages descended from a few language "families," the largest of which are Caddoan and Siouan. Estimates are made about the length of time it took speakers of a language, who subsequently separated and lived apart, to develop mutually unintelligible languages. Both the archaeological and the linguistic methods used to reconstruct past ways of life are informative. Yet it must be noted that by the time these native people were encountered by Europeans, there had been considerable interaction among peoples of different archaeological "traditions," and sometimes groups of people speaking several different languages formed a new community.

On the Southern Plains, at least some peoples from the Custer, Washita, and Panhandle archaeological traditions relocated in the upper Arkansas River valley and developed what archaeologists refer to as the Great Bend tradition sometime between 1400 and 1500. These people were speakers of Caddoan languages. According to linguists, originally an ancestral population occupied villages on the forested eastern margins of the plains at least as long ago as 4,000 years. As groups broke off from this population and moved northwest, they settled in different regions and their languages changed over time and eventually became distinct. Linguists divide Caddoan languages into northern and southern branches. The Southern Caddoan speakers settled in and adjacent to the southeastern corner of the Great Plains along and southwest of the Red River; their descendants became known as "**Caddo**" (that is, several autonomous groups often referred to as Caddo) and were encountered by De Soto in 1541. The members of the Northern branch eventually became speakers of the Wichita, Kitsai, Pawnee, and Arikara languages, and their descendants are so named. "**Wichita**" (and possibly "**Kitsai**") were living in the farming villages of the Great Bend tradition. "**Pawnee**" were on the Loup River by about 1500, and their villages were descendant from the Central Plains tradition. Other people whose villages were once part of the Central Plains tradition went farther north and were in central South Dakota at least by 1500 and in contact with the Middle Missouri peoples whose way of life they influenced; they are generally accepted to have been "**Arikara**," as the Pawnee and Arikara languages became distinct during this period of time.[11]

There also are sites on the Southern Plains that date from about 1675 A.D. and that archaeologists refer to as the Dismal River tradition. The people living in these villages and campsites on the upper Canadian River and other upland regions in western Kansas, Colorado, and Nebraska grew corn and other crops but also obtained much of their subsistence from hunting the buffalo. Based largely on Spanish accounts, the occupants of these villages are generally accepted to be eastern "**Apaches**," Athapaskan speakers descended from a larger group of people who settled throughout the Southwest in the fifteenth century, established close relations with Pueblo peoples, located in different areas, and over time developed different languages. The Dismal River people lived in small houses made with a pole frame and covered with grass or hide; some of these structures and the baking pits associated with them had similarities to houses in the Southwest. They made pottery that was similar to pottery of the upper Rio Grande area, and they traded with the Great Bend and Lower Loup settlements. They, like the Apaches described in Spanish documents in the late seventeenth century, had horses.[12]

The peoples of the Middle Missouri farming tradition were the ancestors of the "**Mandan**" and "**Hidatsa**," encountered in the early eighteenth century in the same vicinity as the Middle Missouri sites. These people were speakers of Siouan languages. Over time Siouan speakers dispersed widely in eastern North America. Many of them moved from the Eastern Woodlands onto the Northeastern Periphery of the Great Plains after Europeans arrived in North America; some apparently were there in the Plains Woodland era, if not before. Some speakers of Siouan languages settled in the Southeast and the Ohio River valley. Others settled in the upper Mississippi valley. Gradually different, mutually unintelligible languages developed from a proto-Siouan language. One group that split off eventually divided into Mandan speakers and Hidatsa speakers. They migrated to the Middle Missouri region, the Mandan preceding the Hidatsa by several centuries. Another group of Siouan speakers included the **Iowa, Otoe**, and **Missouria**. These people have been associated with the Oneota archaeological tradition, although there were no European visitors in the Oneota villages excavated by archaeologists, so identifications are less certain. The people known as Oneota once were embroiled in relations with Cahokia and moved into the upper Mississippi River valley in northwestern Illinois and southern Wisconsin about 1,000 A.D. Oneota sites also are found in Iowa, Minnesota, and Missouri. They are fortified villages with pole-and-brush wigwams. These villagers grew some corn and other crops but also hunted. Their pottery was shell-tempered. By 1300 the Oneota peoples dominated the southeastern part of the Northeastern Periphery. They produced and traded catlinite pipe-stone throughout the Plains. By 1500 they probably had started to move west toward the border of Iowa and South Dakota. Some archaeologists believe that they were ancestral to the Iowa, Otoe, and Missouria. Just exactly when people associated with the Oneota tradition arrived west of the Missouri River in eastern Nebraska and northeast Kansas is controversial. Conservatively, the move is dated to the seventeenth century. Another group of Siouan speakers (the **Omaha**, **Ponca**, "**Osage**," **Kaw**, and the **Quapaw**, who located in Arkansas) are also associated with the southern Oneota tradition.[13]

The nomadic peoples who lived on the upland Plains at the time of European entry arrived at different times and represented a variety of cultural and linguistic traditions including Siouan, Algonquian, and Numic. No upland peoples encountered by Europeans can be shown to be descended from Paleo-Indian or Archaic archaeological traditions. Nomadic Siouan speakers developed distinct languages over time: Stoney (spoken by the "**Stoney**" people); Assiniboine (spoken by "**Assiniboine**"); and Sioux or Dakota, which had three dialects (eastern, spoken by "**Santee**"; central, spoken by "**Yankton**" and "**Yanktonai**"; western, spoken by **Teton**—see "**Sioux**"). Some archaeologists argue that some of these peoples (particularly the Assiniboine or Assiniboine speakers) were descendants of the Plains Woodland groups who were in the Northeastern Periphery in 800–900 A.D. The Siouan-speaking "**Crow**" split off from the Hidatsa villages and moved west to the upper Missouri River area, but there is no agreement on when this happened.[14]

Another family of languages is Algonquian. Proto-Algonquian speakers subdivided over time as they dispersed throughout the Canadian subarctic and Great Lakes regions and eastward and became identified as "**Cree**," **Blackfeet**, **Piegan**, **Blood**, "**Arapaho**," **Gros Ventre**, and "**Cheyenne**." Proto-Algonquian languages evolved into Eastern Central (a group of languages that included Cree); Blackfoot (spoken by the Blackfeet, Piegan, and Blood peoples); Arapahoan (with Arapaho and Gros Ventre dialects); and Cheyenne. The Blackfoot and Arapahoan speakers were encountered in the Saskatchewan River country in the seventeenth century, but how long they had been there is uncertain. They had not been together in the region for very long because their languages were quite distinct. The "Cheyenne" lived just to the east of the Northeastern Periphery until they were forced west by intertribal warfare in the seventeenth century. Cree speakers were north of the parkland area in Manitoba and Saskatchewan and had been there since at least the Woodlands era.[15]

Speakers of Numic (a branch of the Uto-Aztecan languages) included the "**Comanche**" and the "**Shoshone**," who moved onto the Great Plains from the west in the very early eighteenth century. Other Uto-Aztecan speakers remained west of the Plains. Finally, it is possible that the "**Kiowa**" moved onto the Great Plains from the Southwest because the Kiowa language belongs to a group descended from a proto language known as Kiowa-Tanoan, which includes Kiowa and several languages spoken in the Eastern Pueblos, including Jemez, Taos, Picuris, and Piro. This may have happened in the seventeenth century when many peoples in the region relocated to escape the Spanish regime.[16]

When Europeans first entered the Plains, they encountered basically two different kinds of adaptations among the native peoples there. Riverine horticultural villages were established in the tall grass prairie along the Missouri River and its tributaries and along other rivers that flowed east into the lower Mississippi River through the Southern Plains. These autonomous villages sometimes allied. Some of the villages were fortified and all had hunting territories not too far away, where the people walked to hunt buffalo once or twice a year. Most of the year they tended their crops. These village societies were stratified to varying degrees; that is, hereditary elites held important political and religious leadership positions and were responsible for the fortunes of the village and expected to help maintain the poorer households. The other adaptation was of the nomadic buffalo hunting peoples who lived in the upland regions of the Plains in small bands. They hunted the buffalo on foot, following the herds' seasonal moves, using dogs to transport their belongings. In the late spring to the fall, bands came together for ceremonies that helped unify and reassure the participants. Leadership was earned by achievement and personal qualities, not inherited, and social relations were egalitarian. There was room for individual innovation in religious ritual. The villagers and the nomadic peoples came into contact with one another, especially at trade centers and trade fairs where they exchanged agricultural and other products for the products of the hunt.

The history of the native peoples of the Great Plains is a dynamic one in which there has been great social flux. Through trade, travel, intermarriage, and alliance there has been an exchange of peoples, ideas, and technologies. Groups split off from larger populations and combined with others. Remnants of diverse peoples, speaking a variety of languages and representing different **cultural traditions**, were absorbed by larger populations, and all contributed to new social orders and cultural traditions. Thus, native communities known today are modern developments. These societies all changed in response to ecological and political conditions prior to the coming of Europeans. They represent a long process of social, cultural, and linguistic reorganization.

Like the native peoples, Europeans entered the Great Plains from different directions. The Spanish and French entered the Southern Plains; somewhat later, the French ventured onto the Central Plains. North of Nebraska on the Northern Plains (in the vicinity of Middle Missouri villages and the Northeastern Periphery), French traders were the first to make contact, followed by the English. Europeans relied on the help of native peoples to explore and initiate trade on the Plains. Trading relationships became essential to the colonial economies of the European nation-states and transformed the lives of native peoples in the region.

NOTES

1. Waldo R. Wedel, *Prehistoric Man on the Great Plains* (Norman: University of Oklahoma Press, 1961), 20–25, 34–39, 44–45.
2. Ibid., 25, 40, 278–79.
3. Jesse D. Jennings, "Origins," in *Ancient North Americans*, ed. Jesse D. Jennings (San Francisco: W. H. Freeman, 1983), 27, 29, 30, 62, 63; Wedel, *Prehistoric Man*, 46–59; Waldo R. Wedel, "The Prehistoric Plains," in *Ancient North Americans*, ed. Jesse D. Jennings (San Francisco: W. H. Freeman, 1983), 210–11; Dean R. Snow, "The First Americans and the Differentiation of Hunter-Gatherer Cultures," in *Cambridge History of Native People of North America* 1 (Cambridge: Cambridge University Press, 1996), 131–32.
4. Wedel, *Prehistoric Man*, 3–13, 60–64; Wedel, "Prehistoric Plains," 212–15; Snow, 166.
5. Wedel, "Prehistoric Plains," 215–24; Brian M. Fagan, *Ancient North America: The Archaeology of a Continent* (London: Thames and Hudson, 2000), 121–28.
6. Wedel, "Prehistoric Plains," 224–28; Fagan, 137–40.
7. Wedel, "Prehistoric Plains," 229; Fagan, 141–46.
8. Wedel, "Prehistoric Plains," 229–31; Wedel, *Prehistoric Man*, 160, 168–93, 208; Fagan, 137, 143–45.
9. Wedel, "Prehistoric Plains," 231–32; Wedel, *Prehistoric Man*, 80, 94–102; Fagan, 141–42; Patricia J. O'Brien, "The Central Lowlands Plains: An Overview A.D. 500–1500," in *Plains Indians, A.D. 500–1500: The Archaeological Past of Historic Groups*, ed. Karl H. Schlesier (Norman: University of Oklahoma Press, 1994), 212–16.
10. Wedel, "Prehistoric Plains," 232–34; Fagan, 145–46; Wedel, *Prehistoric Man*, 139–44; Jack L. Hofman, "The Plains Villages: The Custer Phase," 287–305, Robert E. Bell, "The Plains Villages: The Washita River," 307–24, and Christopher Lintz, "The Plains Villages: Antelope Creek," 325–46, in *Prehistory of Oklahoma*, ed. Robert E. Bell (Orlando: Academic Press, 1984).
11. Wedel, "Prehistoric Plains," 233; Wedel, *Prehistoric Man*, 105–11, 131–32; O'Brien, 222; Roger T. Grange, "An Archeological View of Pawnee Origins," *Nebraska History* 60 (Summer 1979): 134–60; Ives Goddard, "Introduction," 4–8, and "Classification," 319–20, in *Languages*, vol. 17, ed. Ives Goddard, in *Handbook of North American Indians*, ed. William C. Sturtevant (Washington, DC: Smithsonian Institution Press, 1996).
12. Wedel, "Prehistoric Plains," 233; Wedel, *Prehistoric Man*, 111–17; Jack L. Hofman, "The Western Protohistoric: A Summary of the Edwards and Wheeler Complexes," in *Prehistory of Oklahoma*, ed. Robert E. Bell (Orlando: Academic Press, 1984), 359.
13. Goddard, "Introduction," 4–8; Goddard, "Classification," 322; Wedel, "Prehistoric Plains," 224–28, 233–34; Wedel, *Prehistoric Man*, 102–11, 117–20, 126; R. Peter Winham and Edward J. Lueck, "Cultures of the Middle Missouri," 162, and Michael Gregg, "Archaeological Complexes of the Northeastern Plains and Prairie-Woodland Border, A.D.

500–1500," 89, 93–94, in *Plains Indians*, A.D. 500–1500: *The Archaeological Past of Historic Groups*, ed. Karl H. Schlesier (Norman: University of Oklahoma Press, 1994), 162; James B. Griffin, "The Midlands," in *Ancient North Americans*, ed. Jesse D. Jennings (San Francisco: W. H. Freeman, 1983), 289, 292–93.

14. Goddard, "Introduction," 8; Goddard, "Classification," 322.

15. J. Roderick Vickers, "Cultures of the Northwestern Plains: From the Boreal Forest Edge to Milk River," in *Plains Indians*, A.D. 500–1500: *The Archaeological Past of Historic Groups*, ed. Karl H. Schlesier (Norman: University of Oklahoma Press, 1994), 24, 28, 33; Gregg, 93; Wedel, *Prehistoric Man*, 237; Goddard, "Introduction," 4–8; Goddard, "Classification," 318–19.

16. Goddard, "Introduction," 4–8; Goddard, "Classification," 321.

CHAPTER 2

Encounters with Europeans: Trade Relations

The Spanish entered the Plains in the mid-sixteenth century, and the French and the British followed. Impelled by nationalism and a desire for profit, all three competed for Indian trade and slaves. On the Southern Plains, Spain and France established trading posts; on the lower Missouri River, French traders competed with Spanish interests, as well as British traders who entered the Illinois country from their base in Carolina. On the Northern Plains, French and British traders from Canada vied for the native hunters' furs. Guns sold by the French and the British, as well as the incorporation of horses brought by the Spanish, revolutionized the lives of the native peoples on the Plains in the seventeenth and eighteenth centuries. The "**Comanche**," "**Osage**," "**Teton Sioux**," "**Cree**," and "**Assiniboine**" capitalized on their strategic position in trade relations to expand their territory and dominate neighboring groups. Thus, as the nature of warfare was transformed, native life, including demographic patterns, economic and family life, political organization, and religion, changed dramatically. And the histories of the European nation-states became linked to the histories of the native peoples in North America.[1]

THE SOUTHERN PLAINS

On the Southern Plains, the lives of the "**Caddo**," "**Wichita**," "**Apache**," and Comanche changed significantly after the Spanish and the French created a market for slaves. Centuries before the Europeans came, the Caddo and the Wichita were well established. The Apache moved into the Southwest about 1450, then onto the Southern Plains, where the Spaniards encountered them a century later. Between 1350 and 1540 the Caddo were settled along rivers and streams between the Trinity and Red River country in what is now eastern Texas, southeastern Oklahoma, northeastern Louisiana, and southwestern Arkansas. The Caddo lived in small towns and surrounding farmsteads. Each community had a chief (*caddi*) whose position was hereditary, and communities were loyal to a priest-chief (*xinesi*) who conducted religious ceremonies on behalf of several towns and who lived in a larger civic-ceremonial center. The priest-chief's position was hereditary. Caddo society was organized into **matrilineal clans,** ranked internally and in relation to one another. Chiefs came from high-ranking clans and had ritual duties; they could be either male or female, but as an elite group inherited their position in society from males. Councils of leaders from the clans participated with the *caddis* in governing the towns. Commoners could rise to the status of war chief through achievements in battle. The Caddo lived in dome-shaped grass- and cane-covered structures. Good farmers, they grew two varieties of maize, beans, and squash, as well as other crops. They hunted white-tailed deer and other small game to supplement this diet, and black bear for oil and skins. The priest-chief represented the supreme power of creation, as did the sun and fire; the *xinesi*'s duty was to guard the sacred fire in the temple for which he was responsible and conduct ceremonies to perpetuate the agricultural cycle. The Caddo engaged in an extensive trade network reaching west to the Southwest and east to the Mississippi River valley. By the mid-fifteenth century the population of all the Caddo towns may have been as high as 200,000.[2]

In 1541 Hernando **de Soto** (see **De Soto**) and Luis **Moscoso** de Alvarado traveled toward the territory of the Caddo on the bend of the Red River. The first native people encountered in what is now western Arkansas engaged De Soto in battle. They may have been Caddo and probably had heard accounts of Spanish atrocities farther east. Subsequently, while wintering on the west bank of the Mississippi River, De Soto died and Moscoso surreptitiously buried him to prevent Indians from learning that Christians were not, in fact, immortal; then the party continued westward. In July 1542 Moscoso passed through the Red River heartland of Caddo country and into northeastern Texas. He fought Caddo warriors before reaching the Red River. Victorious, Moscoso tortured a captive and sent him to the local *caddi* to demand guides. The Spanish burned houses and crops, seized food and other supplies, and killed the guides after they were no longer needed. When Moscoso reached the villages of the Hasinai division of the Caddo in what is now eastern Texas, he looted them and took captives, whom he tortured. Finally, after failing to find the wealthy cities for which he had been searching, he and his party returned to the Mississippi River. At about the same time, Francisco Vásquez de **Coronado** (see **Coronado**), guided by a Wichita slave (see **slavery**), traveled from Pecos Pueblo in the Southwest onto the Southern Plains, where the Apache were settled (see map 2). He continued east to the bend of the Arkansas River, where he visited Wichitas. Juan de Oñate, who established a Spanish colony in New Mexico in 1598, visited the Wichita again in 1601. The Spaniards were disappointed in the lack of potential for mineral and other development of this country; thus, they largely ignored the Southern Plains until almost a century later. The potential for trade and missionary work and fear of French advancement on the Southern Plains eventually led the Spanish to establish posts in the country of the Hasinai in Texas in 1690.[3]

At pueblo trade fairs, Spanish settlements, and the Texas outposts, the Spanish gave manufactured goods, including knives and sword blades, lace and cloth, bells and silver spoons (used by native people for decoration, along with Spanish coins), and stock—particularly horses and mules—for buffalo and antelope hides and captives (whom they used as slave labor in the settlements in the Southwest and in the mining provinces to the south). Slave raids dislocated and decimated native communities that lived in terror of being attacked yet, if they had the means, sought to profit from the trade in captives. Spanish policy prohibited the sale of guns to Indians. Metal technology gradually supplemented or replaced tools made from bone or stone, but of most utility to native peoples were the horses and mules.

During the fifteenth century, Apache peoples had moved into New Mexico and eastward into the upland Plains in what is now Texas, Oklahoma, Kansas, and Colorado. The Apache raided Caddo, "**Kitsai**," and Wichita villages for food and property, and they also took captives, whom they sold along with meat and hides in **Pueblo** towns in the Southwest. They also interfered with the Caddo trade network, as well as that of the Wichita traders who had to travel through Apache territory to reach the pueblo trade centers. The Apache who lived to the north and east of the pueblos farmed for part of the year and hunted bison when they were not tending to their crops. After Spanish colonists in New Mexico began to allow Pueblo Indians to ride horses to herd their livestock, Apaches obtained horses in the pueblos and settlements by trading or by raiding for them. In the **Pueblo Revolt** against the Spanish in 1680, much of the colonists' livestock was abandoned, so horses and mules were available in larger numbers. Once the Apache became equestrian they became especially efficient raiders of the Caddo and Wichita villages, taking numerous captives to sell to Pueblo people and Spanish colonists. In 1719 they controlled the area between the Red River and the South Platte in the upland Plains, effectively raiding the Wichita on the bend of the Arkansas River and eastward on its tributaries and the Caddo groups in eastern Texas, as well as other peoples within reach.[4]

By the time of European settlement in the late seventeenth century, the Caddo had suffered severe population loss due to epidemics that followed the Spaniards' entry into the Southwest and Southeast. Now numbering perhaps 10,000, they had reorganized into three loose confederacies: 3,500 Kadohada-cho at the bend of the Red River, living in four politically independent groups; 2,000 Natchitoche farther down the Red River in three groups; and 4,500 Hasinai in at least nine groups between the Neches and Sabine rivers.[5]

By the mid-seventeenth century, the Caddo had horses as well as cloth and medal items from Indian middlemen, particularly **Jumanos**, who attended trade fairs in Hasinai villages in eastern Texas. Caddos traded pottery, baskets, bows made of pliable bois d'arc, and salt to the nomadic Plains peoples who brought Spanish goods from the Southwest. The acquisition of the horse led to a change in the Caddo economy. Before, they largely had hunted deer and bear. Buffalo were less important because their range was 80 miles west near

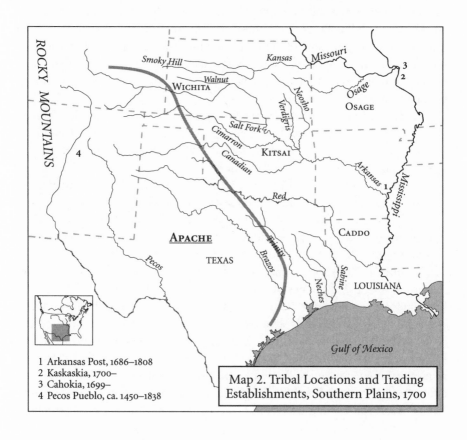

1 Arkansas Post, 1686–1808
2 Kaskaskia, 1700–
3 Cahokia, 1699–
4 Pecos Pueblo, ca. 1450–1838

Map 2. Tribal Locations and Trading Establishments, Southern Plains, 1700

the Brazos River or far up the Red River. Sometimes buffalo were hunted on foot in the winter; dogs transported the meat back to Caddo villages. After the Caddo had horses, buffalo hunts became more frequent, for they could reach the buffalo range quickly and transport large quantities of meat. The Caddo began to raid the Apache to augment their supply of horses, changing their emphasis from sporadic wars of revenge to frequent raiding parties in order to obtain stock. By the end of the seventeenth century, horses were common in the Caddo villages. Henri de **Tonti** on a foray from the Illinois country in 1690 noted that Hasinai families each had four or five horses. The Caddos farther northeast had fewer.[6]

In 1700 France and Spain agreed on a boundary between the country of the Kadohadacho and Natchitoche, recognized as French, and Hasinai country, claimed by the Spanish (in fact, missions were briefly established there in the 1690s). Thus the Caddo occupied a strategic position between the Spanish and French and could play each off against the other while maintaining a large measure of independence and the ability to bargain over prices. By 1700 the Caddo also were experiencing devastating attacks by the well-armed **Chicka-saw** to the east (who raided them for captives to sell to the British), as well as the effects of European diseases. In the second decade of the century, the Kado-hadacho numbered about 1,000; the Natchitoche, 500; the Hasinai, 1,500. Caddo groups began to combine and absorb remnants of weaker ones. The Caddo eagerly sought trade with the French, who, unlike the Spanish, would sell guns and ammunition to them.[7]

France was eager to establish a base among the Caddo and Wichita in order to stop British penetration into the interior of North America and to eventually establish trade with the Southwest. In 1684 Réné-Robert Cavelier, Sieur de **La Salle**, came via the Illinois River to the Mississippi River and down to the Gulf of Mexico, naming the Mississippi basin Louisiana. He built a fort on the Illinois River and later visited the Caddo country. He reached the Hasinai, and he and his party were housed, fed, and welcomed in a **calumet ceremony** by Hasinai leaders bringing gifts of horses and food. La Salle stayed three or four days trading, being careful not to offend his hosts. Life with the Hasinai was so pleasant that four of La Salle's men deserted and took up residence with them. La Salle visited the Hasinai again in 1687 and was murdered by some of his own men who became disgruntled during the expedition. The Hasinai possessed many horses (called *cavali* after the Spanish word *caballo*), having received them in trade from middlemen (most probably Jumanos, among others). French colonies subsequently were established in Louisiana near the gulf, where the colonists provided a market for horses and mules, produce, and slaves purchased from Indian allies. Arkansas Post was established on the lower Mississippi at the mouth of the Arkansas River in 1686 by Henri de Tonti and

French traders from Canada, and from there individual traders went to trade with native peoples living to the west (see map 2). On Tonti's visit to the Caddo in 1690, he returned two Caddo women who had been enslaved; he was well received, for the Caddo hoped to get French assistance against their enemies. From their base in Louisiana, traders made forays into Caddo country. Jean-Baptiste Le Moyne, Sieur de Bienville, traveled up the Red River and met the Natchitoche, participated in a calumet ceremony to make peace, and continued on to meet some of the Kadohadacho. Louis Juchereau de Saint-Denis, a member of Bienville's expedition, returned later and established trade relations with all three of the Caddo confederacies. He established a trading post (Natchitoches) in 1713 (see map 3). Saint-Denis remained influential in Caddo country for 40 years. Bénard de **La Harpe** established a post (Nassonite) among the Kadohadacho at the Nasoni village in 1719 and, with the help of the Caddo, journeyed on to the Wichita villages to the northwest. The Caddo provided horses, salt, produce and products of the hunt, and slaves, as well as pottery created in a European style. From the French they received guns and ammunition, metal tools (including axes, knives, and needles), cloth, and luxury items including glass beads and rings. From time to time Frenchmen joined Caddo warriors in retaliatory attacks on the Caddo's enemies, and they provided annual presents to the Caddo confederacies, including special gifts to the high-ranking leaders (see **medals**). French traders often married Caddo women, and French creole communities began to develop.[8]

Threatened by the French activity among the Caddo and motivated by reforms in Indian policy in Spain that stressed conversion of natives to Christianity, the Spanish briefly reestablished missions in Hasinai country from 1716 to 1721 and a presidio near the Adaes village (Los Adaes) in eastern Texas in 1721 (see map 3). While graciously welcoming the Spanish and accepting their presents and trade goods, the Hasinai refused to congregate around the missions and to reject their native religion. The Spanish presence was too weak to compel them. But epidemics resulted from the Spanish contact, contributing to the population decline in the early eighteenth century. Thus, while access to French guns helped the Caddo resist attacks by the Apache from the west, the Osage from the northeast, and other groups from the east, the Caddo continued to be at a disadvantage in their struggle against their enemies. At mid-century, the Kadohadacho combined their villages, with two groups absorbing the other two, and the Hasinai confederacy reorganized its eight groups into four.[9]

French trade transformed the lives of the Caddo. They increased their hunting activities to produce more buffalo skins, deer chamois, and bear fat to sell to the French along with their corn surplus. They adopted saddles and bridles and used buffalo-hide tepees when hunting buffalo on the plains. Steel hatchets and knives replaced those of stone, and the Caddo became dependent on tools such as scissors, awls, screws, and flints for fire. European shirts, blankets, and hats largely replaced hide and fiber apparel. Glass beads, combs, vermilion (for face paint), and mirrors were in great demand. The Caddo used European goods in innovative ways: bells served as mortars for grinding corn, scissors worked to cut up kettles to make arrowheads, and mirrors became ornaments or scrapers. The need for horses and captives to sell to the French led to a new emphasis on raiding and on the sale rather than the execution of captives. French instruction in the use of guns, as well as the guns themselves, helped the Caddo in offensive and defensive military engagements. Native religion continued to be important in Caddo life (for example, in **first fruit ceremonies**), although the elaborate ceremonies underwent simplification so as to allow the Caddo to be more flexible in accommodating to their changing world. The Caddo may have lost faith in the priest-chiefs because of their inability to deal with health problems and military reversals. Commoners had access to wealth from trade, which worked to undermine the hierarchy. *Caddi*-based government continued to provide stable leadership and effective diplomacy in dealing with the French and Spanish throughout most of the eighteenth century, but the influence of the *xinesi* declined and leadership positions in general were based more on secular than on sacred authority. In fact, as small communities became absorbed by larger ones, strong *caddis* who represented many communities emerged and maintained diplomatic relations with Europeans. Caddo trade fairs continued to draw nomadic peoples as well as the Wichita, who came for French goods as well as traditional products. The Caddo also established trade relations with the Comanche and served as intermediaries between them and the French, as well as between the Wichita and the French. By the latter half of the century, the Caddo were acting as intermediaries between these two tribes and the Spanish as well.[10]

In the latter half of the eighteenth century, Caddo fortunes began to decline. After the French were defeated by the British in the **Seven Years' War**, Louisiana was transferred to Spanish control and the Caddo were dependent on Spanish assistance. Spanish officials allowed French-American traders to provide trade goods to the Caddo, but by this time the more numerous and better-armed Osage were threatening the Caddo's hold on the lower Red River and the supply of guns was limited in Caddo country. In the province of Texas, Spanish officials opposed the gun trade, but the officials in Louisiana prevailed and, liberally dispensing trade goods including guns, retained the services of the Caddo as intermediaries with the tribes to their west (see **Tinhiouen**). The Caddo received annual presents from the Texas officials as well as those in Louisiana, and the Caddo chiefs received the symbols of office, including medals, flags, and special clothing. By the last two decades of the century, the Caddo position was precarious. They had continued to lose population to attacks from the Osage from the north and the **Choctaw** from the east, as well as to an epidemic in 1777. Intermarriage with other peoples helped offset losses, but their numbers declined to the point that the Spanish no longer were solicitous with presents. Spain was not able to provide them with needed trade goods and protection from enemies, in large part because attention was diverted to war against Britain in the 1770s. In 1788 the Kadohadacho consolidated and began moving downstream to a lower point on the Red River, retreating in the face of Osage attacks. Some Kitsai moved southeastward, closer to the Caddo, for the greater protection of all these villages. Finally, in 1800 the Kadohadacho left their Red River village and moved 35 miles farther west to Caddo Lake. By 1800, the Natchitoche numbered fewer than 100; the Hasinai, about 650; the Kadohadacho, fewer than 800.[11]

The effect of trade relations on the Wichita peoples was just as dramatic. Before the arrival of the Spanish among the Wichita and Kitsai in the mid-sixteenth century, the Wichita-speaking people had long occupied the Southern Plains in Kansas and Oklahoma. When Coronado met the Wichita they were established in the Arkansas River valley in buffalo country, probably as far north as the Smoky Hill River. Like the Caddo, the Wichita built grass-covered pole-frame houses that were home to matrilineal extended families. They built their villages in the river valley and had a combined farming and buffalo-hunting economy. Crops were planted, harvested, and stored in the spring and summer; villages left to live on the Plains in hide tepees and hunt bison in the fall. The Wichita grew two varieties of corn, beans, and squash. They prepared mats of dried strips of pumpkin and dried tobacco to trade at pueblos in the Southwest, as well as bois d'arc wood, salt, dried buffalo meat, and buffalo hides. They obtained some food, obsidian, and turquoise at the pueblos. Although their focus on agricultural ceremonies was quite similar to the Caddo religion, the Wichita were more egalitarian than the Caddo (perhaps because of their greater emphasis on bison hunting and warfare, particularly in the wake of the Apache attacks from the west). The village leaders earned their positions of authority through war exploits, and religious societies were open to all.[12]

The Spanish first contacted the Wichita in 1541. A Wichita captive led Coronado from the Southwest to Wichita villages on the great bend of the Arkansas River. Coronado was hoping to find the legendary "Quivara," a land of great wealth. He left the area disappointed and, in his frustration, killed his guide. Estimates of Wichita population at this time vary widely, from 38,000 to 150,000. From Spanish accounts in the mid-sixteenth century, there were at least 25 villages of perhaps 1,000 residents each. The Wichita groups were organized in two divisions. The Tawakoni were on Cow Creek and the Little Arkansas, the Taovaya were on Cottonwood Creek, and the Guichita were on the lower Walnut River. A second group, the Iscari, were southwest of the others on the upper

Canadian and Red rivers. The Kitsai, a group with a similar way of life and a language closely related to that of the Wichita, lived apart farther down the Arkansas River, near the mouths of the Verdigris and Neosho rivers. In 1601 Juan de Oñate traveled to the Canadian River from the Southwest and then to the Iscari on the Salt Fork of the Arkansas River. He made note of an economy based on farming and buffalo hunting as he traveled eastward to the Walnut River visiting various Wichita villages. Sometime after Oñate's visit, the Wichita acquired horses and learned how to raise and manage them.[13]

There were other Spanish visits, but the most significant effects of the Spanish presence were the introduction of the horse into the Wichita way of life and population loss from European diseases. The Wichita began to hunt buffalo on horseback, which made possible larger concentrations of population and probably led to hunts in which the entire village participated. Attacks from mounted Apaches and Osages armed with muskets also encouraged the Wichita to combine villages in the late seventeenth century and to construct elaborate fortifications. Contact with the Spanish influenced the technology of war. The Wichitas made rawhide armor for their horses and incorporated the lance (with an attached sword blade) into their weaponry. Revenge-based warfare, in which captives were often killed in the Wichita villages, gave way to an emphasis on raiding for horses. Captives also were taken, to sell either to Pueblo peoples or to the French or to use to ransom Wichita captives (see **slavery**).[14]

The first official contact between the Wichita and the French was not until 1719, but there may have been French-Canadian traders, or more likely Indian middlemen, before that. In 1719 La Harpe reached Wichita villages and opened regular trade relations. The people were informed of La Harpe's visit and had assembled representatives from many villages to greet him. He was welcomed with a calumet ceremony and assured that the Wichita wanted an alliance with the French and the trade such an alliance would bring. A French flag flew in Wichita villages in subsequent years. La Harpe found that there were fewer Wichita than in the sixteenth century and that some villages had consolidated. That same year, Claude-Charles **Dutisné** came from the French settlement of Kaskaskia to visit Wichita villages. At this time the Wichita had only six guns, which were highly prized, and not all warriors had horses. Once trade relations were established, the Wichita built paired villages at convenient spots for trading and operated marketplaces that attracted nomadic groups as well as French traders. Attacks from Osages and others led to a gradual movement south in the Arkansas River basin both to distance themselves from Osage raiders and to get closer to the French trading posts where trade goods were more plentiful. By 1719 the Kitsai had moved from the lower Arkansas River to the Red River valley, and by 1737 Wichita villages had started moving south toward the Red River. In the 1740s French **voyageurs** and hunters went up to trade with Wichitas still living on the Arkansas River, and several took up residence in their villages to trade for salted meat and hunt for hides, bear oil, and tallow. At mid-century the Wichita were very important in the commerce of Louisiana and were well armed and wealthy in horses. The French supplied them with guns and other trade goods, and by allying with the Comanche in 1746, the Wichita were able to trade guns for horses and to jointly prey upon the Apache (the Lipan especially) south of the Red River for stock and captives. In 1751 smallpox and measles decimated the Wichita, which encouraged more relocation and consolidation of villages. By 1758 none of the Wichita villages were still located on the Arkansas River; they had all moved to the Red River and to the Sabine River in Texas. The supply of French goods declined after the Seven Years' War, which also put the Wichita at a disadvantage in relation to the Osage.[15]

By the late 1780s the Osage had intensified their attacks on the weakened Wichita and had driven them south of the Arkansas River valley to the Red River west of the western **Cross Timbers**, where there were still many buffalo. The Taovaya village there was a busy market, with the Comanche adjacent on the west bringing horses and captives and the French traders' boats coming from Spanish Louisiana. On the Red River, the Wichita continued to raid the Apache to the south and to experience attacks from the Osage to the north. The Wichita concentrated on making an alliance with the Spanish in order to influence their trade policies and get their assistance against the Osage and Apache. Important Wichita chiefs tried to cultivate the Spanish officials to this end (see **Quiscat**), offering to broker a peace between the Spanish and the Comanche and returning Spanish captives (sometimes for a price) they obtained from the Comanche. They even invited the Spanish to establish a mission among them. But Spain was in the process of attempting to make peace with the Apache in Texas, which led to hostilities with the Wichita. In order to stop raiding on the Plains, the Spanish curtailed trade with the Wichita; traders from Louisiana were not allowed to sell guns or buy horses and captives from Indians (Spain abolished Indian slavery in Louisiana, where African slaves were numerous). Instead they concentrated on buying deerskins and pelts. The Spanish continued to recognize and issue medals to Wichita chiefs and to give annual presents, including guns, but these gifts were inadequate for the Indians' needs. These policy changes made it difficult for the Wichita villages to defend themselves. Some illicit trade with French-American and British traders and Indian middlemen from the Missouri River took place, but by the 1770s the better-armed and more numerous Osage were well established in the Arkansas River valley and were pounding the Wichita. Some Wichita and Kitsai villages began to combine and move farther south into Texas. Several settled on the Trinity and Brazos rivers. Epidemics in 1777 and 1801 killed as many as one

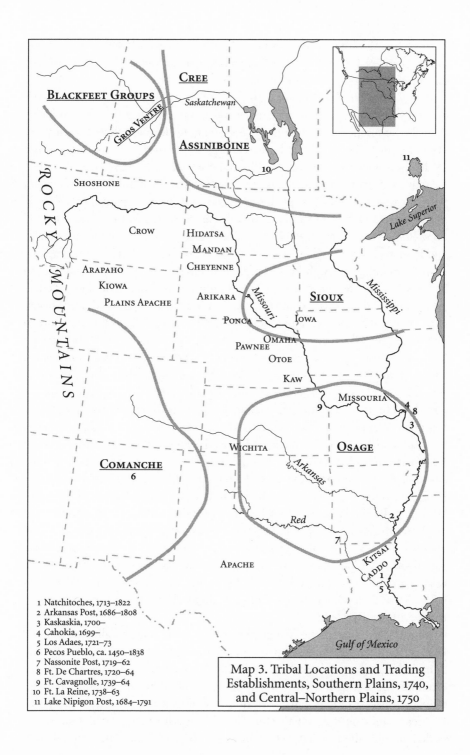

CREE

BLACKFEET GROUPS

GROS VENTRE

Saskatchewan

ASSINIBOINE

10

ROCKY MOUNTAINS

SHOSHONE

CROW

HIDATSA

MANDAN

CHEYENNE

ARAPAHO

KIOWA

PLAINS APACHE

ARIKARA

PONCA

Missouri

11

Lake Superior

SIOUX

Mississippi

IOWA

OMAHA

PAWNEE

OTOE

KAW

MISSOURIA

9

4 8

3

WICHITA

OSAGE

COMANCHE

6

Arkansas

Red

2

7

KITSAI

CADDO

1

APACHE

5

1 Natchitoches, 1713–1822
2 Arkansas Post, 1686–1808
3 Kaskaskia, 1700–
4 Cahokia, 1699–
5 Los Adaes, 1721–73
6 Pecos Pueblo, ca. 1450–1838
7 Nassonite Post, 1719–62
8 Ft. De Chartres, 1720–64
9 Ft. Cavagnolle, 1739–64
10 Ft. La Reine, 1738–63
11 Lake Nipigon Post, 1684–1791

Gulf of Mexico

Map 3. Tribal Locations and Trading
Establishments, Southern Plains, 1740,
and Central–Northern Plains, 1750

third of the Wichita. In desperation, they raided Spanish settlements in the 1790s to replenish their horse herds and take captives, many of whom were held for ransom or adopted by Wichita families.[16]

The Comanche fared better than their allies. They were a nomadic group, generally less susceptible to epidemics and more difficult for raiders to locate than the semisedentary Wichita. The Comanche formerly lived in southern Wyoming in small bands that hunted and gathered in the mountainous country. In about 1706 they entered the Plains in the company of the "**Ute**." The Ute lived in small groups in the mountain valleys of Colorado, hunting antelope on the plateaus and trading at pueblos for corn and beans. Spanish and Pueblo traders took pack trains to Ute camps for pelts. Attracted by the horses, the Ute drew closer to the Spanish settlements in the 1670s. They began to learn to raise and manage horses, so they reoriented their economy to buffalo hunting and, in order to obtain enough horses for their needs, began raiding the pueblos in the 1690s. The Ute traded some horses to the Comanche. Soon after, the two peoples formed an alliance and, in addition to raiding in New Mexico, began to challenge the Apache, raiding them and driving them from their territory in Colorado and Oklahoma. The Comanche knew the location of the Apache farming communities, made surprise attacks, and seized captives and horses. These Comanche peoples became expert horsemen and lived by bison hunting. They may have numbered as many as 24,000 and were organized into politically independent bands led by charismatic men with good war records (see **warfare**). At mid-eighteenth century, the Comanche were in three divisions: Cuchanec or Eastern Comanche, who lived between the upper Arkansas and Red rivers east of New Mexico; Yamparica or Western Comanche, between the Arkansas River and northern Colorado to the northeast of the Pueblos; Yupe or Jupe, north of the Yamparica, between the Arkansas River and southern Wyoming. By the late 1730s, they had dissolved their alliance with the Ute and displaced the Apache north and east of New Mexico, and they controlled the area from the South Platte southeast to the headwaters of the Canadian and Red rivers. The Comanche also pushed the "**Kiowa**" and **Plains Apache** (see also "**Apache**"), who probably joined the Kiowa sometime after being dislocated by the Comanche, eastward from the upper Platte River during the mid-eighteenth century.[17]

The Eastern Comanche (Cuchanec or Kotsoteka) made an alliance with the Wichita on their east and prospered by trading horses and captives for French guns and manufactured goods, as well as the Wichita products they enjoyed (for example, the pumpkin mats). Being more mobile than the Wichita, the Comanche escaped serious damage from Osage attacks and were less susceptible to disease; they extended their range into Texas with their Wichita allies and raided not only the Lipan Apache there but also Spanish settlers, who were perceived to be Apache allies. The Comanche reportedly lost two thirds of their population in the 1779–80 smallpox epidemic, which may have given new impetus to raiding, for many captives were adopted by Comanche families rather than being traded. In 1786, with the help of Wichita chiefs, the Comanche made peace with the Spanish in Texas and selected the most influential of their band chiefs to represent them in dealings with Spanish officials. They sought to trade regularly in the Spanish settlements and to enlist Spanish aid in fighting the Apache and Osage. The Western Comanche both raided and traded in New Mexico, as well as with native people from the Missouri River villages and the nomadic Kiowa, who had access to French goods from the lower Missouri area. Comanche trade in meat, hides (used to make harness, as well as other items), and captives was important to the New Mexico economy; for this reason, the Spanish tolerated some raiding. The Comanche also often returned Spanish captives for ransom rather than selling them. The Western Comanche established a formal peace with the Spanish in New Mexico and selected a principal chief who received a cane of office (see **medal**) and gifts to distribute. He dealt with the Spanish on behalf of other bands. This kind of political centralization was an innovative reaction to the wider political society of the times. In the 1790s or just after the turn of the century, the Comanche made peace with the Kiowa and their Plains Apache allies and allowed them to share their territory, thereby strengthening their hold on the upland Southern Plains.[18]

THE LOWER MISSOURI RIVER REGION

In the late seventeenth century, in an effort to halt British expansion and to develop trade with native peoples, French traders began moving south from the Great Lakes down into the Mississippi River valley. They enticed natives in the vicinity to trade beaver pelts and captives for flintlock muskets and other manufactured goods. Groups that had hitherto lived in relative peace now came into conflict. The **Illinois** tribes and the Sioux, pressed by other groups to the east, attempted to push the **Iowa** and other Siouan-speaking peoples westward in the late seventeenth and early eighteenth centuries to prevent their trading directly with the French. As trade middlemen and eventually as raiders, Illinois and Sioux groups protected their own positions as they expanded west. In the 1680s the French were in the lower Missouri River region, trading with Siouan-speaking people there: the 7,000 Osage on the Osage River, the **Kaw** near the mouth of the Kansas River, and the **Missouria** near the mouth of the Missouri River. The French got deer and bear skins and buffalo tongues from these peoples and gradually came to rely on them for large numbers of horses and captives who were enslaved in the French colonies.

The Osage were located where they could control the waterways west and expand into the Southern Plains where, with the advantage of both horses and guns, they raided the Wichita, Caddo, and Comanche relentlessly. Both the French at Cahokia settlement and Fort De Chartres (see map 3) and the English traders in Illinois country courted the numerous Osage. Throughout most of the eighteenth century, the smaller Siouan-speaking groups (the Iowa, **Otoe**, **Omaha**, and **Ponca**) had to accept Osage domination to trade with the French and were repeatedly attacked by Illinois peoples and Sioux raiders from east of the Missouri River. The "**Pawnee**" were far upstream from the Osage and numbered more than 10,000. They were organized in two politically autonomous divisions when Europeans entered the Plains. The Skiri (or Skidi) bands included several independent villages, and there were three Southern bands. The Skiri in the Loup River area and the Southern bands on the lower Platte River and Republican fork of the Kansas River were sometimes hostile to each other. Pawnee groups were periodically friendly with the Wichita, from whom they obtained many horses and mules, which they traded for a few guns and other goods from independent French traders or native middlemen. They were not heavily involved in the fur trade in the early eighteenth century; rather, they protected their hold on the Loup and middle Platte rivers and expanded the buffalo-hunting component of their economy.[19]

The Osage lived in several large villages on the Osage River and the small allied Kaw village was to their north when first encountered by French traders coming up the Missouri River in the 1680s. The Osage subsequently worked to obtain a monopoly on the trade by trying to bar traders from reaching groups to their west along the Missouri and south along the Arkansas River. Able to take advantage of the market for horses and slaves and very well armed, they and the Kaw raided groups with less access to trade goods, particularly the Caddo, Wichita, and Pawnee. In 1700 one Osage village moved north to the Missouri River in order to better position itself in relation to the trade route. The French Canadian trader Étienne Véniard, sieur de Bourgmont, married to a Missouria woman, worked out of Fort Orleans (1723–26), which he built near the Missouria people. Bourgmont tried to arrange peace between the Osage, their allies the Missouria, and their other Siouan-speaking neighbors. In the 1730s and 1740s the small Kaw village, allied and subordinate to the Osage, helped block French access to groups to the west, particularly the Comanche (although the Comanche alliance with the Wichita enabled them to hold their own on the upland Southern Plains). The Osage's strength and strategic position enabled them to play the French off against English interests in Illinois country, where the Osage retained peaceful relations with the Illinois peoples. And when French supplies were diminished due to wars east of the Mississippi or in Europe, the traders gave preference to the Osage. In the 1740s the French

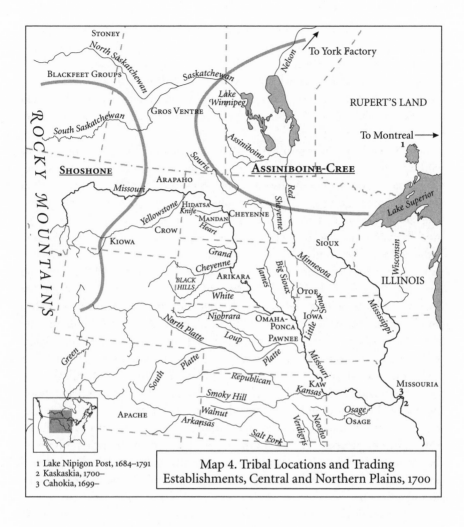

1 Lake Nipigon Post, 1684–1791
2 Kaskaskia, 1700–
3 Cahokia, 1699–

Map 4. Tribal Locations and Trading
Establishments, Central and Northern Plains, 1700

expanded, building Fort Cavagnolle (Cavaghial) in 1739 near the Kaw on the
Missouri River (see map 3). They also began to trade directly with some
Pawnee and to travel to the Southern Plains. The start of the Seven Years' War
in 1754 forced the French to redirect their resources.[20]

The Missouria probably arrived on the Missouri River in the 1670s, where
they established themselves and traded with the French, using booty from raids
on the Wichita and other peoples. They allied with the more numerous Osage
to secure their position in the region until the end of the century. The Otoe
and Iowa followed, moving from northwestern Iowa, where they were harassed
by groups to the east (especially the "**Yankton**" and Teton Sioux), to the mouth
of the Big Sioux River in about 1685. The Omaha and Ponca located north of

there a few years later, the Ponca splitting off and moving farther west. To escape attacks from the Illinois country, in 1714 the Omaha moved north to the mouth of the White River (where they were in close association with the "**Arikara**"), but later moved back down to the Missouri River in Nebraska, where they had more access to guns. These small villages struggled to hold their own in the region, careful not to alienate the Osage or, if hostilities occurred, to reestablish peace.[21]

The Seven Years' War resulted in the replacement of French administrators with Spanish officials, but the French and French-American employees continued trading on the lower Missouri. The Osage produced more fur pelts than any of the other groups and they continued to receive preferential treatment. The Osage also traded with the English based east of the Mississippi River; thus, they continued to be well armed and were able to displace the Wichita and Caddo on the Southern Plains, expanding into the middle Arkansas River valley, where they obtained furs. Although Spain tried to curtail the slave and horse trade, the English were good customers. St. Louis was built in 1764 under Spanish authority and served as a marketplace for the Osage and other native peoples on the lower Missouri. In 1795 French trader **Auguste Chouteau**, who married an Osage woman, constructed Fort Carondelet among the Osage, which reinforced their dominance in the region. The other villagers fared less well. Epidemics drastically reduced the populations of these small villages, and they were unable to defend themselves against attacks from Yankton and Teton Sioux and the Illinois raiders. In 1798 the remnants of the Missouria fled west to settle in other villages, most joining with the Otoe on the lower Platte River. Although they prospered briefly in the 1770s, due to their strategic position on the Missouri River (see **Blackbird**), the Omaha also were displaced and moved west for a few years after the 1801–02 smallpox epidemic reduced their population significantly.[22]

Trade relations affected Osage social and political organization as well as allowed them to expand their territory. Acquisition of the horse and expansion into the Southern Plains led the Osage to increase the importance of buffalo hunting in their subsistence pattern. Before their extensive involvement in raiding, the Osage had made periodic war expeditions, generally to revenge a killing of one of their own. These expeditions were controlled by elderly religious leaders who had to approve the mission, select the leader, and conduct lengthy ceremonies before the war party departed. Because of the economic advantage that horse and slave raids brought in the eighteenth century, **patrilineal clans** assumed the right to authorize raiding parties without lengthy ceremonies. Ambitious young men, not part of the elite organization that formerly controlled military and other political organizations, engaged in frequent raids and became wealthy. However, war expeditions were dangerous and a party

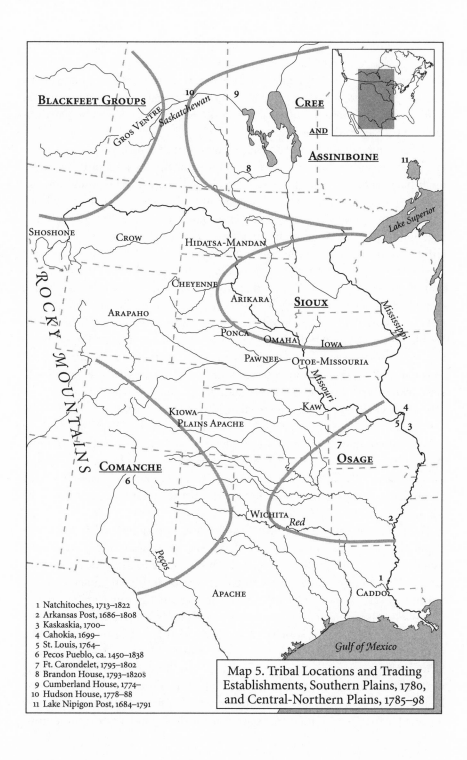

BLACKFEET GROUPS

GROS VENTRE

Saskatchewan

10   9

CREE

AND

ASSINIBOINE

11

Lake Superior

SHOSHONE

CROW

HIDATSA-MANDAN

8

CHEYENNE

ARIKARA

SIOUX

Mississippi

ARAPAHO

PONCA

OMAHA

IOWA

PAWNEE

OTOE-MISSOURIA

Missouri

KAW

4

5 3

KIOWA
PLAINS APACHE

7

OSAGE

COMANCHE

6

WICHITA

Red

2

Pecos

APACHE

CADDO

1

Gulf of Mexico

ROCKY MOUNTAINS

1 Natchitoches, 1713–1822
2 Arkansas Post, 1686–1808
3 Kaskaskia, 1700–
4 Cahokia, 1699–
5 St. Louis, 1764–
6 Pecos Pueblo, ca. 1450–1838
7 Ft. Carondelet, 1795–1802
8 Brandon House, 1793–1820s
9 Cumberland House, 1774–
10 Hudson House, 1778–88
11 Lake Nipigon Post, 1684–1791

Map 5. Tribal Locations and Trading
Establishments, Southern Plains, 1780,
and Central-Northern Plains, 1785–98

might experience heavy casualties. Before the intense raiding activity, the Osage residence pattern had been patrilocal. This meant that a village whose young men were killed in a raid would be left without hunters and defenders. The Osage altered the residence pattern to a matrilocal one so that the men in a village would be from many different patrilineal clans; thus, if a war party was lost, the village would lose only a few men.[23]

Osage political organization was an expression of religious belief. **Wakonta**, the all-pervading life force, was manifested in the sky and earth realms, a dualism reflected in the organization of Osage society into two **moieties**. Before their extensive involvement in trade with Europeans, villages had two chiefs, each representing one moiety and each with different responsibilities. A council of elderly ritual authorities who had earned their positions by mastering various levels of ceremonial knowledge made most of the important decisions. Villages had joint decision-making institutions through the combination of the elders' councils. Chieftainship was hereditary through the clans; council membership was largely confined to men from the most important, wealthy clans. Political organization changed dramatically during the eighteenth century. The elderly ritual leaders attempted to integrate the economic changes into the ceremonial organization, for example, in building a ceremony around metal. The opportunity for new wealth presented by trade with Europeans allowed young men to challenge the hereditary leaders and, at the turn of the century, create separate villages under new leadership. Traders also preferred to deal with one designated leader rather than with a large body of village representatives, so the chief of the Sky Moiety often became the official representative and his power was augmented through his connections in the trade (see **Pawhuska**; **Claremore**). The other Siouan-speaking village groups had similar social organizations and experienced similar changes in the eighteenth century.[24]

By the late eighteenth century, warfare and epidemics had reduced the population of the Pawnee, although they were still more numerous than the Siouan groups. Villages had amalgamated so that the Skiri occupied one village and each of the three Southern bands occupied its own village. The acquisition of the horse had led to efforts to expand hunting territory to the southwest, where they came into conflict with nomadic peoples. One of the Southern villages moved somewhat north and east to get easier access to the traders and the trade in guns. Their leaders visited St. Louis and established formal relations with the Spanish officials there. Chieftainship was hereditary from father to son, and chiefs came from high-status families. **Tiratwahat**, the highest power representative of an all-pervasive life force, validated chiefs' authority, for they represented this power on earth. In the eighteenth century,

the traditional chiefs maintained their control over young warriors and commoners. Major transformations in Pawnee life would come in the nineteenth
century.[25]

THE NORTHERN PLAINS

Before the European explorers and traders came, the Northern Plains was the
home of several semisedentary peoples, who farmed and hunted buffalo, and
several nomadic hunting peoples. The village people and the nomadic hunters
engaged in trade at Mandan and Arikara villages and at trade fairs, for example,
in the Black Hills and on the Green River in "**Shoshone**" country. French and
British traders were competing for the prime pelts in Canada, and they entered
the already established trading network on the Northern Plains at least by the
early eighteenth century. The effects of trade with Europeans and the diffusion
of the horse from the Southern to the Northern Plains had far-reaching effects,
just as in the country to the south.

In the late seventeenth century, the "**Mandan**," who actually were different
groups who had arrived in the upper Missouri River valley at different times,
lived in several independent villages along the Missouri River in the vicinity of
the Heart River. To the north on the Knife River were the "**Hidatsa**," who
joined the Mandan, coming by way of what is now eastern North Dakota. The
political divisions of the Hidatsa were the Awaxawi; the Awatixa, who were in
close contact with the nomadic "Mountain Crow" who had separated at some
point in the past from the Awatixa village to live by hunting the buffalo and who
ranged as far west as the Yellowstone River; and the Hidatsa proper, who were
in contact with a splinter group known as the "River Crow," who also had taken
up the nomadic life. In fact, groups of villagers sometimes journeyed out onto
the upper Plains to hunt for long periods of time. The region in which the villages were situated was "a kind of elongated oasis," where the river meandered
back and forth across a densely wooded floodplain on which corn, beans,
squash, and sunflowers were grown. Varieties of corn were developed that were
resistant to drought, wind, cold, and frost. The villages were built on the terrace
rim above the floodplain. In the summer, hunters went west to hunt buffalo; in
the winter, buffalo frequented the timbered river valley. Sometime after 1400
ancestors of the Arikara (who had separated from the Skiri Pawnee farther
south) moved into the Big Bend area of the upper Missouri River south of
where the Mandan were established. Mutual borrowings of ideas and customs
occurred, including the adoption of the round earth lodge by the Mandan. By
the early 1600s the Mandan had withdrawn to the Heart River area, leaving the

Big Bend region to the Arikara. The small Mandan settlements in northern South Dakota and southern North Dakota combined into fewer, larger fortified ones as Mandan territory contracted.[26]

By the late seventeenth century Mandan villages were the most important trade centers on the Northern Plains, where groups from many regions (the Great Lakes, the Gulf Coast, and the upper Missouri River, for example) came to trade. Mandan and Hidatsa farmers exchanged their own corn, beans, squash, and sunflower seed and goods they obtained from others for the dried meat, dressed hides, and flour made from prairie turnips brought by nomadic peoples. Arikara villages were busy trading centers as well, where nomadic peoples came for corn and tobacco. A complex social and political organization had evolved in the Mandan villages, focusing on religious ceremonies in a central plaza, matrilineal clans, and **age-graded societies**. In each village, clans had sacred **medicine bundles** that were inherited by the wealthy elite males. The nomadic groups who visited or contacted parties from the Mandan, Hidatsa, and Arikara villages at trade fairs were "**Crow**," Kiowa, "**Cree**," and Assiniboine, probably "**Arapaho**," and possibly Blackfoot-speaking bands.[27]

The horse spread to the nomadic tribes in the early eighteenth century. The Shoshone received horses in trade from the Comanche, probably at a trade fair on Green River. Peoples from the plateau area at the eastern edge of the Rocky Mountains also traded there. The Shoshone, wealthy in horses, began to expand out onto the Plains, hunting buffalo on horseback in western Wyoming and Montana, threatening Blackfeet who ventured south of the Saskatchewan River, and fighting Kiowa and others in the vicinity of the Black Hills (see map 4). They traded horses to the Crow, who took them to the Mandan and Hidatsa villages. Horses were probably traded by the Pawnee or Kiowa to the Arapaho near the Black Hills; they also could have been obtained through raiding. The Blackfeet and their **Gros Ventre** allies (see **Blackfeet confederacy**) acquired horses through contacts with the plateau peoples near the upper Saskatchewan River or from the Arapaho to the south. The horse transformed the lives of the nomadic hunters. To use the Blackfeet as an example, prior to their acquisition of the horse, they hunted buffalo communally on foot, driving the animals into pounds or over cliffs. The meat was shared among all the participants. Social relations were egalitarian. Warfare was sporadic, largely motivated by revenge, and casualties were not high. With the horse they could travel farther for buffalo, and hunters could ride beside the herd shooting the animals they preferred. Large quantities of meat could be transported by horses back to camp. The size of bands increased, and ceremonial life became more elaborate when regalia could be transported on horses and food stores could be acquired for large camps over several weeks. Horse ownership created a less egalitarian society, with a large gap between those wealthy and those poor in horses. Wealthy individuals generously provided for the poor, who then were obligated to their benefactors; thus, leaders maintained a following through distributing wealth generously. The demand for horses led to an emphasis on raiding for horses and weaponry suited to mounted combat.[28]

In the late seventeenth century, nomadic Cree groups were on the northwestern shore of Lake Superior and on the lower Red River; Assiniboines were to the south in southern Manitoba and Ontario and in northern Minnesota, where they hunted, fished, and gathered wild plant foods. The French had founded Quebec in 1608 and were well established to the east and southeast, using the **Ottawa** and other middlemen to trade with the Cree and the Assiniboine. In 1668 the British formed the Hudson's Bay Company, and it was granted a royal charter in 1670. From posts on the bay (particularly from York Factory), Britain competed with France for the Indian trade in pelts. The British traded guns to the Cree, and subsequently the Assiniboine allied with the Cree against the Sioux to the south and southeast. The French pushed westward in the late seventeenth and early eighteenth centuries, traveling by water along the St. Lawrence River and the Great Lakes, building posts and sending individual traders to native villages north and west of the lakes. The French built Lake Nipigon Post in Assiniboine country in 1684 to divert the Cree and Assiniboine from the bay (see map 4), but these peoples were in a position to control all canoe routes. They could play the French and British off against each other and they acted as middlemen in the trade with **Chipewyan** groups to the north, the Blackfeet groups to the west, and the Mandan to the south. The Cree and the Assiniboine used the manufactured goods they received from the British and French, then traded them for a markup in price. In the Mandan and Hidatsa villages, nomadic groups brought products of the hunt (and horses by 1741) and exchanged them for food grown in the villages and other trade items received by the villages, including a small amount of European goods. The village traders prospered as brokers by controlling the prices. Occasionally there were attacks by Cree and Assiniboine, and there is evidence that captives were taken.[29]

French traders reached the Mandan and Hidatsa villages in the 1730s and began direct trade, which the Assiniboine tried to thwart as best they could. In 1738 Sieur de La Vérendrye led an expedition departing from the Assiniboine River. He was the commander of the interior posts, which went as far as Lake Superior. La Vérendrye established Fort La Reine in Assiniboine country and was the first Frenchman of record to visit the Mandan (see map 3). His report was handicapped by lack of an interpreter, for the man he was relying on eloped with a woman in the party of Assiniboines accompanying him. La Vérendrye's sons visited in 1741 and 1742, and afterward French traders began regular trade in the Mandan and Hidatsa villages, some marrying and living there year-round. A post was established nearer the villages at the mouth of the Souris River in 1755. In the trade the standard of value was the Made Beaver (one prime beaver skin). The Mandan and Hidatsa provided wolf and fox skins and some beaver pelts, which were exported to Europe. Buffalo hides, meat, corn, fat, dogs, and captured women were largely for the Canadian market. Dogs were more useful in winter and were cheaper to care for than horses. The women usually were purchased by the traders as consorts or wives. The traders traveled to the villages on horseback in the fall and spring when the pelts were best and came on foot in the winter, using dogs to transport goods. The French trade provided some guns, powder, shot, tobacco, axes, knives, chisels, awls, and "luxury" items.[30]

After the Seven Years' War, several independent French trading companies formed a partnership with headquarters in Montreal. This North West Company dominated the trade on the upper Missouri River from a post on the Souris River and on the Saskatchewan River by a string of posts on both branches of the river. The Hudson's Bay Company attempted to compete by expanding west, building posts in the Red River valley and on the Assiniboine River in the 1780s and 1790s. Brandon House was built on the Assiniboine in 1793, from which trading expeditions went to the Mandan and Hidatsa villages. Cumberland House was established in 1774 on the Saskatchewan River, and in 1778 Hudson House was built farther upriver near the Gros Ventre and the eastern range of the Blackfeet confederacy (see map 5).[31]

These new posts threatened the role of the Cree and Assiniboine middlemen. Blackfeet and Gros Ventre began trading directly, bringing primarily provisions and horses as well as some skins (mainly wolf). The smallpox epidemic of 1780–81 weakened the Cree and Assiniboine, which made direct access to the Blackfeet confederacy especially important, and traders courted their leaders with gifts. Wealth in luxury goods, such as Brazilian tobacco, became a prerequisite for leadership, and the competition among traders to attract hunters contributed to the fission of large bands and to the development of rituals to formalize the redistribution of wealth. The Cree and Assiniboine responded to the construction of posts in Blackfeet country by making war on the Blackfeet confederacy. Better armed, they pounded the Gros Ventre and more eastern Blackfeet bands during the 1780s and 1790s. Eventually the Gros Ventre were displaced from the forks of the Saskatchewan and the Blackfeet driven more to the southwest. The Cree and Assiniboine began provisioning the posts on the Saskatchewan River. The weakened Gros Ventre became more dependent on the Blackfeet, which eventually led to their splitting off from the confederacy. As the Cree pushed into the Saskatchewan territory, some of the more southern bands relied more on hunting buffalo and became known as **Plains Cree**. The epidemic of 1780 devastated the Shoshone so that the mounted and armed

Blackfeet and Gros Ventre were able to drive them from Montana and move there to escape the constant Cree attacks (see map 5).[32]

The Mandan and Hidatsa also suffered from the smallpox epidemic of 1780–81, losing probably 68 percent of their population of 11,500. Regular attacks by the Teton also cut into the population and led to malnutrition by preventing them from hunting and gardening. The surviving Mandan combined their villages and amalgamated on the Knife River with the surviving Hidatsa villages. Before 1780 there were 24 Mandan and Hidatsa villages (a population of probably 12,000). Afterward, there were 3,750 in five villages. They also reorganized their political, kinship, and religious life to cope with their new circumstances. After the smallpox epidemic the thirteen Mandan clans were reduced to nine. In some clans the female members all died and the clan became extinct. Where there were a few survivors, they joined a larger clan of the same moiety. Rules for the transfer of bundles within the clans were altered, and where there were multiple bundles in a village made up of remnants of several villages, one bundle was used and the others not transferred. In this way, the Mandans perpetuated their ceremonial system despite the devastating effects of the epidemic.[33]

The Teton Sioux moved into the upper Missouri area and gradually came to dominate other peoples in the region. In the late seventeenth and early eighteenth centuries they lived on the prairies of Minnesota, where they secured their position by a ready supply of British guns from their "**Santee**" allies to their east. They kept the Cree and Assiniboine to the north of the headwaters of the Minnesota River and set about driving the Omaha, Iowa, Otoe, Missouria, and "**Cheyenne**" west toward the Missouri River. Once in control of this territory, they trapped beaver in the winter, hunted buffalo in the summer, and took their furs to the Santee trade fair in the spring. The Teton had some horses in 1707 and began moving to the Missouri River, where they settled for a time with the Arikara and continued to act as middlemen in the trade, bringing horses and other goods to the Santee fair where they obtained guns and other goods to bring back to the upper Missouri River area. By the late eighteenth century, traders from St. Louis were threatening the Teton's position. The Teton attacked traders before they could get to the Arikara and beyond and they harassed the villages farther downriver. From St. Louis, the French traders had reached the Arikara in the 1740s and the Spanish also went to the Arikara villages, but the traders' attempt to travel to the Mandan and Hidatsa was thwarted by Arikara and Teton Sioux, who wanted to protect their advantage. The smallpox epidemic of 1780 affected the Teton slightly, but it destroyed the ability of the Arikara, Mandan and Hidatsa, and Omaha to resist their attacks. Thus, the Teton controlled the trade on the Missouri River by the turn of the century. Some bands began moving west as far as the Yellowstone and up the Cheyenne River (see map 5). They shifted their emphasis from hunting beaver to full-time buffalo hunting and horse raiding. The "**Yanktonai**" and Yankton, allies of the Teton, remained east of the Missouri River on the Little Sioux River.[34]

The Cheyenne had been living near the mouth of the Wisconsin River in 1673, but pressure from the Cree and Assiniboine as well as the Teton and Yanktonai forced them to southern Minnesota. They were living in villages where they farmed and hunted. From southwestern Minnesota and southeastern South Dakota on the Minnesota River they were forced to move again; in 1700 they had villages on the Sheyenne River in North Dakota. They obtained horses and began moving toward the Missouri River, where some settled in the mid-eighteenth century on Porcupine Creek in North Dakota. By 1780 they had affiliated with the Arikara on the Grand River in South Dakota, and there they allied with a related group, the Sutai. Some Cheyenne bands moved west along the Cheyenne River toward the Black Hills in the upland Plains, where they made contact with the Arapaho and the Kiowa (who had allied with the Comanche and could make raids into Mexico to obtain horses) and served as middlemen in the trade between these nomadic peoples and the villages on the Missouri River. They gradually became a fully nomadic society, hunting buffalo year-round. Some Cheyenne bands married into Teton bands and took on a new identity, Cheyenne-Sioux, though they were still loosely allied with the Cheyenne. This facilitated an accommodation with the Teton, still to the east nearer the Missouri River. Cheyenne brought horses and products of the hunt to villages and trade fairs to exchange for manufactured goods, including guns.[35]

In 1803 the United States purchased Louisiana, and the fur trade passed to the control of Americans. The semisedentary horticultural villages (Caddo, Wichita, Pawnee, Arikara, Mandan, Hidatsa, and the Siouan-speaking villages on the lower Missouri) all had relocated to varying degrees and constricted their territory to escape attacks from enemies. Absorption of remnants of different peoples and amalgamations of villages during these tumultuous times led to the construction of new cultural identities. The village peoples embarked on a struggle during the nineteenth century to protect their remaining land base from American settlers pushing west across the Missouri into Kansas, Nebraska, and Texas. These settlers were not interested in trade, but rather wanted to dispossess native peoples of their land. Thus, the village peoples bore the brunt of the westward expansion of the United States in the early nineteenth century.

NOTES

1. Elizabeth John provides an overview of trade relations on the Southern Plains in *Storms Brewed in Other Men's Worlds* (Norman: University of Oklahoma Press, 1996), 64, 74, 129,

134, 151, 158–64, 187–92, 196–99, 218–23, 247, 255. For the central Missouri River region, see A. P. Nasatir, *Before Lewis and Clark: Documents Illustrating the History of the Missouri*, 2 vols. (St. Louis: St. Louis Historical Documents Foundation, 1952), 1–115. For the Northern Plains, see W. Raymond Wood and Thomas D. Thiessen, *Early Fur Trade on the Northern Plains: Canadian Traders Among the Mandan and Hidatsa Indians, 1738–1818* (Norman: University of Oklahoma Press, 1985), 3–74; Arthur J. Ray, *Indians in the Fur Trade: Their Role as Trappers, Hunters and Middlemen in the Lands Southwest of Hudson Bay, 1660–1870* (Toronto: University of Toronto Press, 1974),11–23; Olive Patricia Dickason, *Canada's First Nations: A History of Founding Peoples from Earliest Times* (Norman: University of Oklahoma Press, 1992), 138–146, 192–201.

2. Timothy K. Perttula, *"The Caddo Nation": Archaeological and Ethnohistoric Perspectives* (Austin: University of Texas Press, 1992), 13–18, 85; David La Vere, *The Caddo Chiefdoms: Caddo Economics and Politics, 700–1835* (Lincoln: University of Nebraska Press, 1998), 10–22, 29; Cecile Carter, *Caddo Indians: Where We Come From* (Norman: University of Oklahoma Press, 1995), 33–37, 64–68, 79–80 (and see the origin story, 73–76).

3. John, *Storms*, 20–21; Carter, 20–25; F. Todd Smith, *The Caddo Indians: Tribes at the Convergence of Empires, 1542–1854* (College Station: Texas A & M Press, 1995), 3.

4. John, *Storms*, 54–64, 70–71.

5. John, *Storms*, 165–69; Smith, *Caddo*, 8–14.

6. John, *Storms*, 79, 165–71, 189; Carter, 60.

7. Smith, *Caddo*, 37.

8. Carter, 26–32, 103; John, *Storms*, 198–203, 210–11; La Vere, 60, 65, 69. For a discussion of the bicultural community, see La Vere, 81–86.

9. Carter, 110–21; Smith, *Caddo*, 54.

10. Ibid., 37, 40, 44, 52–55; La Vere, 41, 49, 55, 64, 66, 105–6, 108–15; George Sabo III, "Reordering Their World: A Caddoan Ethnohistory," in *Visions and Revisions: Ethnohistoric Perspectives on Southern Cultures*, ed. George Sabo III and William M. Schneider (Athens and London: University of Georgia Press, 1987), 38, 39, 43.

11. Smith, *Caddo*, 63–83; Carter, 179–92, 206–14, 217; La Vere, 78, 80, 92–104, 106–8, 120–21, 124.

12. F. Todd Smith, *The Wichita Indians: Traders of Texas and the Southern Plains, 1540–1845* (College Station: Texas A & M Press, 2000), 3–9.

13. Ibid., 8–13; Mildred Mott Wedel, "The Wichita Indians in the Arkansas River Basin," in *Plains Indian Studies: A Collection of Essays in Honor of John C. Ewers and Waldo R. Wedel*, ed. Douglas H. Ubelaker and Herman J. Viola (Washington, D.C.: Smithsonian Contributions to Anthropology 30, 1982), 118–34.

14. Ibid.

15. Smith, *Wichita*, 15–17, 20–26; John, *Storms*, 218–21, 279, 304–5; Elizabeth Ann Harper, "Taovayas in Frontier Trade and Diplomacy, 1719–1768," *Chronicles of Oklahoma* 31 (1953): 268–89, 272.

16. Smith, *Wichita*, 27, 35–91; Wedel, 118–34; Elizabeth Ann Harper, "Taovayas in Frontier Trade and Diplomacy, 1769–1779," *Southwestern Historical Quarterly* 57 (1953): 181–201; Elizabeth Ann Harper, "Taovayas in Frontier Trade and Diplomacy, 1779–1835," *Panhandle-Plains Historical Review* 26 (1953): 41–72.

17. John, *Storms*, 95, 117–21, 226–32, 236, 244–45, 250–51, 266–67, 290, 313; Elizabeth A. H. John, ed., "Inside the Comancheria, 1785: The Diary of Pedro Vial and Francisco Xavier Chaves," trans. Aden Benavides Jr., *Southwestern Historical Quarterly* 98 (1994): 27–56;

Thomas W. Kavanagh, *Comanche Political History: An Ethnohistorical Perspective, 1706–1875* (Lincoln: University of Nebraska Press, 1996), 90.

18. John, *Storms*, 316–17, 338; John, "Inside the Comancheria," 27–56; Stanley Noyes, *Los Comanches: The Horse People, 1751–1845* (Albuquerque: University of New Mexico Press, 1993), 11–12, 22, 24–25, 57–59, 61, 70, 79–80; Kavanagh, 81–83, 94–105, 109, 111–13, 116, 121, 146–48.

19. Gilbert C. Din and A. P. Nasatir, *The Imperial Osage: Spanish-Indian Diplomacy in the Mississippi Valley* (Norman: University of Oklahoma Press, 1983), 23–53; Willard H. Rollings, *The Osage: An Ethnohistorical Study of Hegemony on the Prairie-Plains* (Columbia: University of Missouri Press, 1992), 96–153; John L. Champe and Franklin Fenenga, "Notes on the Pawnee," in *Pawnee and Kansa (Kaw) Indians, American Indian Ethnohistory: Plains Indians*, ed. David Agee Horr (New York: Garland, 1974), 17, 39, 41–42, 47–49; Douglas R. Parks, "Bands and Villages of the Arikara and Pawnee," *Nebraska History* 60 (1979): 214–39, 229–37.

20. Garrick A. Bailey, "Changes in Osage Social Organization, 1673–1906," *University of Oregon Anthropological Papers* 5 (1973): 1–122, 33–40; William E. Unrau, *The Kansa Indians: A History of the Wind People, 1673–1873* (Norman: University of Oklahoma Press, 1971), 13, 25, 39, 52–79.

21. Berlin Basil Chapman, "The Prehistoric and Historic Habitat of the Missouri and Oto Indians," in *History of the Otoe and Missouria Lands, American Indian Ethnohistory: Plains Indians*, ed. David Agee Horr (New York: Garland, 1974), 35, 45–46; G. Hubert Smith, "Ethnohistorical Report on the Omaha People," *Omaha Indians, American Indian Ethnohistory: Plains Indians*, ed. David Agee Horr (New York: Garland, 1974), 23–242.

22. Bailey, "Changes," 39–40, 50; John M. O'Shea and John Ludwickson, *Archaeology and Ethnohistory of the Omaha Indians: The Big Village Site* (Lincoln: University of Nebraska Press, 1992), 17–32; Unrau, 41.

23. Bailey, "Changes," 27, 42–45.

24. Ibid., 42–45; John J. Mathews, *The Osages: Children of the Middle Waters* (Norman: University of Oklahoma Press, 1961), 233.

25. James R. Murie, *Ceremonies of the Pawnee*, 2 vols., ed. Douglas R. Parks, Smithsonian Contributions to Anthropology 27 (Washington, D.C.: Smithsonian Institution Press, 1981), 1:1, 7, 10–11; David J. Wishart, *An Unspeakable Sadness: The Dispossession of the Nebraska Indians* (Lincoln: University of Nebraska Press, 1994), 253n87.

26. Alfred W. Bowers, *Hidatsa Social and Ceremonial Organization* (Lincoln: University of Nebraska Press, 1992 [1963]), 15–16, 19, 22; Roy W. Meyer, *The Village Indians of the Upper Missouri: The Mandans, Hidatsas, and Arikaras* (Lincoln: University of Nebraska Press, 1977), 1–3, 8–11 (quoted, p. 1), 15; Edward M. Bruner, "Mandan," in *Perspectives in American Indian Culture Change*, ed. Edward H. Spicer (Chicago: University of Chicago Press, 1961), 188–89, 192–205.

27. Meyer, 15–16.

28. John C. Ewers, *The Horse in Blackfoot Indian Culture with Comparative Material from Other Western Tribes* (Washington, D.C.: Smithsonian Institution Press, 1980 [1955]), 299–322.

29. Wood and Thiessen, 6–9, 20–21, 57, 63; Ray, 3–6, 11–14, 23, 69.

30. Wood and Thiessen, 20, 22, 25, 56; Meyer, 18–26.

31. Wood and Thiessen, 12; Ray, 126–27.

32. Ibid., 98–99, 102–4, 140–41; Loretta Fowler, *Shared Symbols, Contested Meanings: Gros Ventre Culture and History, 1778–1984* (Ithaca: Cornell University Press, 1987), 24–27, 34–39, 41–47.

33. Wood and Thiessen, 6–8, 20, 27–28, 46, 48, 71–72, 74; Meyer, 14, 26–31; Bruner, 230.

34. Richard White, "The Winning of the West: The Expansion of the Western Sioux in the Eighteenth and Nineteenth Centuries," *Journal of American History* 65 (1978): 319–43, 321–27.

35. John H. Moore, *The Cheyenne Nation: A Social and Demographic History* (Lincoln: University of Nebraska Press, 1987), 200.

CHAPTER 3

American Expansion:
Trade and Treaties

The acquisition of Louisiana by the United States in 1803 paved the way for American expansion westward. American traders pushed west of the Missouri River and, without European rivals, had the edge in bargaining with native hunters. The settlers who followed the traders in the 1840s did not become kinsmen and partners in commercial enterprise, as had their predecessors. They viewed Indians as alien impediments to the settlement of the west. The farming peoples in the tall-grass prairie region felt the brunt of the entry of settlers and of immigrant Indians driven from their homes east of the Missouri River. These peoples were friendly to Americans, but their plight was ignored as the United States tried to placate the numerous Teton, bent on expanding west and driving other peoples from the buffalo range. The United States made several peace treaties, followed by land cession treaties as the circumstances of native groups worsened over time. Nomadic peoples on the Southern, Central and Northern Plains adopted a friendly or hostile stance toward Americans after 1850, depending on the effect of immigration on their hunting territory. On the Southern Plains, Osage dominance of the region gradually ended and they withdrew to the north. The Wichita moved their villages farther west and affiliated with the Caddo, who had moved onto the plains after their lands were overrun. Comanche and Kiowa prosperity continued unabated until the flow of settler traffic to California and Oregon began to disturb the buffalo herds in the upland

Plains in the 1840s. On the Central and Northern Plains, the farming villages consolidated and tried to withstand hostility from settlers and the aggressive Sioux. By the 1860s the survival of the nomadic Cheyenne, Arapaho, and Teton Sioux on the Central Plains was threatened by the westward migration, and they took military action to defend their territory. Nomadic groups on the Northern Plains were the last to face the trespass of American settlers. By the 1870s all the native peoples were settled on reservations, economically dependent on the United States yet determined to maintain their way of life in a changed world.

THE SOUTHERN PLAINS

After the **Louisiana Purchase** the United States worked on moving Indians from the **Eastern Woodlands** into Osage territory, even encouraging warfare with the Osage. Large numbers of Eastern Indians moved into southern Missouri and northern Arkansas, a region important to Osage subsistence. This immigration had begun in the 1790s as the United States encouraged Eastern tribes, such as the **Delaware** and the **Shawnee**, to move west. The Osage began withdrawing to the west; the Little Osage abandoned their village on the Missouri River and moved westward to join other Osage on the Osage River. The trader **Auguste Chouteau** built a post on the Arkansas River and encouraged Osage to move southwest. A village led by **Claremore**, the principal peace chief, settled there. In 1808 the Osage were pressured to cede southern Missouri and northern Arkansas, and the Arkansas village agreed to cessions in 1809. By this time large numbers of **Cherokee** were moving into Osage territory and attacking them. In 1817 the Cherokee destroyed Claremore's village on the Arkansas River. The Osage had little choice but to cede more territory in 1818 for the Cherokee settlers. Even then the federal government failed to protect the Osage from the Cherokee attacks. In 1822 the Osage began to negotiate for peace; they agreed in 1825 to cede all their land in Missouri and Arkansas. They retained a strip 50 miles wide in eastern Kansas for a reservation.[1]

The Osage's circumstances worsened after the **Indian Removal Act** of 1830 resulted in more native peoples from the Southeast moving into Osage territory. By 1840, 73,000 Eastern Indians had settled in eastern Oklahoma and Kansas, outnumbering the 5,500 Osage. The increased population resulted in the extermination of much of the game in the area. The Osage continued to hunt in the Arkansas River region, challenging the Comanche and Kiowa to their west. Probably in an effort to intimidate the Kiowa, they attacked a village when most of the men were away hunting, killed the women and children, cut off their heads, and left them in pots for their men to find when they returned. This Cut-Throat massacre in the Wichita Mountains aggravated the hostile relationship

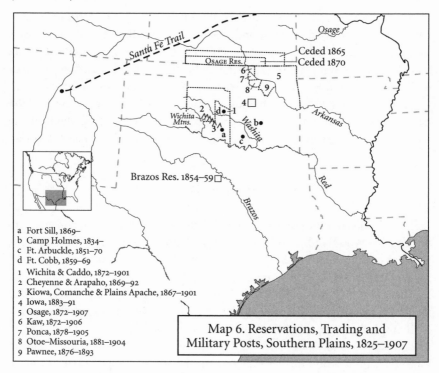

a Fort Sill, 1869–
b Camp Holmes, 1834–
c Ft. Arbuckle, 1851–70
d Ft. Cobb, 1859–69
1 Wichita & Caddo, 1872–1901
2 Cheyenne & Arapaho, 1869–92
3 Kiowa, Comanche & Plains Apache, 1867–1901
4 Iowa, 1883–91
5 Osage, 1872–1907
6 Kaw, 1872–1906
7 Ponca, 1878–1905
8 Otoe–Missouria, 1881–1904
9 Pawnee, 1876–1893

Map 6. Reservations, Trading and Military Posts, Southern Plains, 1825–1907

between the Osage and the Comanche and Kiowa (see map 6). The scarcity of game and internal competition between leaders led to the separation of the large Osage villages into several smaller ones. In 1839 there were eight villages, whereas in 1802 there had been three. The buffalo robe replaced furs as a major trade item, which was an additional incentive for remaining near the buffalo country. Young warriors became increasingly influential in the villages as they struggled to defend the Osage's position in southeast Kansas and northeast Oklahoma. By 1839 their military dominance of the region was broken. The Osage on the Arkansas River agreed to move to the reservation in Kansas, where they would receive regular issues of food. They remained there for 30 years, except during the Civil War when life was disrupted by war conditions. Union and Confederate sympathizers competed for Osage support. The Great Osage village signed a treaty with the Confederacy in 1861 but did not actually take up arms. Outlaws on the Kansas frontier raided settlements, making it impossible for the Osage to remain on the reservation. Some bands fled to the **Creek** and Cherokee Nations. Some went to a Union stronghold. All the bands joined together for bison hunts when they could. The Osage all returned to the reservation when conditions allowed.[2]

Before the Civil War, pressure was mounting to open the northern section of **Indian Territory** (what became Nebraska and Kansas after 1854) to settlement. After the war, in 1865 the United States pressured the Osage to cede the eastern part of their reservation. The Osage needed the **annuity payments** from the cession, for hostile Cheyennes interfered with their buffalo hunts in the Smoky Hill and Republican River area and settlers were trespassing and stealing their property. Delays in receiving the payments and increasing pressure to open land to settlers led the Osage to agree to another cession in 1869. They ceded their reservation in Kansas and agreed to move south to Indian Territory to a new reservation that adjoined it. Before Congress could arrange for the removal, settlers moved into Osage villages and appropriated their homes and property. In 1872 the Osage settled on their new reservation (see map 6).[3]

In the early nineteenth century, the Wichita were in Spanish Texas and traded in their villages on the Brazos River with the Spanish and with the Americans who came to their fortified villages on the Red River. They played these rivals off against each other. By 1810 Osage attacks and the decline in buffalo due to the influx of Americans were damaging enough that Wichita villages began to move south from the Red to the Brazos River. The Wichita raided Spanish settlements in Texas in order to obtain horses and other goods. When Mexico won independence from Spain in 1821, Mexican officials were unable to prevent such raids. These officials had encouraged American colonists to settle in eastern Texas, and the settlers, as well as immigrant Indians from the Southeast, were targets of Wichita raiders.[4]

Not long after the turn of the century, Caddo people, the Kadohadacho, began moving from Louisiana into Texas east of the Wichita. They had lived on the eastern border of the Plains and had welcomed the Americans to Louisiana in the early nineteenth century, hoping to obtain trade goods and protection from the hostile peoples who were raiding their villages in the Red River valley. Attacks from Osage and Eastern peoples such as the **Choctaw**, who had been encouraged to leave the Southeast by the federal government, contributed to population decline. At this time the Hasinai and Anadako divisions of the Caddo were living in Texas east of the Wichita, and they continued to maintain friendly relations with the Spanish. The plight of the Kadohadacho worsened after 1812. Although President Thomas Jefferson had guaranteed them title to their land, Americans moved into the Red River territory and began to exterminate the game in the woodlands and nearby prairie. Louisiana became a state in 1812, and even though the Kadohadacho had supported the United States in the War of 1812, federal officials did nothing to stop the trespass. The Kadohadacho expressed willingness to sell some land in return for a guarantee that they could retain the remainder. By 1819, 14,000 settlers were in Kadohadacho country and Arkansas had become a territory. Choctaws and others from east of the Mississippi, as well as

Americans, moved into the area, prepared to make war to stay there. The Kado-hadacho had absorbed small remnant populations, as well as some Kitsai, to strengthen their numbers, and they had established farming communities with grass houses, crops, chickens, and hogs. But their circumstances deteriorated to the point that the larger Kadohadacho settlements, led by **Dehahuit**, the princi-pal *caddi* from 1800 to 1833, moved to Texas before the 1820s to escape attacks. They had adopted some European clothing and learned European languages, yet maintained their commitment to Caddo ceremonies. In Texas the Caddo groups tried to establish good relations with Spanish officials and often served as intermediaries in Spanish-Wichita relations.[5]

In their villages the Wichita, who needed to raid to obtain horses and items to trade, were vulnerable to counterattack. Settlers drove them and the Kitsai from eastern and central Texas. As Anglo-American immigration into Texas surged in the 1820s and 1830s, large numbers of Indians from the Southeast and Caddo peoples competed for the diminishing game. Caddo traveled as far west as the Washita River to hunt. More Kadohadacho moved into Texas after 1835, when they were pressured into ceding all their lands in the United States (Louisiana); some went to Indian Territory and settled east of the Wichita there. The United States failed to pay the money they had agreed on for the land, yet sold it for four times as much as they had promised the Kadohadacho. The de-teriorating conditions led to the Wichitas moving farther from the areas of set-tlement. Thus, by 1830 the Taovaya had established two villages near the Wi-chita Mountains in the Red River valley near the mouth of the Washita River, and the Tawakoni and Wako had moved from the Brazos River to join them there. The Wichita had to continue raiding the settlers in Texas in order to ob-tain horses and mules to trade to Americans on the Red River and to Pawnees from north of the Platte River. The Americans wanted to suppress intertribal conflict because it interfered with trade. With the assistance of a captive Wichi-ta woman whom they ransomed from the Osage, a treaty council was held with the Wichita, Kiowa, Choctaw, and Delaware (an immigrant tribe) at Camp Holmes in Indian Territory in 1835 (see map 6). The Wichita agreed to peace-ful relations with the United States and, with the encouragement of the com-missioners, planned to raid Mexico for stock. The Wichita villages were east of the Wichita Mountains and on Cache Creek near Fort Sill in Indian Territory. They traded robes, horses, and mules at Camp Holmes and at a trading post at the mouth of the Washita River. Some Wichitas on the Red River raided into Texas and others, living in Texas, tried to maintain peaceful relations.[6]

After Anglo-Americans in Texas revolted and established the Republic of Texas in 1836, settlers attacked and destroyed Wichita villages. In the 1840s some Wichitas made retaliatory raids, despite several peace councils. The Caddo struggled to survive in Texas during this time. They were in three groups: 500 Kadohadacho, 225 Hasinai, and 250 Anadako. Most were in Hasinai country where Anglo-Americans trespassed on their lands and harassed them. The Texas Rangers, organized in 1835, reflected settler opinion and took every opportunity to attack the Caddo. Although they tried to be peacemakers, the Caddo often were blamed for raids conducted by Wichitas, Comanches, and Kiowas. Some joined with the Choctaw and **Chickasaw** in Indian Territory and some settled near the Wichita there. In 1843 and 1844, those who remained in Texas signed peace treaties with Texas, and many moved back to settle on the Brazos River with small groups of Kitsai and Delaware.[7]

In 1845 a peace treaty was signed by the Wichita and the Comanche with the Republic of Texas, but the following year the United States annexed Texas and assumed responsibility for the protection of Indians and the maintenance of peace, although Texans did not grant native people rights to land. Texas Rangers actively assumed the peacekeeping role because United States troops were engaged in a war with Mexico. Still Wichita raiders continued to steal stock. The treaty goods promised by the United States did not arrive and settlers continued to trespass, undermining the Wichita's ability to support themselves. The Caddo faced the constant threat of attack, despite promises of protection from the United States. They moved their villages farther up the Brazos River away from settlers. Some Wichita and Caddo villages combined for better defense on the Brazos River, but Rangers often attacked them despite treaty guarantees. Some Wichitas on the Brazos began moving north of the Red River to join the Wichita there. By 1851 the Caddo population in Texas had dropped to 476; some had gone north to Indian Territory.[8]

By the 1850s the United States had committed to establishing reservations for native peoples, rather than merely removing them from territory coveted by settlers. A reservation was established for several Wichita and Caddo villages on the upper Brazos River near Fort Belknap, and they relocated there in 1854 (see map 6). Caddo people from the Anadako and Hasinai divisions settled on the eastern portion of the reservation and the Kadohadacho to their west. Some Delaware and Shawnee allies moved there. Caddo *caddis* from elite families continued to provide strong leadership. **Iesh** (or Jose Maria) was the most important *caddi* during the reservation years. The Caddo tried to raise livestock and farmed traditional crops (corn, beans, melons, pumpkins) as well as wheat. They tried to hunt, but the Comanche blocked their way to the buffalo country. Two groups of Wichita, the Waco and the Tawakoni, settled on the west side of the reservation. Still, they were under almost constant attack from Texans, as well as from Comanche and Kiowa warriors. Some Caddos fled to Indian Territory and joined others there. The reservation in Texas was surrounded by settlers a few years after it was established; only twelve families of settlers lived nearby in 1854; by 1857, 150 families were there. They blamed the Brazos

Indians for the raids of others, despite the fact that on three occasions, in 1856, 1858, and 1859, Caddos and Wichitas joined Rangers and U.S. troops to attack Comanche villages. A series of murders of Caddos by settlers in 1858 led to the recognition on the part of the United States that the reservation community would have to be moved to Indian Territory.[9]

Wichita villages (Taovaya and others), some Kitsai, and some Caddo already were in the lower Washita River valley near Fort Arbuckle (see map 6) when the United States moved to establish a reservation for them and other native people there. Despite the fact that the area was part of the Wichita homeland, this land had been assigned to the Choctaw and the Chickasaw in return for their lands in the Southeast; thus, the United States leased land from the Choctaw and Chickasaw in order to establish a reservation there for the Wichita and others. The threat of annihilation of the Brazos reservation people by settlers led the United States to evacuate the reservation and move the Wichita, along with the Caddo and others, north to the Red River Wichita community in the "Leased District." The trip from the Brazos reservation in 1859, referred to by historians as another "trail of tears," was 150 miles and took 17 days.[10]

The Wichita and Caddo living in Indian Territory and some Kitsai and Delaware (associated with the Caddo) were asked to proceed to the Leased District and choose the best area for settlement. The Texas groups later approved these selections. The Wichita Agency was established and Fort Cobb built in 1859 (see map 6). Both groups arrived at the agency within days of each other. The Wichita settled on the south bank of the Washita River in two villages. The three Caddo bands with affiliated families of Delaware chose to settle on the north bank of the river. The Caddo were in three divisions: the Kadohadacho, the combined Hasinai and Anadako (or Nadoco) from the Brazos, and the White Beads (those who had been living near Fort Arbuckle). Attacks from Comanche and Kiowa were always a threat. Fort Cobb was built three miles west of the Wichita Agency to help protect the agency and its residents, who began rebuilding their homes and farms in the river valley.[11]

Just three years after their arrival, the Civil War (1861–65) started and the troops from Fort Cobb left, only to be replaced by militia from Texas. Soon after, the Caddo and Wichita fled north to Kansas, where they lived under the protection of the Union forces and tried to support themselves by selling their cattle and cattle they rustled. Some Caddos joined a Southern Comanche group; groups from the Kansas settlement joined them for the spring hunt along the Arkansas River. They were in Kansas five years, and the Caddo began to forge a common identity as well as one based on band. Similarly, the Wichita began to organize as pan-Wichita. Conditions were difficult and probably one fourth of the population died. The agency on the Washita River was burned by Union troops. In 1867 the Wichita and the Caddo moved back to the

Leased District and began to rebuild their community at Wichita Agency. In 1872 they agreed on reservation boundaries.[12]

Nearby, the Comanche, the Kiowa, and the allied Plains Apache were soon to begin reservation life as well, although they resisted reservation settlement much longer. The Comanche had prospered by hunting and raiding in the early nineteenth century, just as they had before. They traded in New Mexico and Texas and raided deep into Mexico. The Spanish, anxious to remain on good terms, tolerated raids on Spanish settlements north of Mexico. The Americans and the Spanish both courted the Comanche and sought their trade by giving the head chiefs gifts and provisions. The Comanche were numerous; despite population loss from a smallpox epidemic in 1816, they numbered close to 20,000 in 1838. Their alliance with the Kiowa helped them fight off incursions into their hunting territory from tribes to the east. Mexican independence in 1821 did not affect their circumstances; they continued to raid and accept presents from Mexican officials. David Burnet, who knew the Comanche in the 1820s, described a Comanche raiding party to Mexico thus. Each warrior set out on a riding pony and leading a war pony. The party arrived at its destination at night and established camp, leaving their horses with their wives or male companions. They went into the settlement stealthily by moonlight on their war ponies to look for stock and captives (and, if the opportunity presented itself, to take a scalp). They seized as many horses as possible and made for the Rio Grande, riding night and day. Americans bought as many horses and mules as the Comanche could produce. The Comanche also did a business in captives, ransoming many of them back to their home communities in Mexico, New Mexico, and Texas. In 1830, they held probably 500 Mexican captives. Others were adopted into the Comanche community, helping to maintain the population. The Comanche had to compete for buffalo in the 1830s as Cheyenne and Arapaho and other groups adversely affected by United States expansion moved into their territory. In the late 1830s the Comanche and Kiowa were at war with the Cheyenne and Arapaho, but in 1840 they made peace and became allies.[13]

In 1835 when Anglo-Texans revolted against Mexico and founded the Republic of Texas, these settlers traded with the Comanche for horses, grease, meat, and furs and encouraged them to raid into Mexico for the stock the Texans wanted. The trail from Missouri to Santa Fe (see **Santa Fe Trail**) was heavily traveled and helped the merchants in Missouri prosper. The threat of Comanche and Kiowa raids on the trail led to a peace treaty with several tribes, including the Comanche, signed at Camp Holmes in 1835, in which the United States agreed to work to curtail intertribal warfare and raiding north of Mexico. But the settlers—35,000 between the Brazos and Colorado rivers— began to disrupt Comanche hunting as they entered the buffalo range, and the

Anglo-Texans were inherently hostile to native peoples, unwilling to negotiate or coexist. Comanches sometimes raided settlements in Texas and took captives. In 1840 the Southern Comanche bands attempted to make peace with the Texans, offering to return captives. The peace delegation of men, women, and children were invited into the council house at San Antonio, then massacred there under a flag of truce. This "Council House massacre" soured Comanche-Texas relations and led to years of revenge raids, many led by **Buffalo Hump**. Not only were the Comanche at odds with the Texans then, but incursions from the immigrant Indians and the desperate Osages threatened Comanche prosperity.[14]

In 1846 the United States annexed Texas and provoked a war with Mexico. Efforts were made by the Americans to establish peaceful relations with the Comanche, in large part to facilitate the war effort. The various Comanche bands sometimes took opposing stances toward the Texas settlements. Some Comanches and Kiowas raided, then hurried north beyond the Red River. Raids into Mexico were common. Other Comanches traded and attended local rodeos. The United States made a treaty in 1846 that guaranteed protection to the Comanche and arranged for the return of captives, and the Comanche and Kiowa ceased raiding on the Santa Fe Trail for a while. In 1849 Americans began streaming west through Comanche and Kiowa territory toward the gold fields in California. The wagon trains along the Platte River brought smallpox and cholera (see **Oregon Trail**), and the Comanche lost thousands of people to disease. In order to try to prevent Comanche attacks on the emigrants and raids into Mexico (which the United States had promised to end at the close of the war), the United States organized another peace council at Fort Atkinson in 1853. Using Mexican captives as interpreters, 9,000 Comanches with their Kiowa and Plains Apache allies met with the commissioners. The Comanche agreed to allow the road west in return for provisions to compensate them for their losses. The United States hoped to settle the southern bands on a reservation near the Caddo and the Wichita on the Brazos and, by protecting them from attack, prevent them from attacking settlers. But the Comanche were wary of American promises, and only a few families settled there. Attacks from Americans eventually drove the Brazos River Comanche north across the Red River near the Wichita at Fort Cobb in 1859. Most northern bands were still moving from camp to camp, raiding for horses and captives and hunting. The Comanche and their allies did what they could to protect their buffalo range, fighting the better-armed Eastern Indians. They extracted tolls from the emigrants on the trails west. The Civil War brought some relief as troops were removed from the West. By 1864 the Comanche were raiding the Texas frontier again, and they joined with the Cheyenne and the Arapaho in a general war on the Southern and Central Plains in retaliation for a massacre of Cheyennes and Arapahos on Sand Creek in Colorado in 1864 (see map 7). In 1865 the Comanche were forced by fear of army reprisals to cede their territory in Colorado, Kansas, and New Mexico in return for a reservation in another part of their territory. The raiding for stock and captives continued. Another treaty council was held on Medicine Lodge Creek in 1867 (see **Medicine Lodge Creek Treaty**). **Ten Bears** was the Comanche spokesman and **Satanta** spoke for the Kiowa. The boundaries of the reservation were set within the Leased District in southwestern Oklahoma between the Red and Washita rivers. Reservation life began in 1868, but the Comanche, the Kiowa, and the Plains Apache still hunted for most of their subsistence (see map 6). Not until the buffalo disappeared from the Southern Plains in the late 1870s did the Comanche have to adjust their way of life to the reservation system.[15]

THE CENTRAL PLAINS/LOWER MISSOURI RIVER

After the United States purchased Louisiana from France in 1803, the native peoples along the lower Missouri faced new challenges, as had the native peoples on the Southern Plains. The newly acquired land presented an opportunity for the westward expansion of American settlers, the removal of native peoples from the east to the area west of the Missouri River, and the expansion of trade. At the same time, the large Teton population was continuing its westward expansion, dislodging or harassing groups in its path. Travel over wagon roads westward along the Platte River, as well as the Santa Fe Trail, in the 1840s disturbed the bison, driving them away from the ranges they habitually occupied. The village peoples—Kaw, Otoe, Missouria, Iowa, Omaha, Ponca, and Pawnee—bore the brunt of the population movements in the early nineteenth century, while the nomadic peoples faced displacement at mid-century.[16]

Before 1807 the St. Louis fur trade was confined to the lower reaches of the Missouri River and focused on the Kaw (and the Osage, who were south of their Kaw allies), Otoe, Ponca, and Omaha. In 1807 Manuel Lisa of the Missouri Fur Company helped to expand the trade by his foray into Crow country in the upland Northern Plains. As American traders moved northwest and west, they dealt directly with nomadic peoples, thus bypassing the village middlemen. The defeat of the British in the War of 1812 largely removed them as competitors for the Indian trade in the region. American trade companies maintained posts along the lower Missouri and continued to distribute gifts there in order to placate the villagers. The post at Council Bluffs (Fort Lisa) (1812–19) and later Bellevue was within reach of the Omaha, Otoe, Missouria, Iowa, and Pawnee. Another post, built at Cedar Island in 1809, served the numerous Teton and Yankton Sioux, who were becoming the dominant military power in the lower Missouri region (see map 7). In 1824 **William**

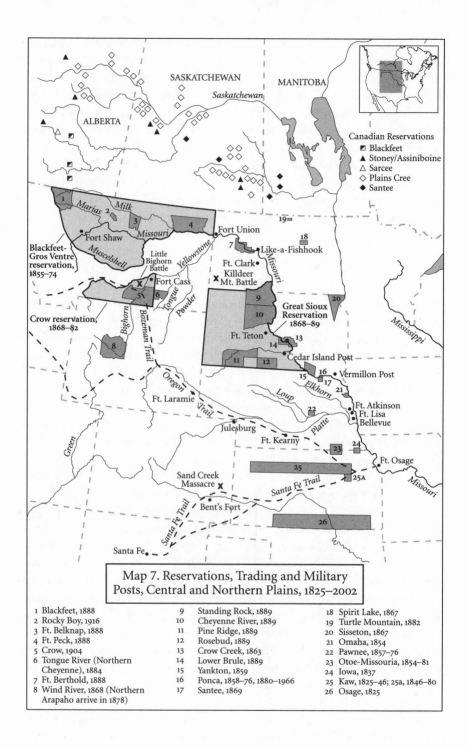

Canadian Reservations
- ◩ Blackfeet
- ▲ Stoney/Assiniboine
- △ Sarcee
- ◇ Plains Cree
- ◆ Santee

SASKATCHEWAN

MANITOBA

ALBERTA

Saskatchewan

Blackfeet-Gros Ventre reservation, 1855–74

Fort Shaw

Marias *Milk*

Missouri

Muscelshell

Little Bighorn Battle

Crow reservation, 1868–82

X Fort Cass

Bighorn

Tongue

Powder

Bozeman Trail

Fort Union

7

Like-a-Fishhook

Ft. Clark
Killdeer
X Mt. Battle

18

19

Great Sioux Reservation 1868–89

9

10

Ft. Teton

13

14

Cedar Island Post

11   12

20

Mississippi

15   16   17   21

Vermillon Post

Elkhorn

Loup

22

Ft. Atkinson
Ft. Lisa
Bellevue

Platte

Ft. Laramie

Oregon Trail

Julesburg

Ft. Kearny

23   24

Ft. Osage

25

25A

Missouri

Sand Creek Massacre X

Santa Fe Trail

Bent's Fort

26

Santa Fe Trail

Santa Fe

Green

Map 7. Reservations, Trading and Military Posts, Central and Northern Plains, 1825–2002

1 Blackfeet, 1888
2 Rocky Boy, 1916
3 Ft. Belknap, 1888
4 Ft. Peck, 1888
5 Crow, 1904
6 Tongue River (Northern Cheyenne), 1884
7 Ft. Berthold, 1888
8 Wind River, 1868 (Northern Arapaho arrive in 1878)

9 Standing Rock, 1889
10 Cheyenne River, 1889
11 Pine Ridge, 1889
12 Rosebud, 1889
13 Crow Creek, 1863
14 Lower Brule, 1889
15 Yankton, 1859
16 Ponca, 1858–76, 1880–1966
17 Santee, 1869

18 Spirit Lake, 1867
19 Turtle Mountain, 1882
20 Sisseton, 1867
21 Omaha, 1854
22 Pawnee, 1857–76
23 Otoe-Missouria, 1854–81
24 Iowa, 1837
25 Kaw, 1825–46; 25a, 1846–80
26 Osage, 1825

Ashley financed trappers who flocked to the western edge of the Plains along the Green and Snake rivers and obtained furs themselves, squeezing out the native hunters. Furs were shipped overland along the Platte River to St. Louis, a route later followed by settlers moving west. These developments also minimized the role of the peoples of the lower Missouri region in the fur trade of the 1820s. All the Prairie Plains village people continued to plant their crops, hunt buffalo, and hold ceremonies that supported these activities. Epidemics had decimated the village populations by 1804, but during the next two decades their numbers increased. In 1804 the Otoe were about 500 and the Missouria, 300; in 1820, together they numbered 1,200; the Omaha were 900 in 1804 and 2,000 in 1820; the Ponca, 250 in 1804 and 1,000 in 1820; the Pawnee increased from 4,800 in 1804 to 10,000 in 1820.[17]

After 1826, the **American Fur Company** obtained a monopoly and controlled the trade, so Indian hunters could not count on a liberal distribution of gifts or good prices for pelts and hides. The Teton effectively barred the villagers' access to buffalo herds that were gradually moving west, so the Otoe-Missouria and Omaha (closest to the Missouri River) became increasingly dependent on the traders. Marriages between Otoe, Missouria, and Omaha women and traders helped ensure access to goods. The federal government opened the Upper Missouri Agency at Bellevue; it became a source of supplies as hunger became a problem for the Omaha, Otoe, and Missouria. The Pawnee and Ponca lived to the west near the buffalo country and retained more independence, although the Ponca had to subordinate themselves to the Teton in order to continue their hunts and reorganized their society to adapt to the nomadic life.[18]

In the 1830s the market for beaver pelts collapsed (for the silk hat had become fashionable) and the buffalo robe became the preferred article of trade. Traders focused on establishing posts along the Upper Missouri River on the Northern Plains and in the upland areas of the Platte valley, where they traded with nomadic peoples. The village peoples were hard pressed to obtain buffalo near their villages or to compete with the Teton and other nomadic groups in the upland area where buffalo herds had migrated in the wake of the wave of settlers moving from east to west. Epidemics of smallpox in 1831 and 1837–38, as well as other diseases, decimated the village populations. As David Wishart puts it in *An Unspeakable Sadness*, influenza, whooping cough, and cholera "landed on the Indians like breakers on a beach." Teton raids also took a heavy toll. By the 1850s the Pawnee, Otoe-Missouria, and Omaha had lost 50 to 60 percent of their population and the Ponca, 33 percent. The effect of these changes on the Indian trade was the villagers' increased dependency on American traders and officials. Manufactured tools and utensils had replaced those made of stone, bone, hide, and pottery. Broadcloth, decorated with glass beads, brought the wearer status, and guns still were a necessity. Traders interfered in village politics, sometimes favoring men who were viewed as unqualified to represent their peers. Over-hunting of adjacent territory made for more intense competition in the more westerly buffalo range, and intertribal warfare escalated.[19]

The United States made treaties of peace with the Prairie-Plains villages, largely to secure a trade advantage in 1817–18, 1822, and 1825. As American trav-elers and settlers began to cross the Missouri toward the Southwest and toward California and Oregon, the United States attempted to move the Kaw and Pawnee away from the routes and secured other cessions from the Otoe-Missouria and Omaha in the 1830s to make room for immigrant Indians just east of the Missouri River. In 1854 Congress passed the Kansas-Nebraska Act, which created the territories of Kansas and Nebraska out of the northern part of Indian Territory. To make room for settlers, native peoples in Kansas and Ne-braska were pressured to cede land and settle on even smaller reservations.

The United States needed to relocate Eastern tribes that were being forced from their homes by settlers. A treaty council was held in 1830 at Prairie du Chien (see **Treaty of Prairie du Chien**), where representatives of the Otoe-Missouria and Omaha were pressured to give up their claim to lands east of the Missouri River. Although they retained the right to hunt in this region, Eastern tribes effectively moved in and prevented them from doing so. Again in 1833 the Otoe-Missouria were pressured to cede some of their land in Nebraska to im-migrant Indians. They were by this time dependent on the federal government for supplies and on the wild plants in the region for much of their food. These circumstances were compounded by population loss and the death of the prin-cipal chief Ietan in 1837. The Missouria village drew off from the Otoe and the Otoe split into three separate villages, weakening their ability to negotiate. Still vulnerable to Sioux attacks and under pressure to cede more land, they became further impoverished when their **annuity payments** expired in 1850. Thus, they agreed in 1854 to sell most of their land and move onto a small reservation on the Big Blue River on the Kansas-Nebraska line. The Otoe-Missouria were the first of the Nebraska tribes to settle on a reservation in 1855 (see map 7). They rebuilt their earth lodges and tried to farm and hunt. Vaccination helped pre-vent further population loss from smallpox, yet in 1861 the Otoe-Missouria numbered but 708.[20]

The Omaha had lost their advantage in the trade at the beginning of the nineteenth century. A smallpox epidemic in 1801 and relentless attacks from the Teton Sioux and others on their village on the Missouri River made their accommodation to the Americans necessary. They attempted to hunt buffalo to the west of their village in order to buy guns, and Manuel Lisa of the Missouri Fur Company built a fort nearby and married an Omaha woman "of some fame" in 1814. A formal peace treaty was made with the United States in 1815, and the Omaha ceded land to the United States in 1820 for the establishment of a military post, Fort Atkinson. But the American alliance could not protect them from the Sioux and they abandoned their village, moving west to the Elkhorn River closer to the buffalo range, where they lived for fourteen years (1820–34). They took their buffalo robes to the Missouri River in the winter and became increasingly dependent on the trade. The Sauk, expanding into the lands east of the Missouri, began to try to destroy them and take over the buffalo range. In 1830 the Omaha ceded rights to their lands east of the Missouri River, which already were overrun by Eastern tribes. They briefly returned to their village on the Missouri in 1834, for the Sauk had been defeated by the United States in the **Black Hawk War** of 1832, but by the 1840s the Teton were attacking them relentlessly and they were driven back to the Elkhorn River. Their annuities had expired in 1840, their numbers were reduced from a cholera epidemic in 1836, and they were marginal to the trade as they were unable to contest other tribes for the buffalo range. They needed to cede land in order to get annual supplies from the United States. In 1845, they relocated near the Bellevue agency, where Fort Lisa was moved in 1823, and ceded most of their land in 1854 in return for a small reservation on the Missouri River and for annuities (see map 7).[21]

By the time of Lewis and Clark's visit (see **Lewis and Clark expedition**), the Kaw had recently abandoned their village on the Missouri and moved farther up the Kansas River to the mouth of the Blue Earth River, where they planted corn, beans, and pumpkins and made buffalo hunts to the west. This move did not free them from attacks, for the buffalo range was crowded, and even though they sometimes joined with Osage to the south and east, they had to compete with the more numerous Pawnee and the nomadic Cheyenne and Arapaho. The nearest trading post was the government **factory** Fort Osage (1808–19) near the mouth of the Kansas River (see map 7). Intermarriages between Osage and Kaw and between Kaw women and some of the traders helped ensure the Kaw access to the trade. They sold mostly deerskins. When Missouri became a state in 1821, the traffic from the Missouri frontier through Kaw country to Santa Fe increased and the federal government began to pressure the Kaw to cede land. They were subjected to a demonstration from Major Stephen Long's expedition in 1819 that was designed to intimidate them. Sailing up to meet the Kaw just above the mouth of the Kansas River, Long's steamboat's bow was shaped like a scaly serpent and the smoke from the ship bellowed from the serpent's nostrils. At dusk Long fired shells and rockets into the sky. In 1825 the Kaw ceded all their claims to land except a small strip in Kansas. The federal government, influenced by the trader Chouteau, recognized White Plume, the son of Osage chief Pawhuska and a Kaw woman, as head chief; thereafter, political dissension among rival chiefs undermined the Kaw's effort to negotiate.

The United States ignored many of the 1825 treaty provisions calling for support of the Kaw, and proximity to settlers led to more deaths from disease, despite the federal government's efforts to vaccinate Indians for smallpox. By the 1830s the Kaw had moved closer to the agency and the federal troops at Fort Leavenworth, where they could get supplies. They built villages in the easternmost part of their territory, settling in four villages from Mission Creek eastward to the agency on the Kansas River, and attempted to compete for buffalo with the Pawnee. They suffered from smallpox in 1831 and 1833 and again in 1839. In 1846 the Kaw were pressured by the United States to cede more land and were awarded a small reservation in Kansas on the Neosho River near the Santa Fe Trail, where they stayed until pressured to remove to Indian Territory in the 1870s (see map 7). They struggled to survive on this Neosho reservation, for traders and American squatters overran their land. When Kansas Territory was opened in 1854, trespassing escalated. In 1859 they were pressured into ceding some of the reservation land. Another smallpox epidemic during 1853–55 and poverty born of the exploitation by settlers and others contributed to a gradual decline in population.[22]

The Pawnee initially were in a better position than the less numerous Kaw and other villagers to their east and southeast. When Lewis and Clark visited the Pawnee on their 1804–06 expedition, the Southern or South Band villages were on the south bank of the Platte and they hunted high up the Platte and the Smoky Hill Rivers, still good buffalo range. They exchanged beaver pelts for the goods they needed from Americans. Soon after the Lewis and Clark expedition, the South Bands moved north, some to the Loup River. The Skiri village, decimated by smallpox in 1801, was on the Loup River, farther removed from trade. All the Pawnee numbered about 9,000. They grew corn, beans, and pumpkins and continued to make two extended hunts and to raid to the southwest, taking horses from the Comanche and other nomadic peoples as well as Spanish settlements. Teton raids began to take their toll, and the Pawnee signed treaties of peace with the United States in 1818 and 1825 and became more receptive to American demands that they curtail raiding that threatened trade along the Santa Fe Trail. The Pawnee needed guns and other trade goods from the Americans and in the 1820s were trading large numbers of buffalo robes to the traders who traveled to their villages. Even the more remote Skiri saw a need to be on good terms with the Americans to obtain trade goods. Thus, **Petalesharro**, the son of a chief, freed a Comanche captive before she could be killed in 1816. A Pawnee delegation was taken on a tour of Eastern cities in 1821 to impress them with the power of the United States. By the 1830s the Pawnee faced attacks by the Teton from the northeast, the Cheyenne and Arapaho from the west, and the Comanche and Kiowa from the south. Their hunts were less successful, and while they were away the Teton raided their villages and stole stored crops. Thus, the Pawnee also began to rely on the United States for protection and became increasingly dependent. In 1833 they ceded their lands south of the Platte River in south central Nebraska and northwestern Kansas (reserving their rights to hunt there) and built a village for the South Bands on the Loup River; the Skiri relocated nearby. But Teton Sioux attacks were unrelenting and the federal government did not protect the Pawnee as it had agreed to do. A smallpox epidemic (spread by several Sioux captives in 1838) killed many; some were saved by a federal vaccination program. The Pawnee moved farther east, closer to United States troops, in the 1840s, but government agents who settled with them could do nothing to protect them from the Sioux attacks that prevented their farming and hunting activity. The Pawnee, suffering from hunger, began to collect tolls from the settlers moving west along the Oregon (or Overland) Trail along the Platte River. In 1848 the Pawnee ceded more lands north of the Platte (a strip along the Oregon Trail) and increased their dependence on government supplies.

In 1857 the United States pressured the Pawnee to cede all their land except for a small reservation on the Loup River and, in return, promised protection (see map 7). But protection and adequate support for relocation to the reservation were not forthcoming after the Pawnee moved their villages in 1859. In the 1860s they were constantly attacked by Teton, Cheyenne, and Arapaho. Pawnee men scouted for the army against these enemies. Despite this assistance, the United States neglected the Pawnee, and their circumstances continued to worsen.[23]

Between 1873 and 1880 the Euroamerican population in Nebraska increased by 500,000. The pressure to open Indian reservations there and in Kansas to settlement led to the expulsion of the Kaw, Ponca, Pawnee, and Otoe-Missouria from their homeland to Indian Territory. In some cases, these village peoples were eager to go, for pressure on the land hindered their efforts to farm and attacks from the Teton made hunting very risky. The Kaw were the first to leave, followed by the Pawnee.

The Kaw wanted to remain on their reservation in Kansas, but the Cheyenne and the Arapaho prevented them from hunting successfully west of their villages, and they continued to have trouble with hostile American trespassers. They faced starvation and began to negotiate with the United States to move to Indian Territory, where they believed they would be more secure economically. In 1872 Congress agreed to sell their reservation in Kansas and move the Kaw to Indian Territory, where they would select a site for their reservation. The Osage already had a reservation they had purchased from the Cherokee, and they sold part of it to the Kaw. In 1873, 533 Kaw arrived indebted to the Osage until their reservation land was sold, whereupon they protested that the price they eventually received was outrageously low (see map 6).[24]

The Pawnee suffered terribly from raids by the Oglala and Brule Teton Sioux, and their population declined dramatically. The attacks prevented the Pawnee from farming and hunting successfully. They got no protection from the United States, for federal officials were attempting to placate the Sioux by providing them with guns and other supplies, while ignoring the needs of "friendly" tribes. Settlers trespassed on their reservation, stealing timber and otherwise interfering with the Pawnee. Hunger and malnutrition made them desperate. In 1873 a group of about 500 Pawnee from two South bands were encouraged by their chief, whose advice carried the weight of ritual authority, to migrate south to Indian Territory. They went to the Wichita agency, where they were welcomed as allies by the small Wichita population. The remainder of the Pawnee agreed in a treaty council in 1874 to sell their reservation in Nebraska and move south; the United States promised to pay the expenses of resettlement but reneged. The Pawnee land in Indian Territory was purchased from the Cherokee and Creek (who had received it after ceding their lands in the Southeast) with the proceeds of the sale of the Nebraska lands. The Pawnee bands all relocated there in 1875 and established separate villages, rebuilding earth lodges and planting with the seeds from their medicine bundles (see map 6).[25]

In 1858 the Ponca ceded most of their hunting territory in northwestern Nebraska. In the 1870s the eight Ponca bands lived in three villages at the eastern end of their reservation, as far away from the Teton as they could get (map 7). Like the Pawnee they faced starvation; the Brule raided them weekly, and the nearby troops refused to engage the Teton. Settlers allied with the Ponca against the Teton, but federal removal policy took precedence over the wishes of the settlers, and Congress initiated preparations for the removal in 1876. The Ponca resisted this pressure, shutting "themselves up in their lodges and houses" and wailing "through the night," as Wishart describes. Troops were sent in, and they threatened to shoot the Ponca chiefs if the Ponca did not leave; some chiefs were arrested, including **Standing Bear**. By the summer of 1877 the Ponca had moved to Indian Territory and camped on the **Quapaw** reservation, impoverished, until they were moved west to land that eventually was to become their new reservation. A small group led by Standing Bear made their way back to Nebraska in the winter of 1879. They took refuge with the Omaha, and some with the Yankton on the north bank of the Missouri River. Standing Bear's party was arrested, but there followed a public outcry led by a group of humanitarian reformers, which helped reverse the government's harsh treatment of the Ponca. In a federal court, Standing Bear was declared a "person" with the legal right to settle in Nebraska. In 1880 this small group of Poncas settled in Nebraska on a portion of their old reservation carved out of the Great Sioux Reservation (see map 7) and, known as the Northern Ponca, became politically autonomous and safe from attack from the Sioux, now recently defeated by the U.S. Army. The old Ponca reservation in Nebraska was sold in 1881 and with these funds a reservation was purchased from the Cherokee for the Southern Ponca (see map 6).[26]

The Otoe and Missouria resented federal officials' efforts to interfere with their way of life. In 1873 they began to request that the government buy their reservation and relocate them in Indian Territory where they might farm and hunt. Part of the reservation was sold in 1876 but the Otoe and Missouria received little benefit. In 1880 some of the 400 Otoe-Missouria moved to Indian Territory and in 1881 the rest followed. With the proceeds from the sale of the remainder of their reservation in Nebraska, the federal government bought the land for their reservation in Indian Territory. There they rebuilt their earth lodges and tried to live as before. The Iowa also relocated from the lower Missouri area to Indian Territory in the 1880s. A large segment of them had joined the Otoe-Missouria during the early nineteenth century. Other Iowa had lived east of the Missouri, where they had to subordinate themselves to the immigrant Sauk who moved into their territory from the east. After Missouri had become a state in 1821, in 1824 and 1830 they were pressured to sell their land in Missouri and Iowa. In 1836 the Iowa gave up all their land east of the Missouri River and moved west of the river to a small reservation on the Kansas-Nebraska border where they remained until 1854, when they ceded most of this reservation. After 1877 some moved to Indian Territory; they were assigned a reservation in 1883.[27]

With the exception of the small Northern Ponca group, only the Omaha managed to retain a reservation in Nebraska. The Omaha were regarded by the government as a people committed to self-support through farming. In fact, they produced a surplus of crops and, though poor, they were better off than the Pawnee, Ponca, and Otoe-Missouria. This success was reinforced by more liberal federal assistance than the other village peoples received in Nebraska. Humanitarian reformers, galvanized by the plight of the Ponca, worked diligently in Washington to protect the Omaha's rights to their lands in Nebraska. One advocate, Thomas Henry Tibbles, was married to **Susette La Flesche**, the daughter of an Omaha chief. Attempting to win good will, the Omaha were receptive to the establishment of schools; in 1872 they sold some land at the western border of their reservation, and in 1874 they sold additional land for a reservation for the **Winnebago,** who moved there from Wisconsin. The Omaha did not receive full payment for these lands. In 1882 anthropologist **Alice Fletcher**, also a friend of the La Flesche family, succeeded in getting Congress to grant individuals title to their farmlands. At this time the Omaha sold more of the western portion of their reservation.[28]

While the villagers were in decline, the nomadic groups (Cheyenne, Arapaho, and Teton Sioux) prospered in the early nineteenth century. The expansion of the Teton affected the Arapaho and Cheyenne as well as the villagers. Numbering upwards of 13,000, the Teton had arrived in the Missouri River valley in seven autonomous divisions (see **"Sioux"**) that sometimes assisted one another in conflicts with other groups. The Oglala were in the vanguard of the movement west; the Brule and Minneconjou generally were to their east. The other four bands, including the Hunkpapa, ranged to the northwest. Maintaining a marketplace for nomadic groups in the upland plains, the Arikaras had barred Teton expansion in the late eighteenth century, but by the 1790s the Arikara were in decline and moved north to the Northern Plains. Thereafter, the Teton began to dominate the Missouri River trade. They and the Yankton Sioux, who followed the Teton to the Missouri River, harassed the villagers on the lower Missouri, prevented American traders from bypassing them to reach new markets, and began to try to take possession of the buffalo range, making hunting difficult for the villagers.[29]

The Cheyenne were middlemen in the trade between the nomadic Arapaho and the Arikara villages at the turn of the century. The Arapaho ranged from southern Montana to the Black Hills and south to the upper North and South Platte region. When the numerous Teton Sioux began to expand west into the Black Hills, Cheyenne bands and the more numerous Arapaho allied and withdrew from the Black Hills toward the upper Platte. At this time the Arapaho bands were in northern and southern divisions, as were the Cheyenne. In these population movements, the Crow were pushed to the northwest to the Big Horn River (see **The Northern Plains**) and the Pawnee were attacked between the forks of the Platte River and the upper Republican River. The Cheyenne and the Arapaho established peace with the Teton Sioux and formed an uneasy alliance, making room for the Sioux on the Platte and expanding southward, where they came into conflict with the Kiowa, the Comanche, and the Plains Apache on the Southern Plains in the late 1820s.[30]

Relations with Americans were fairly friendly; in 1815 a peace treaty was signed with the Teton on the Missouri River and in 1825 the Teton, Yankton, and Yanktonai Sioux agreed to trade exclusively with American traders. When the demand for buffalo robes increased dramatically in the 1820s, several trading posts were built in the country of the Teton Sioux, Cheyenne, and Arapaho. Many posts of varying spans of occupancy were established by the American Fur Company; the most important were Fort Laramie and Fort Teton. The latter was built in 1817 at the mouth of the Bad or Teton River. Fort Teton became Fort Tecumseh (1822–31), which was succeeded by Fort Pierre (1831–55). Fort Laramie (1834–49) was on the North Platte in southeastern Wyoming. Oglala and Brule traded regularly there, as did the northern divisions of the Arapaho and the Cheyenne. Competitors of the American Fur Company, brothers William and Charles Bent and their partner Ceran St.Vrain, established posts on the South Platte and Arkansas rivers in 1833 and 1835 to attract the Southern Cheyenne and Arapaho (see map 7). **William Bent** married a Cheyenne woman, Owl Woman, the daughter of an important religious leader. The trade in buffalo robes made the nomadic peoples wealthy in trade goods and led to significant social change.[31]

By the late 1840s the situation of these peoples began to worsen. A cholera epidemic in 1849, followed by smallpox, cut into the population of the Arapaho and the Cheyenne, as well as other groups. The Cheyenne and the Arapaho had made peace with the Comanche, Kiowa, and Plains Apache in 1840 and begun to extend their hunts southward. But the traffic along the Santa Fe Trail, where it followed the Arkansas River, and the Oregon Trail (to Oregon and the gold fields in California) had begun to drive the buffalo away, for it wore away grazing land and timber. The Oglala and Brule and the Cheyenne and Arapaho were adversely affected when almost 158,000 emigrants passed through their hunting territory in the 1840s. In 1849 the federal government built Fort Kearney and purchased Fort Laramie and stationed troops to try to prevent trouble between Indians and Americans who came into contact. Travelers along the routes were subject to tolls collected by groups of Indians, and sometimes were robbed. The United States also sought to make peace treaties.[32]

In 1851 a council was held near Fort Laramie in which Arapaho, Cheyenne, and several bands of Teton Sioux camped alongside Assiniboine, Crow, Shoshone, Mandan, Hidatsa, and Arikara from north of the Platte River. This was a gathering of about 10,000 Indians. One thousand Sioux warriors paraded on horseback, singing, through the camps in columns four abreast. The Cheyenne parade followed. The government attempted to secure consent to travel through (not settle in) the tribal territories and to curtail intertribal warfare. Federal officials also insisted that the Teton, Cheyenne, and Arapaho each select a head chief to act as representative and spokesman. The Teton, organized into many politically autonomous bands, were uncomfortable with this kind of centralization of authority, and the man selected was assassinated subsequent to the treaty council. The Arapaho had a theocratic tradition that helped validate intermediary chieftainship: Arapaho men were organized into **age-graded societies** supervised by elderly priests, and wives were incorporated into this ceremonial structure. Decisions made by priests (one of whom kept the tribal **medicine bundle**, the Flat Pipe) had supernatural sanction and obligated all the Arapaho. Thus, when the priests validated the selection of the chiefs, they could count on cooperation. The Cheyenne **military societies** drew men from different bands, but often individuals joined the society of a close relative. The societies were competitive and largely self-governing. The tribal religious ceremonies were directed by priests and policed by one of the military societies. Tribal medicine bundles helped provide a charter for conduct and a symbol of identity, but the priests of the two bundles (Medicine Hat and Arrows) could not make decisions on behalf of all the Cheyenne. Hoping to mobilize support for the treaty, the Cheyenne selected their Arrow bundle keeper as head chief.[33]

Peace lasted until 1854, when troops provoked a clash near Fort Laramie. Some Minneconjou seized a ferry near the fort in frustration over problems resulting from the traffic westward. Troops retaliated and in the melee killed some Minneconjou warriors. In response a warrior shot a cow belonging to an emigrant. The chief of his band attempted to settle the matter as required by the 1851 treaty, but soldiers provoked a fight with a camp of Brule near the post. In the incident, the chief of the Brule was killed and the warriors in the camp returned fire. All the soldiers were killed (see **Grattan Massacre**). For several months afterward the Teton made revenge attacks on the road, attacking mail wagons and stealing horses. The Cheyenne tried to stay away from the Platte road, but they were angry that the annuities (see **annuity payments**) promised in the treaty did not arrive. Months later, the United States retaliated against the Teton. General **William Harney** ordered "friendly" Sioux, Cheyenne, and Arapaho to Fort Laramie and tried to attack the bands still hunting on the plains. A camp of Brule not involved in the Grattan incident was attacked and possibly 136 killed; the others were taken captive. In the fight the Brule warrior **Spotted Tail** was wounded twice from bullets and twice from saber cuts. Harney demanded that any warriors involved in the raiding surrender, presumably for execution by federal officials. Spotted Tail was taken into custody; he was pardoned by President F. Pierce and spent 1855 under guard at Fort Leavenworth, where he became convinced that war with the United States was not feasible. He returned to his people in 1856. Peace was restored that year, and Harney obtained promises from the Sioux to remain at peace with the United States.[34]

Meanwhile, although the Cheyenne tried to stay away from the troubles on the Platte River, they were becoming increasingly frustrated and had resorted to collecting tolls on the roads again. Of particular concern was the fact that roads were being built through their good hunting ground on the Smoky Hill and Republican rivers and settlers, in violation of the treaty, were occupying the Smoky Hill region. Professional buffalo hunters were killing buffalo for the hides, leaving the meat to rot—in a time when it was increasingly difficult to hunt successfully due to the traffic through the area. As the grievances mounted, a fissure developed between Cheyennes who believed that they had to remain at peace with the Americans and those who felt that war was the best solution. At this time the Northern and Southern Cheyenne became politically autonomous, with the former bands withdrawing north of the Platte, joining with the Oglala and Northern Arapaho, and committing to defending the buffalo range there. During the late 1850s and early 1860s, Cheyenne relations with the United States were intermittently hostile: Cheyenne would raid for booty to supplement their resources; peace chiefs (that is, men committed to maintaining peace within their society and responsible for arranging peace with outside groups) would attempt to smooth over the incidents; army officers would overreact and attack the Cheyenne indiscriminately; peace chiefs would lose credibility; and the cycle would begin again. The Arapaho took little part in the Cheyenne raids during 1856. They struggled to stay on good terms with the Americans in 1857 as well.[35]

Just a few months later in 1858–59, after gold was discovered in Colorado in the best winter range of the Arapaho, this area was invaded by 150,000 miners who traveled to Colorado along the buffalo range of the Republican and Smoky Hill rivers as well as the Platte road. The Cheyenne and Arapaho found it more difficult to hunt buffalo. The Arapaho suffered severe population loss from smallpox and cholera when prospectors and adventurers flooded into their territory and began to establish towns. The miners cared nothing for the treaty rights of the Arapaho and Cheyenne. The Arapaho head chief **Little Raven** worked diligently to keep the peace, but the Southern Arapaho and Cheyenne bands found it increasingly difficult to obtain enough game to prevent hunger. Settlers in Colorado, eager to evict Indians from the area and reacting with anger and fear to the news of the **Sioux Uprising** in Minnesota, pressed for cession treaties and paid little attention to the rights of the Arapaho and Cheyenne on these lands guaranteed to them in the 1851 treaty. Some Cheyenne chiefs as well as Little Raven tried to negotiate for a reservation in the area. In 1861, at the Treaty of Fort Wise, the Arapaho chiefs and the Cheyenne peace chiefs agreed to cede much of the 1851 territory and accept a reservation within the upper Arkansas region if they were guaranteed protection. But the treaty provisions were not followed by the United States, and thus they did not settle there. Cheyenne **Dog Soldiers** rejected the agreement and continued to defend their right to live and hunt in the Smoky Hill area. Military posts were built in response to the escalating discord. There were a series of incidents in which Cheyennes raided settlers (illegally occupying their territory) for booty and subsequently were attacked by the United States army, after which they retaliated. The Arapaho generally refrained from participating in the Cheyenne skirmishes, but occasionally stole stock from settlers for food. After the troops withdrew in response to the outbreak of the Civil War, local militias formed, committed to exterminating the Indians in Colorado Territory. Cheyenne peace chief **Black Kettle** tried to get protection from the federal government in return for guaranteeing peaceful relations. The Arapaho followed the orders of federal and territorial officials and, along with Black Kettle's and other peace chiefs' bands, went to camp on Sand Creek. There, Black Kettle's camp and some Arapahos with him were attacked by Colorado militia on November 29, 1864. This killing and mutilation of scores of men, women, and children led to an Indian war in the Platte valley and adjacent areas in which Teton joined the Arapaho and Cheyenne, as did some Comanche and Kiowa, in retaliating for the **Sand Creek Massacre**. Travelers, settlers, and miners were at risk during this time, as Indians attacked ranches, stagecoaches, telegraph stations, and the town of Julesberg.[36]

The Southern Arapaho made peace with the United States in 1865, as did a number of Cheyenne peace chiefs. Little Raven and Black Kettle represented their followers in agreeing to accept a reservation south of the Arkansas and cede the rest of the land assigned to them in 1851, although they retained the right to hunt between the Arkansas and Platte rivers. But many of the other Cheyenne bands took no part in the treaty council of October 1865. Other Cheyenne (see **Dog Soldiers**), reeling from continued attacks by the army on their camps, continued to retaliate when they could. Trespassing settlers in the Smoky Hill region threatened the subsistence of the Cheyenne and the Arapaho, who in response harassed settlers there. Peaceful relations characterized 1866, but in the spring of 1867 the army provoked the Cheyenne into another period of warfare. The Arapaho tried to stay south of the region where the Cheyenne and the troops came into conflict. General **W. S. Hancock** and Lt. Colonel George Custer located a camp of Cheyenne and Sioux and advanced, sending the women and children into a panic. The warriors formed a line between the troops and the village, and the chiefs met with Hancock and tried to persuade him to hold a council at some distance from the village. But the general surrounded the village, the occupants of which had fled during the chiefs' negotiations. Custer pursued them and Hancock had their village — 111 Cheyenne lodges and 140 Teton lodges and their contents — burned. In retaliation the Cheyenne began raids on the Republican and Smoky Hill valleys and attacked troops when they encountered them. Public pressure against respecting treaty rights encouraged the army to exterminate the Cheyenne and Arapaho. However, Congress decided to establish another peace commission and negotiate a settlement with the tribes. Another peace council was held at Medicine Lodge Creek (see **Medicine Lodge Creek Treaty**) in October 1867. The Arapaho protected the commissioners and the provisions they brought for the participants, and they asked to be treated separately from the Cheyenne.[37]

The Southern Arapaho and some Cheyenne bands led by Black Kettle made peace and agreed to leave southern Wyoming and Colorado for a reservation in Indian Territory between the Cimarron and Arkansas rivers where they could hunt undisturbed. Cheyenne bands hunting in the Republican River valley came into conflict with settlers there in the summer of 1868, and troops pursued Cheyenne camps. After several skirmishes, the army ordered peaceful bands to go to Fort Cobb on the Washita River and prepared to exterminate the bands out hunting on the prairie. The Arapaho, led by Little Raven, and the Cheyenne under Black Kettle and the peace chiefs went to the Fort Cobb vicinity and tried to get assurances of protection. But Custer led his troops toward the Washita River and with the help of Osage scouts attacked Black Kettle's camp in November 1868. The lodges and horses were destroyed, and women and children were killed while running away. Farther down the river were the Arapaho camps, other Cheyenne camps, and some Kiowa and Comanche visitors. They rode to Black Kettle's rescue and Custer retreated. The Arapaho and most of the Cheyenne fled south to the Wichita Mountains. Subsequently, Custer took several Cheyenne chiefs hostage under a flag of truce while pursuing Cheyenne camps. The survivors agreed to settle on a reservation south of the Arkansas River. The Dog Soldier band fled north and, with the help of Pawnee scouts, were intercepted by Major E. A. Carr and defeated. Survivors surrendered to the army and prepared to remove to the reservation. Little Raven and other leaders objected to the location of this reservation, and in response, in the fall of 1869 President Ulysses S. Grant set aside a reservation at another location in what is now west central Oklahoma for the Southern Arapaho and Southern Cheyenne (see map 6). By 1870 the Southern Arapaho and the Cheyenne were regularly visiting the reservation for supplies. The Teton (except for Spotted Tail's Brule), Northern Cheyenne, and Northern Arapaho had already moved north to the buffalo range in the Powder River and Big Horn River area where they fought the army on the Northern Plains.[38]

During the Indian wars of the mid-1860s and 1870s the army relied on Indian scouts and auxiliaries, not only Osage and Pawnee, in virtually every theater and conflict in the west. In 1866 Congress provided for indeterminate enlistments of Indians, which, unlike those of other soldiers, could be terminated if a soldier wished. Scouts wore moccasins and used their own horses but were issued a uniform and a repeating carbine rifle. They enabled the army to accommodate to the local terrain and natives' tactics; commanders depended on Indian soldiers in matters of mobility, concealment, and surprise. Sometimes Indian scouts as well as auxiliaries engaged in combat. Native men enlisted to help their people's position in relation to the United States and to more effectively combat enemy tribes, as well as to help themselves achieve prominence in their own society through acts of bravery. Scouting provided a man with extra rations for his family at the agency, and a scout could keep horses and other property seized from the enemy.[39]

THE NORTHERN PLAINS

The Northern Plains was home to several nomadic peoples and to the Mandan, Hidatsa, and Arikara villagers on the upper Missouri River. The entry of American traders marked the beginning of the decline of the villagers, as in the lower

Missouri region. The nomadic groups prospered at first, then some were adversely affected by the overland trail and the opening of new trails into Montana in the 1860s. These groups divided along "friendly"–"hostile" lines, largely depending on whether American or Sioux trespass was the more disadvantageous. By the 1870s all the nomadic groups had to make peace with the United States and accept settlement on reservations.

When Lewis and Clark went up the Missouri River in 1804–05, they learned that the Arikara had consolidated into three villages above the mouth of the Grand River. Progressing upriver, they spent time at the villages of the Mandan and the Hidatsa. The latter had consolidated their villages into three, which they located near the mouth of the Knife River. The Mandan had built two villages south of the mouth of the Knife. One village represented the consolidation of two and the other of seven Mandan villages. Until the smallpox epidemic of 1837, the Mandan and Hidatsa lived much as they had in the late eighteenth century. Their earth lodges were built and owned by the women in the **matrilineal clans** that, along with a **moiety** system, formed the basis of social organization. Families moved to smaller lodges in the timbered bottom land in the winter. Women grew several varieties of corn, beans, squash, and sunflowers. Men hunted, focusing on the bison, and fish were an important source of food. Buffalo carcasses also were retrieved from the river in the spring. Metal technology obtained from traders had been adopted, but in Mandan sacred ritual the pre-trade technology was used: for example, the shoulder-blade bone hoe rather than a hoe with a metal blade. The combination of villages had led to political reorganization, though in ways compatible with tradition. For example, the Hidatsa had village councils on matters of war; in the early nineteenth century these were combined into one war council. A hierarchy of tribal bundles that were used in ceremonies and owned by representatives of clans and villages and dramatic reenactments of creation stories occupied much of the villagers' time. Adults also were organized into age-graded societies for men and women, one of which, the men's Black Mouths society, was common to both Mandan and Hidatsa and served to police their respective villages. The Arikara villages were arranged like those of the Mandan and Hidatsa. Farming was somewhat more important to them than hunting, and fishing in the river was a regular activity. The Arikara did not have clans; rather, kinship was organized bilaterally. The houses and crops passed through the female line and ritual status through the male line. Elite families furnished the leaders, as in Mandan and Hidatsa villages. The consolidation of Arikara villages brought about serious political conflicts because a large number of chiefs from different bands vied for political position. The origin stories of the Arikara differed from those of the Mandan and Hidatsa, but their ceremonies also were dramatizations of those events. The Arikara had three kinds of medicine bundles: village bundles important in agriculture, medicine society bundles central to curing rites, and household bundles dedicated to the regeneration of corn. Arikara medicine societies drew males from all the bands, as did the numerous societies with military and social functions, including the Black Mouth society.[40]

After the Lewis and Clark expedition, American traders began to push up the Missouri and past the Mandan and Hidatsa villages to try to trap and trade directly on the upper Missouri. The British became less active in the region after the War of 1812, so Americans controlled the trade. Posts were maintained near the Mandan and Hidatsa even while the traders expanded. The villages remained trade centers, drawing Cree and Assiniboine from Canada and the nomadic Crow and Cheyenne and others from the west. The Indians traded corn to the Americans. Disease and attacks from the northern Teton, Yanktonai, and Yankton Sioux continued to result in population losses. In 1834 the Sioux destroyed two of the Hidatsa villages, and the residents moved into the Mandan villages. The Hidatsa raided other peoples even west of the foothills of the Rockies and returned with captive women and children to incorporate into their villages or, in the case of the women, to sell to employees of the trade companies. **Sacajawea** was such a captive, sold to the trader Toussaint Charbonneau, who took her as consort. The Hidatsa also refused alcohol and spent more time on the hunt than the Mandan, which may have spared them some of the effects of the diseases brought by the traders. The Arikara faced more serious problems. They tried to stop traders from going upriver, in order to defend their position as middlemen and to stop tribes to the north and west from getting guns. The Teton dominated them in trade and drove the buffalo away from their villages so that the Arikara would buy meat and hides from them. Eventually, attacks by the Teton forced them to consolidate into two villages by 1811. In 1823 they attacked an American trading party, which resulted in a punitive expedition led by General Henry Leavenworth from Fort Atkinson, assisted by 750 Teton and Yankton warriors. The Arikara temporarily fled the Missouri River area. In 1825 General Henry Atkinson (see **Atkinson-O'Fallon expedition**) made treaties of peace with the Mandan, Hidatsa, and Arikara and secured promises that the villagers would trade exclusively with Americans. The Arikara returned to their villages on the Missouri and remained there until 1833 when, plagued by the Teton and in economic decline, they moved to the Skiri village on the Loup for two years, then lived as nomadic hunters for two years, eventually returning to the Missouri River in the vicinity of the Mandan villages in 1837.[41]

By the 1830s the trade in buffalo robes had supplanted the trade in beaver pelts. Fort Union, built at the mouth of the Yellowstone River in 1829 near the Crow and Assiniboine, became the pivot of the American Fur Company trade on the upper Missouri, and in 1832 it could be reached by steamboat, which allowed for a heavier trade in robes. Fort Clark was established at the Mandan and Hidatsa villages in 1831 (see map 7), but the villagers' trade was secondary. The director of the post was married to a Mandan woman, as were many other employees, so they were still able to obtain trade goods, and the federal government often appointed the company's men as Indian agents who distributed goods from the government. In 1837 the Mandan, Hidatsa, and Arikara contracted smallpox from the traders. The Mandan may have lost as much as 90 percent of their population. Throughout the epidemic the Sioux kept up attacks on the villages. One Mandan village was burned by the Teton in 1839 and the survivors subordinated themselves to a band of Sioux whose leader was part Mandan, his mother having been a captive. The Arikara moved into the second Mandan village. The Hidatsa eventually relocated north and in 1845 founded Like-a-Fishhook village (see map 7), higher up the Missouri. Mandans gradually joined them there, and the American Fur Company built Fort Berthold to serve this new village and maintained Fort Clark for the Arikara. By this time the Mandan and Hidatsa needed supplies from the United States to offset their reduced ability to make a living from farming and hunting, for the Teton continued to plunder their crops and ambush hunting parties. The Mandan and Hidatsa also had to adjust their ceremonial life by altering rules for the transmission of bundles in order to ensure that bundles were cared for, combining clan memberships and, after 1837, discontinuing moiety exogamy. Possibly as few as 23 Mandan males survived the 1837 epidemic. Mandan women married men from other groups, but the husbands had to agree to accept adoption into Mandan society and to rear children as Mandan. Ceremonial life became more intensive, as they looked to supernatural sources of power to rebuild their society. The Mandan and Hidatsa each maintained their own section of Like-a-Fishhook village, but gradually the Hidatsa participated in Mandan ceremonies and their clans became equated.[42]

Lewis and Clark did not visit the camps of the nomadic Crow, Gros Ventre, and Blackfeet. Except for the Crow, who retained some aspects of Hidatsa social organization, these nomadic groups had bilateral descent systems (in which individuals could count equally on their father's and mother's relatives), which helped them maintain flexibility in the size of their bands. Their camps moved throughout the year in response to needs of pasture for horses and access to buffalo. The tepee was easily transported by horses, and meat and plant foods were preserved by drying methods. These tribes each had one or more **medicine bundle**s that linked them to their creation and symbolized their covenant with supernatural forces. They came together at least once a year for a religious ceremony, the features of which varied by tribe (see **Sun Dance**). These tribes felt the effects of disease less than the villagers and were less dependent on the traders.

The Crow were separated into three north-to-south divisions at the beginning of the century: the River Crow, the Mountain Crow, and the Kicked in the Bellies (who split off from the Mountain Crow). Among the nomadic groups, the Crow were known to be among the friendliest to Americans. They were also among the wealthiest. Rich in horses obtained largely from Shoshone and other middlemen who were in regular contact with the Comanche, the Crow had large lodges, beautiful hide clothing, and ample mounts for hunting and warfare and for transporting people and household goods. They were eager to establish trade relations with the American fur traders in the early nineteenth century, for they needed guns and ammunition and metal items. Obtaining these in the Hidatsa village was more expensive and required a long trip. They welcomed Manuel Lisa and others. Disinterested in the alcohol that groups on the lower Missouri purchased from the Americans, the Crow instead purchased an ample supply of household utensils and decorative items, including blue glass trade beads. Their beautifully beaded clothing was admired by traders throughout the region. Crow horses were noted for their decorated riding gear. The Crow trapped beaver and brought provisions to the traders, whose goods helped them defend themselves against Blackfeet and Gros Ventre moving south and Cheyenne, Arapaho, and southern Teton moving north into Crow country. The Atkinson-O'Fallon expedition met with Crow representatives in 1825 in a Hidatsa village and tried to ensure their loyalty to American traders. The Crow viewed the Americans as potentially important military allies, for they had recently been defeated in battle by the Teton and Cheyenne, losing 400 people to captivity and about 5,000 lodges with their contents. In 1829 Fort Union was built on the eastern edge of Crow territory, and in 1832 the American Fur Company built Fort Cass in Crow territory (see map 7) and began to purchase buffalo robes in large numbers; the robes were loaded on steamboats and shipped downriver to St. Louis. Crow bands grew in size as they consolidated to be nearer the trading posts. As the Teton began to move into their eastern range and challenge them for hunting territory, military organization took on more importance.[43]

Like the Crow, the Gros Ventre were small in population relative to the other tribes on the Northern Plains. The easternmost group in the Blackfeet confederacy, they bore the brunt of attacks from the allied Cree and Assiniboine. In these circumstances the Gros Ventre developed institutions that promoted an intensely military ethos. Men were motivated to undertake military careers by their incorporation into a moiety system (see **moieties**) whereby men's military societies were associated with either the Wolf or the Star moiety and competed against each other in military exploits; the losers in the competition suffered great embarrassment. Men would choose an "enemy-friend" from the opposite moiety and try to compete with that rival in acts of bravery.

The Gros Ventre and Crow emphasized personal rivalry more than other tribes in the region; the Crow developed a similar kind of institutionalized competition: two military societies became preeminent in the nineteenth century, and they competed against each other. The Gros Ventre also were relatively wealthy in horses (which enabled them to trade large numbers of robes) and, like in Crow society, this wealth was channeled into demonstrations of competitive generosity. In the Gros Ventre case, for example, enemy-friends competed to exhibit generous distribution of property to others.[44]

The Blackfeet groups (three divisions—Blackfeet, Blood, and Piegan—which ranged roughly from north to south) numbered from 16,500 to 20,000 and were allied with the Gros Ventre and **Sarcee**. They traded provisions and horses to the Hudson's Bay Company posts in the Saskatchewan region and vigorously prevented Americans from trapping and trading in northern Montana until the 1830s. They were attempting to prevent Americans from selling guns to their Crow enemies to the south. The Blackfeet robbed Americans and sold their goods to Hudson's Bay Company traders. They also fought the Assiniboine and Cree, allies who were trying to move into northeastern Montana and the Saskatchewan valley to extend their hunting territory. In 1831 the American Fur Company obtained consent from the Blackfeet to build posts in their territory on the condition that the Americans would not hunt but instead would purchase hides and robes from Blackfeet hunters. Robes were in demand in the eastern United States in the 1830s and 1840s for overcoats and sleigh and carriage blankets, and the Blackfeet prospered. For many years the trader in charge of company posts was Alexander Culbertson, married to a Blackfeet (Blood) woman, Medicine Snake Woman. In 1837 the Blackfeet contracted smallpox from their contact with traders and lost two thirds of their population. They were able to recoup losses by adopting and marrying captives in the 1840s.[45]

The Assiniboine were dispersed in small bands throughout the Canadian plains and in Montana and North Dakota on the north side of the Missouri River. Many gradually moved south from Canada into Montana during 1800–37, where they had better access to buffalo and where they engaged the Gros Ventre, Crow, and Blackfeet in intense military conflict. Friendly to traders, they were welcomed by the American Fur Company, which built a fort in 1829 at the mouth of the Yellowstone River. Here, at Fort Union, the Assiniboine traded regularly; they also went north to the Hudson's Bay Company posts and to the **Red River Métis** settlements to trade. Poor in horses, they had to purchase them from traders or raid the Gros Ventre, Blackfeet, and Crow. In 1838 they contracted smallpox from traders and lost more than half of their population. As the trader Edwin Denig, married to an Assiniboine woman, described it, "The dead were daily thrown into the river by cart loads. Others attempted to run away from it. The different roads were dotted with carcasses and occasionally lodges standing in which whole families lay dead. A singular characteristic of this disease was that two-thirds or more died before any eruption appeared. This event was always accompanied by hemorrhages from the mouth and ears." At about the same time, the Teton were pressing them from the east. Comparably small in numbers and weakened by smallpox, the Assiniboine began to try to make peace and ally with the groups to their west in order to hold back the Teton. They also maintained their alliance with the numerous **Plains Cree**, which allowed them easy access to the Hudson's Bay Company traders.[46]

The Sioux groups had pushed to and beyond the Missouri River by the beginning of the nineteenth century. The Yankton ranged on both the northeast and the southwest sides of the river and dominated the trade in the vicinity of Fort Vermillion (see map 7). In several bands, they sometimes allied with other Sioux but generally stayed in the southeastern part of Sioux territory. In 1812 Manuel Lisa opened an agency near their villages where they got supplies to supplement crops and meat from buffalo hunts. As the buffalo gradually moved west, the Yankton had to follow and displace other tribes from the hunting grounds. Eventually, they were dependent on the traders, for the buffalo ranged too far west, and Yankton women became wives of many of the traders in Yankton country. They signed peace treaties with the United States in 1815 and 1825 and were regarded as friendly, avoiding conflict with Americans. They ceded land east of the Missouri in 1830 at the Treaty of Prairie du Chien, and with some Santee allies began to hunt west of the Missouri where they adapted to prairie life, influenced by the Ponca and others. After about 1845 they separated into several smaller bands and, as game became scarce, began to frequent the Missouri River posts regularly. The Yanktonai were less close to the traders and sometimes came in conflict with them. Yanktonai were organized into bands and these bands into two divisions that were politically autonomous, but, like the other Sioux groups, often cooperated, particularly against other tribes. They hunted on both sides of the Missouri River and made war against the Assiniboine and Cree and the Mandan and Hidatsa as they pushed into the buffalo country on the Northern Plains. They continued to trade in Canada during the first part of the century, although they signed the Atkinson-O'Fallon Treaty in 1825. By the 1830s they were trading with the American Fur Company at Fort Pierre. The northern Teton, including the Hunkpapa, also ranged into the Northern Plains, sometimes as far as the Yellowstone, where they fought the Crow and others, as well as the Mandan and Hidatsa. They made alliances with the northern bands of Cheyenne and Arapaho and were generally friendly to American traders. By mid-century, though, relations had begun to sour between the United States and the Sioux.[47]

The northern Teton and the Yankton had representatives at the Fort Laramie Treaty of 1851. That same year the Santee division, still living in Minnesota but sometimes traveling to Yankton territory to hunt, signed a treaty in which they ceded their lands in Minnesota and Iowa and accepted two small reservations on the Minnesota River. These Sioux peoples had had an agency since 1819, and missionaries who settled there developed a writing system for the Sioux language so that Christian literature would be accessible. At about the same time General Harney was retaliating against the southern Teton bands on the Central Plains, some Santee, angered by treaty violations, attacked settlers in the border area between Minnesota and Iowa. Other Santee, fearing United States reprisals, retaliated and drove them west, where they allied with other Sioux. The westward movement of settlers led to more land cessions. In 1858 the Yankton ceded most of their land in Minnesota and eastern Dakota territory in return for a small reservation on the east bank of the Missouri River. Pressed by trespassing settlers and unable to hunt successfully, they opted to maintain peace with the United States, even furnishing scouts in the military engagements between the United States and the western Sioux. That same year the Santee ceded more land. But this did not end their troubles. In frustration over treaty violations and facing starvation, some Santee, aided by a few Yankton and Yanktonai of eastern Dakota, attacked settlers in 1862 and killed some 800 (this was called the **Sioux Uprising**). Forty Santee, some innocent, were executed by the United States, and troops retaliated throughout 1863–64, pursuing Santees who fled west into modern North Dakota (Dakota Territory) and to Canada. Troops indiscriminately attacked northern Teton Sioux, Santee, and Yanktonai at the battle of Killdeer Mountain (see map 7) in July 1864 and destroyed their possessions and lodges. Many Santee fled to Montana and Canada, and some settled on the Yankton reservation on the Missouri River. These events were common knowledge among the Sioux and others on the Northern Plains and reinforced suspicion of the United States's intent and a determination to hold on to the buffalo country west of the Missouri. In 1865 the United States signed the Treaty of Fort Sully with representatives from each of the seven Teton divisions. Some bands agreed to peace and right of way for roads in return for supplies and provisions but may not have understood the terms of the treaty, and many bands were not represented. A reservation was established on the Missouri (Lower Brule). Few Sioux settled there.[48]

The survival of the nomadic groups' way of life was threatened beginning in 1865 when gold was discovered in Montana and the Bozeman Trail was opened from Fort Laramie north to Montana through the Powder River buffalo country. The army built posts in 1865, 1866, and 1867. The Sioux, Northern Cheyenne, and Northern Arapaho harassed the army and the prospectors, killing troops when they could. Assisted by Pawnee and Omaha scouts, the army had fought to defend the posts in the Powder River country but had not been successful in stopping the Sioux and their allies, who, led by **Red Cloud**, prevented the settling of Montana. Groups of northern Teton and Yanktonai also attacked Americans they regarded as interfering with hunting in Montana. Rather than relying only on military strategies, the federal government embarked on a policy of establishing peace and distributing provisions to compensate Indians for the loss of hunting opportunities (see **Grant's peace policy**). In 1868 a peace council was held at Fort Laramie with all the Teton (including the southern Teton, who came north after the 1864–65 war on the Southern Plains), Northern Cheyenne, and Northern Arapaho, and the United States agreed to abandon the forts and close the Bozeman Trail. The Northern Arapaho had suffered heavy losses during the Powder River war and by 1868 were seeking to separate themselves from the Northern Cheyenne and Teton Sioux and make peace with the United States. Northern Cheyenne representatives also signed the treaty but, like the Arapaho, insisted that they had as much right to the Northern Plains country as the Sioux. The goal of the Northern Cheyenne and Arapaho was to obtain reservations in their Northern Plains territory apart from the Sioux and each other and to avoid being sent to Indian Territory. A Great Sioux Reservation was established in South Dakota west of the Missouri with four agencies along the Missouri River where supplies were issued to Sioux, Cheyenne, and Arapaho; the right to hunt in the Powder River country and elsewhere was maintained (see map 7). The buffalo country still was threatened, however, for the federal government then turned its attention to building the Northern Pacific Railroad across the Northern Plains. In 1869 a peace council was held at Fort Buford, where United States representatives met with some Yanktonai and some of the Santee refugees. These people wanted to remain peacefully in Montana where they could hunt. Northern Teton groups in alliance with Yanktonai also were determined to hunt in Montana. The southern Teton, under Red Cloud, were dissatisfied with the location of their agency. The United States, anxious to confine the Teton on reservations, brought a delegation, including Red Cloud and Spotted Tail, to Washington in 1870. Eventually, after another delegation in 1872, the federal government established agencies for the Oglala as well as the Brule on the White River, closer to the buffalo and the traders west of the Missouri River. In 1872 the Northern Cheyenne became involved in a conflict over the custody of one of their two tribal medicine bundles and, during the quarrel, the bundle was damaged. This act was viewed by the Cheyenne as an omen of disaster to come. In fact, for the next six years the fortunes of the Northern Cheyenne declined.[49]

There was relative peace on the Northern Plains from 1869 to 1873. But Congress declared an end to treaty making in 1871 and, thereafter, Plains peoples were to have little leverage in their dealings with the federal government. Many northern Teton and Yanktonai stayed away from the agencies in South Dakota, some returning periodically for supplies but spending most of their time in Montana following the buffalo herds that were concentrated there. Some of the Assiniboine allied with the Sioux in Montana. The Red River Métis challenged the Sioux in northern Montana, coming in large numbers to hunt. The United States attempted to draw the Sioux into the Fort Peck agency, established in 1873 to provide supplies to "friendly" Sioux and win over some of the "hostiles" to agency life. The hostile Sioux in Montana were under the leadership of **Sitting Bull** in the 1870s. They were able to obtain guns and ammunition from the Red River Métis and largely stayed away from the agency. Military surveys in preparation for building the Northern Pacific Railroad through the buffalo country led to skirmishes with Sitting Bull's warriors during 1871–73, and in 1873 George Custer engaged the Sioux in battles twice in the valley of the Yellowstone. Peace commissions and delegations did not pacify the northern Sioux; in fact, some of the southern Teton under **Crazy Horse** joined the resistance in Montana, and the Sioux won a victory in the establishment of an agency for them, outside the Great Sioux Reservation. Relations took a turn for the worse when a military expedition led by General George Custer found gold in the Black Hills (on the Sioux Reservation), which initiated a rush of trespassing miners and led to more skirmishes. The federal government allowed 15,000 miners to trespass on the reservation and began to try to get the Sioux to cede the Black Hills, without success. Therefore, in December 1875 the army asked all Sioux to surrender their horses and guns and threatened military attacks on those who did not. In 1876, with the help of Crow and Arikara scouts, the army attacked camps of Northern Cheyenne and Arapaho and Sioux, destroying their lodges and provisions. The strategy was to launch a winter campaign during which camps could be more easily located and provisions destroyed and to make war on combatants and noncombatants alike. Crow, Shoshone, and Arikara scouts assisted the army, several times saving the troops from being overrun. The war culminated in the defeat of Custer at the **Battle of the Little Bighorn** in the summer of 1876 (see map 7).[50]

In 1876 a peace commission met with the Teton, Northern Cheyenne, and Northern Arapaho to arrange the cession of the Black Hills. The United States threatened to withhold all annuities, by this time necessary to the survival of native people on the Plains. They obtained signatures on the agreement short of the number required by the Treaty of 1868 (three fourths of the men had to agree to make it valid). Many of the Sioux and Arapaho, as well as Pawnee, Crow, and Shoshone men, enlisted as scouts and helped the army renew its campaign against the Northern Cheyenne and "hostile" Sioux, still led by Crazy Horse and Sitting Bull. In doing so, they kept their horses and guns and obtained food and provisions for their families. The Northern Arapaho used their association with army officers to obtain permission to settle on a reservation in Wyoming (see map 7). Military posts were built on the Tongue and

Bighorn rivers to facilitate the war in Yellowstone country. The army attacked and burned Cheyenne villages during the summer of 1876 after the Custer fight, and peace chiefs attempted to negotiate with federal officials for an agency on the Northern Plains; some Cheyenne enlisted as scouts. In November, with help from Cheyenne and Pawnee scouts, the army destroyed the camp of Cheyennes **Little Wolf** and **Dull Knife** on Powder River. All winter the army attacked camps in the Yellowstone valley. In spring 1877 Little Wolf and Dull Knife negotiated the surrender of the Northern Cheyenne, and more Cheyenne men began to scout for the army. The Northern Cheyenne insisted on their right to remain on the Northern Plains, but they were sent to the Southern Cheyenne and Arapaho reservation in Indian Territory in 1878, where they stayed until Little Wolf and Dull Knife led an escape that eventually resulted in their settlement on a reservation in Montana. Many Sioux, led by Sitting Bull, fled to Canada out of reach of the troops. Sitting Bull refused peace overtures from United States officials, whom he distrusted. More Sioux joined him when Crazy Horse was killed while in custody at the agency. The hostiles, numbering perhaps 4,000, periodically came across the border and hunted in Montana. The winter of 1880–81 was particularly harsh and there were few buffalo in Canada. Groups of Sitting Bull's followers began to surrender at the agency and obtain provisions. In January 1881, with the help of Yanktonai, Crow, and Cheyenne scouts, the army began to hunt down and attack Sitting Bull's hostiles. Their lodges were burned and their horses confiscated when they were defeated. In July Sitting Bull surrendered and was placed under guard; he was eventually sent to the Hunkpapa agency on the Great Sioux Reservation.[51]

The army's defeat of the Sioux on the Northern Plains was greatly aided by the "friendly" tribes, including the Crow. Despite the territorial assignments during the negotiation of the Treaty of 1851, where Big Robber of the Kicked in the Bellies was the main spokesman and where the Crow claimed their land in south central Montana and northern Wyoming, Sioux trespassers were a constant threat. Crow territory was invaded by the Sioux from the southeast in the mid-1860s and from the east in the 1870s. Thus it was in their interest to reject Sioux overtures to help fight the Americans and to ally with the United States, even though trespass by miners and others impeded Crow efforts to hunt after the Bozeman Trail opened. Wyoming became a state in 1868, which put pressure on the Crow to cede land. In the Treaty of 1868, they ceded some of their territory north of the Yellowstone and south of Montana but retained the heart of their hunting ground (see map 7). **Sits in the Middle of the Land** was the main intermediary chief at the council. He secured guarantees that the Crow would forever retain the agreed-upon reservation and could hunt outside this area. Despite the loss of territory reserved by the 1851 treaty, the Crow were able to hold on to their lands despite pressure from miners and entrepreneurs who wanted to expel them. Crow scouts helped the army contain the Sioux and end their encroachment on Crow land. The River Crow joined the other divisions at the Crow agency in 1870, where the Crow and troops at the nearby fort had to repel Sioux raids, even on the agency itself.[52]

The Gros Ventre allied with the Crow against the Sioux as they tried to hold their territory in Montana. As part of the Blackfeet confederacy, they participated in the Treaty of 1855, which assigned north central Montana to Blackfeet and Gros Ventre and initiated annuity payments (see map 7). Sioux expansion westward threatened the Gros Ventre as much as their Crow allies, and in the 1870s they also made an alliance with groups of Assiniboine who ranged as far southwest as the Milk River. The Assiniboine also were being attacked by the Sioux and needed to get supplies from the agency established for the Gros Ventre on the Milk River. The Gros Ventre desperately needed these alliances, for they were feuding with one of the Blackfeet divisions during the 1860s and 1870s and could not count on their assistance. In order to maintain good relations with the traders and United States officials, the Gros Ventre granted passage and posts through the upper Missouri valley. American settlement was south of Gros Ventre territory, so they had little problem with trespassers. With the help of Assiniboines, the Gros Ventre were able to hunt successfully in north central Montana into the 1870s. In 1873 a presidential executive order established a reduced reservation, withdrawing the southern part of the 1855 treaty reservation and establishing agencies for the Gros Ventre and Blackfeet. In 1874 more land was removed from the southern portion of the reservation, south of where the Gros Ventre hunted. The southwestern division of the Assiniboine chose to ally with the Gros Ventre to gain access to their hunting territory. They also received many horses, which they desperately needed, through this association. They sometimes went down the Missouri to the Fort Peck agency, where other Assiniboine bands were allied with the agency Sioux.[53]

The Blackfeet did not receive word in time to attend the Fort Laramie Treaty of 1851. Two years later, when newly appointed governor Isaac Stevens traveled through Montana, he initiated negotiations with the Blackfeet through the trader at Fort Union, Alexander Culbertson. Culbertson's wife, Medicine Snake Woman, insisted on helping her husband arrange a council with the Blackfeet: "My husband, where you go I will go, and where you die will I die," she reportedly said. She entertained her people with stories about her visits to St. Louis while her husband conferred with them. The Blackfeet, Blood, and northern Piegan divisions of the Blackfeet confederacy remained mostly in Canada and the southern Piegan ranged in Montana. The peace council was held in October 1855 at the mouth of the Judith River. All three Blackfeet divisions attended, as well as the Gros Ventre and representatives from the Cree and tribes from west of the Rockies who sometimes traveled to the Plains to hunt. Stevens promised that the United States had no designs on their land and agreed that the government would begin annuity payments. All present agreed to maintain peaceful relations. The Blackfeet, having little experience with American foods, threw the flour in the air and shunned the coffee. They continued their raids on Crow and Assiniboine but remained friendly to Americans until the 1860s when the Bozeman Trail opened the southern part of their range to miners and other Americans trespassing on the treaty lands on their way to the gold fields. Incidents of violence on both sides from 1865 to 1870 led to the construction of Fort Shaw in Blackfeet territory (see map 7), and early in 1870 Colonel E. M. Baker led troops to search for and attack Blackfeet wherever he found them. Baker attacked a village of a friendly chief on the Marias River, killed 173 men, women, and children, and captured 140 women and children and 300 horses, then burned the lodges and provisions. In the Eastern press, the "massacre on the Marias" was condemned and Congress changed its mind about transferring the Bureau of Indian Affairs from the Department of the Interior back to the Department of War. The Blackfeet, at the time suffering from smallpox, did not retaliate but began ranging into the north, many staying in Canada. They also refused overtures from the Sioux to join in fighting the Americans. It was to legalize the trespass of settlers on Blackfeet and Gros Ventre land that President Ulysses S. Grant established a reduced reservation in 1873 north of the Missouri River, but settlers pressed for moving the line north to the Marias and Congress made the change in 1874. The Blackfeet could not hunt regularly in what was formerly the southern section of their reservation, but they still could hunt buffalo and trade robes until the buffalo were gone at the end of the 1870s.[54]

For the friendly villagers—the Mandan, Hidatsa, and Arikara—hunting had ceased to be successful much earlier. The Mandan and Hidatsa sent two representatives to the Fort Laramie Treaty of 1851, including **Four Bears**, the noted Hidatsa chief. The Arikara sent two representatives. The territory assigned them did not include Like-a-Fishhook village, where most of the Mandan and Hidatsa were living. Four years later, the Mandan population was about 252; the Hidatsa, 760; and the Arikara, 840. But they subsequently suffered epidemics and unremitting attacks by the Teton. If the Mandan and Hidatsa went on a hunt, the Teton would rob the village. Medicine bundles and other valuables were left at Fort Berthold for safekeeping. The Mandan and Hidatsa intensified farming but still could not grow enough food. Malnutrition lowered their resistance to disease, and cholera struck in 1851 and 1853 and smallpox in 1856. All three tribes experienced significant population loss. Despite these problems, the United States neglected the agency. Roy Meyer in *The Village Indians of the Upper Missouri* characterizes two of the largely absent agents thus: one was a "drunkard and gambler, already shot through with venereal disease at the age of twenty-seven or twenty-eight," and the other was "a jolly old fellow who preferred brandy but would drink anything." The villagers complained that the Sioux got more supplies than they and continued to make war against them despite the peace treaty of 1851. The Arikara were made even more vulnerable when Fort Clark was abandoned. In 1862 they moved north and established their own section in Like-a-Fishhook, where they had allies against the Teton. The year before, the Sioux had attacked the village and killed Four Bears. The United States ignored the villagers' pleas for help. During the 1860s they became more economically dependent on the government. In 1868 the tribes' agent began to reside with them year-round, but circumstances did not improve. He gave high-quality merchandise sent by the government to the traders in return for inferior goods, which were distributed to the Indians, while the traders sold the quality goods and shared the profits with the agent. The village peoples were outraged and in protest the most important chief, White Shield, an Arikara, refused to sign a receipt for the annuity goods. The Sioux attacked Fort Berthold and burned part of Like-a-Fishhook village in 1862. Arikara and a few Mandan and Hidatsa men were able to enlist as scouts and retaliate, as well as serve as mail carriers, herders, guards, and couriers. The Sioux were particularly aggressive after 1863 when they were attempting to intimidate other tribes into joining them in a war against Americans. Traffic on the Missouri River increased, but the United States did not urge land cessions until 1866, when the Mandan and Hidatsa ceded a small tract on the east bank of the Missouri River. By executive order a large section of the reservation was opened to settlement in 1870 and in the 1880s. The prestige of chiefs and high-status clan offices began to be undercut as the agent bypassed these leaders and distributed annuities and rations directly to households. However, the Mandan, Hidatsa, and Arikara largely retained their ceremonial life and social organization, with some modification. A fourth section of the village was occupied by people with non-Indian spouses. The self-torture component of ceremonies was minimized due to pressure from American officials, and the clan organization continued to undergo consolidation—in 1862 the number of Mandan clans had decreased to four. Mandan and Hidatsa clans and societies became equated, and Mandans and Hidatsas transferred their medicine bundles to each other.[55]

In Canada the movement of settlers westward first affected the Métis (see **Red River Métis**), of French-Indian and British-Indian descent. These people, settled in the valleys of the Red and Assiniboine rivers, faced discrimination from the Hudson's Bay Company after English settlers began to take positions with the company. Many employees with Métis wives abandoned them. The Dominion of Canada, established in 1867, purchased the Hudson's Bay Company lands in 1870 and denied Métis or Indians representation in the territorial government. Métis title to their lands was also in jeopardy. These concerns motivated the Red River resistance movement in 1869, which was forcibly suppressed by Canada. Many well-armed Métis migrated west to Saskatchewan country and to Montana, where they competed for buffalo. By 1870 settlers were prepared to move into the Saskatchewan country and plans were in place to build a railroad through the Canadian plains. The Canadian government, hoping to prevent the expensive Indian wars characteristic of western expansion in the United States, set out to negotiate with the Cree and Assiniboine and the Blackfeet before conflict developed between them and settlers. The buffalo were decreasing dramatically in the late 1870s as the Sioux and Métis from Canada converged on territory already being hunted by others and as professional hunters killed thousands of buffalo for their hides. These hides, not dressed by Indian women, were in demand in the East for commercial leather.[56]

The Canadian government negotiated six treaties with the Plains Cree, the **Plains Ojibwa**, the Assiniboine, the Stoney, and the Blackfeet between 1871 and 1877, obtaining land cessions and assigning native peoples to reserves. Some groups avoided signing until subsequent years. Many Plains Cree and Assiniboine groups led by Piapot and Plains Crees led by **Big Bear** and Little Pine tried to obtain better terms from the Canadians, but supplies were withheld until they capitulated. Big Bear worked to get consolidation of reserve lands to create a stronger political base for the Cree and Assiniboine, but the Canadian government insisted on fragmenting and scattering native peoples on small reserves (see map 7). The North West Mounted Police attempted to intimidate those who resisted the terms of the treaties. By 1882 Big Bear acquiesced to the Canadian terms. Canada refused to negotiate treaties with the Métis. In 1877 it negotiated a treaty and reserves for the three northern divisions of Blackfeet and their Sarcee allies. They selected their reserves near favorite wintering places. The Blackfeet were promised annual supplies, which they needed. They also continued to hunt, raid, trade, and visit their fellow Blackfeet in Montana for several years after the treaty was made.[57]

By the 1870s the United States had succeeded in confining the native peoples of the Plains to reservations where they ostensibly would not be an impediment to American expansion westward (see map 7). But native peoples were not to be left to adapt to reservation life on their own terms.

NOTES

1. Garrick A. Bailey, "Changes in Osage Social Organization, 1673–1906," *University of Oregon Anthropological Papers* 5 (1973): 1–122, 49–56.
2. Ibid., 56–61, 70–71.
3. Ibid., 71–73.
4. F. Todd Smith, *The Wichita Indians: Traders of Texas and the Southern Plains, 1540–1845* (College Station: Texas A & M Press, 2000), 92, 93, 97–98, 101, 103, 106, 110.

5. F. Todd Smith, *The Caddo Indians: Tribes at the Convergence of Empires, 1542–1854* (College Station: Texas A & M Press, 1995), 85, 93, 97, 99, 100, 102–6, 113–15; Cecile Carter, *Caddo Indians: Where We Come From* (Norman: University of Oklahoma Press, 1995), 220–23, 226, 230–32, 238–44, 246, 251–53, 258–59.

6. Smith, *Wichita Indians*, 110–36, 145, 148–53; Carter, 257–59, 264, 266–75; Smith, *Caddo Indians*, 113–15, 118–22, 131–32, 135, 139.

7. Carter, 280, 283–84, 297, 301–6, 312–13; Smith, *Caddo Indians*, 125–26, 130–33, 139, 141, 146–51.

8. Carter, 315–16, 318, 320; Smith, *Caddo Indians*, 154–56, 160–63; F. Todd Smith, *The Caddo, The Wichita and the United States, 1846–1901* (College Station: Texas A & M Press, 1996), 15–17, 19–20, 22, 24, 27, 33.

9. Ibid., 39–47, 50–59, 63, 65–67.

10. Ibid., 65–67, 77–78.

11. Ibid., 70–71, 73, 79–80.

12. Ibid., 82–93.

13. Stanley Noyes, *Los Comanches: The Horse People, 1751–1845* (Albuquerque: University of New Mexico Press, 1993), 111–13, 115, 126, 163, 167, 192, 204, 216; Thomas W. Kavanagh, *Comanche Political History: An Ethnohistorical Perspective, 1706–1875* (Lincoln: University of Nebraska Press, 1996), 155–60, 162–63, 172, 177, 189, 197–98, 230.

14. Ibid., 210, 213, 234–35, 240–41, 243, 248, 250–51, 261–64; Noyes, 134–37, 114, 204, 207, 210–13, 236, 246, 274, 280–89.

15. Kavanagh, 295–98, 324–25, 331, 343–50, 356–60, 364–65, 368, 371, 375, 400, 402, 404–5, 410–18.

16. David J. Wishart, *The Fur Trade of the American West, 1807–1840: A Geographical Synthesis* (Lincoln: University of Nebraska Press, 1979), 42–46; David J. Wishart, *An Unspeakable Sadness: The Dispossession of the Nebraska Indians* (Lincoln: University of Nebraska Press, 1994), 7.

17. Ibid., 7, 39, 41–46, 74.

18. Ibid., 41–43, 75.

19. Ibid., 3, 36, 41–48, 78 (quote on p. 71); Wishart, *Fur Trade*, 62–66, 73, 116–19, 121–27, 161.

20. Wishart, *Unspeakable Sadness*, 59–62, 79–80, 88–90, 111–17.

21. John M. O'Shea and John Ludwickson, *Archaeology and Ethnohistory of the Omaha Indians: The Big Village Site* (Lincoln: University of Nebraska Press, 1992), 31–51 (quote on p. 35); Wishart, *Unspeakable Sadness*, 59–61, 64–66, 68, 77–78, 86–88.

22. William E. Unrau, *The Kansa Indians: A History of the Wind People, 1673–1873* (Norman: University of Oklahoma Press, 1971), 81–93, 98–107, 113, 118–19, 129, 132, 140, 147–48, 150, 159–63 (see also William E. Unrau, *The Kaw People* [Phoenix: Indian Tribal Series, 1975]).

23. John L. Champe, "Notes on the Pawnee," *Pawnee and Kansa (Kaw) Indians*, in *American Indian Ethnohistory: Plains Indians*, ed. David Agee Horr (New York: Garland, 1974), 96, 97, 100, 103, 107, 109; Wishart, *Unspeakable Sadness*, 63–66, 80–83, 90–93, 124–32.

24. Unrau, *Kansa Indians*, 200–15; Unrau, *Kaw People*, 66, 68.

25. Wishart, *Unspeakable Sadness*, 188–202.

26. Ibid., 202–16.

27. Ibid., 188, 216–26; Martha Royce Blaine, *The Ioway Indians* (Norman: University of Oklahoma Press, 1979), 119, 139.

28. Wishart, *Unspeakable Sadness*, 188, 202, 226–38.

29. John C. Ewers, *Teton Dakota: Ethnology and History* (Berkeley, CA: U.S. Department of the Interior, 1937), 7–9.

30. Loretta Fowler, *Arapahoe Politics, 1851–1978: Symbols in Crises of Authority* (Lincoln: University of Nebraska Press, 1982), 15–16, 22–23; Virginia Cole Trenholm, *The Arapahoes, Our People* (Norman: University of Oklahoma Press, 1970), 28, 30, 31, 37, 42, 43, 48, 100, 102.

31. Ewers, *Teton Dakota*, 74–76; Fowler, *Arapahoe Politics*, 23; Trenholm, 102.

32. Fowler, *Arapahoe Politics*, 22–25; George E. Hyde, *Spotted Tail's Folk: A History of the Brule Sioux* (Norman: University of Oklahoma Press, 1961), 39–43.

33. Fowler, *Arapahoe Politics*, 28–34; Hyde, 44–46; Donald J. Berthrong, *The Southern Cheyenne* (Norman: University of Oklahoma Press, 1963), 118–22.

34. Hyde, 48–68; Ewers, *Teton Dakota*, 77–79; James C. Olson, *Red Cloud and the Sioux Problem* (Lincoln: University of Nebraska Press, 1965), 9.

35. Berthrong, 128–42; Trenholm, 145, 147.

36. Hyde, 78, 83, 88–90; Berthrong, 143–227; Trenholm, 148, 153–54, 158–59, 161–63, 166, 168, 171, 174, 177, 184, 197–99.

37. Berthrong, 234–43, 256–88, 292; Trenholm, 212, 217, 219.

38. Berthrong, 289–344; Fowler, *Arapahoe Politics*, 29, 32, 33.

39. Thomas W. Dunlay, *Wolves for the Blue Soldiers: Indian Scouts and Auxiliaries with the United States Army, 1860–90* (Lincoln: University of Nebraska Press, 1982), 8–9, 43–50, 69–90, 95, 200.

40. Roy W. Meyer, *The Village Indians of the Upper Missouri: The Mandans, Hidatsas, and Arikaras* (Lincoln: University of Nebraska Press, 1977), 37, 39, 41–43, 48–50, 54, 59–82; Wishart, *Unspeakable Sadness*, 43, 45; Edward M. Bruner, "Mandan," in *Perspectives in American Indian Culture Change*, ed. Edward H. Spicer (Chicago: University of Chicago Press, 1961), 207–12, 215–18.

41. Meyer, 39, 42, 43, 50–54, 83–89.

42. Bruner, 213–14, 229–33; Meyer, 90–100.

43. Frederick E. Hoxie, *Parading Through History: The Making of the Crow Nation in America, 1805–1935* (Cambridge: Cambridge University Press, 1995), 41, 54, 62–65, 69; William Wildschut and John C. Ewers, *Crow Indian Beadwork: A Descriptive and Historical Study* (Contributions from the Museum of the American Indian, Heye Foundation, v. 16, 1959), 1–3; Norman B. Plummer, "The Crow Tribe of Indians," in *Crow Indians, American Indian Ethnohistory: Plains Indians*, ed. David Agee Horr (New York: Garland, 1974), 90–91.

44. Loretta Fowler, *Shared Symbols, Contested Meanings: Gros Ventre Culture and History, 1778–1984* (Ithaca: Cornell University Press, 1987), 26, 30, 44, 51; Hoxie, *Parading*, 78–80; Robert H. Lowie, *The Crow Indians* (New York: Farrar and Rinehart, 1935), 172–73, 191.

45. John C. Ewers, *The Blackfeet: Raiders on the Northwestern Plains* (Norman: University of Oklahoma Press, 1958), 45, 50–51, 53–56, 60, 69.

46. Edwin Thompson Denig, *Five Indian Tribes of the Upper Missouri: Sioux, Arickaras, Assiniboines, Crees, Crows* (Norman: University of Oklahoma Press, 1961), 64, 69–71, 77, 81, 89–94, 96 (quoted on p. 71).

47. Alan R. Woolworth, "Ethnohistorical Report on the Yankton Sioux," in *Sioux Indians III, American Indian Ethnohistory: Plains Indians*, ed. David Agee Horr (New York: Garland Press, 1974), 24–25, 29, 35, 38, 40, 68, 77–79, 83, 87, 108–9, 113–15, 139–54; Denig, 14–15, 25–36.

48. Woolworth, 155–98, 214, 220–23; Raymond J. DeMallie, "The Sioux in Montana and Dakota Territories: Cultural and Historical Background of the Ogden B. Read Collection," in *Vestiges of a Proud Nation: The Ogden B. Read Northern Plains Indian Collection* (Burlington, VT: Robert Hull Fleming Museum, 1986), 23–25; Robert M. Utley, *Frontiersmen in Blue: The United States Army and the Indian, 1848–1865* (New York: Macmillan, 1967), 263–80, 322–39.

49. Robert M. Utley, *Frontier Regulars: The United States Army and the Indian, 1866–1890* (New York: Macmillan Company, 1973), 93–107, 236–37; Utley, *Frontiersmen in Blue,* 315–332, 336; Olson, *Red Cloud,* 116, 119, 127, 131, 135–41, 144–70; DeMallie, 25, 27; Fowler, *Arapahoe Politics,* 43–47; Peter John Powell, *People of the Sacred Mountain: A History of the Northern Cheyenne Chiefs and Warrior Societies, 1830–1879* (San Francisco: Harper and Row, 1981), 747, 749, 760, 763, 766–67, 791, 813, 816–20, 824–26, 828, 921, 923.

50. DeMallie, 27, 28, 30, 31, 34–38; Utley, *Frontiersmen in Blue,* 237, 247–61, 345.

51. DeMallie, 39, 41–43, 45, 46, 48, 49, 52–54; Utley, *Frontier Regulars,* 273–77, 284–88; Powell, 941, 955, 1048, 1065, 1069; Fowler, *Arapahoe Politics,* 58–67.

52. Hoxie, *Parading,* 82, 83, 86–92, 106, 108–9.

53. Fowler, *Shared Symbols,* 49–50, 198–200.

54. Ewers, *Blackfeet,* 205–52, 263–73.

55. Bruner, 214, 218, 230, 236, 239, 243–45; Meyer, 102–26.

56. Olive Patricia Dickason, *Canada's First Nations: A History of Founding Peoples from Earliest Times* (Norman: University of Oklahoma Press, 1992), 257–83.

57. Ewers, *Blackfeet,* 264–66.

CHAPTER 4

Reservation Life: 1880s–1933

In 1897 two Northern Cheyennes, Spotted Hawk and Little Whirlwind, were tried for murder in a Montana court. Scapegoats for settler antagonism and racism, the men were convicted, despite the fact that their innocence had been established and their families had offered to pay damages to the family of the deceased rancher. This case figured importantly in the establishment of a land base for the Northern Cheyenne and, as we shall see, it illustrates many of the trends of the reservation era. In the 1880s and 1890s, the Plains peoples struggled to demonstrate some level of commitment to assimilation in their dealings with federal officials and, at the same time, to perpetuate a way of life that was meaningful and conducive to their survival in both an economic and a social sense. That struggle was undermined by the relentless movement of settlers and speculators into the region. During the early twentieth century, the reservation lands largely were lost, and native people were left more marginalized than when the reservations were established. Yet native communities and their underlying cultural values persisted in both old and new forms.[1]

THE AMERICANIZATION PROGRAM AND STRATEGIES FOR CULTURAL SURVIVAL, 1880s–1903

By the end of the 1870s, Plains peoples were no longer able to mount military opposition to the westward expansion of the United States. In fact, the decline

of game in the region had led to economic dependency on the U.S. government. Plains peoples had been isolated on reservations, to which often more
than one tribe had been assigned. On the reservations established under President **Grant's peace policy**, "civilization" programs directed by church representatives had failed to make Indians economically self-supporting. Then in
1879 two events led to a reform movement to change public policy toward Indians. The arrest of **Standing Bear** and his followers after their attempted return to their territory in Nebraska aroused public outrage. And the public was
appalled by the massacre of **Dull Knife**'s band of Northern Cheyenne, imprisoned at Fort Robinson after they fled from Indian Territory to return to the
Northern Plains. A group of reformers who called themselves "friends of the Indian," the most influential of whom belonged to the **Indian Rights Association**, joined forces with Western expansionists to develop a program for the assimilation of the Indian ostensibly into mainstream American society, which
would allow for the opening of tribal lands to settlement and the reduction of
federal expenses. At this time the American population in the Western states
was significantly greater than the Indian population and Indian land was coveted by Westerners. The railroads also needed land to expand westward. The
plan was to reduce reservations so that more land would be available for settlement and the remaining reservations would be used to better advantage under
the supervision of federal agents. Individuals were to be separated from tribal
communities, which were based on cooperative forms of economic organization, and extended family organization was to be replaced with nuclear family
organization. Overall, native language and lifeways were to be eradicated in
favor of English, Protestantism, and an American lifestyle. The reformers and
expansionists alike viewed the Euro-American lifestyle as superior and used this
as justification for resorting to force to change Indian lifeways. Thus, Indians,
regarded as inferior, needed the protection and guidance of representatives of
the superior society, whether they realized it or not.[2]

The assimilation program had several components. The reservations were to
be made smaller by cessions of "unused" land. The personal conduct of Indians
was to be brought into conformity with Euro-American ideals through regulations for adults and formal education for children. And missionaries were encouraged to reside in Indian communities, to lead by example and to proselytize.

Bureau of Indian Affairs officials, in cooperation with Congress, began to
reduce the size of the large reservations in the Western states, justifying the cessions largely by claiming that the Indians had more land than they could pro-
ductively use. At first, negotiations were held wherein tribal leaders were
threatened with the loss of food and supplies. The Mandan-Hidatsa-Arikara
reservation was reduced by executive order in 1880, and a land cession commission met with the tribes in 1886 and obtained a cession of two thirds of the

remaining reservation. Negotiations were held with the Blackfeet and the Gros Ventre and associated Assiniboine in 1887 to reduce their reservation in Montana and open up the area for settlement, for the American population in Montana had doubled between 1870 and 1880. The Blackfeet, Fort Belknap, and Fort Peck reservations were created and the remainder of the large Blackfeet–Gros Ventre reservation was ceded (see map 7). In response to pressure from prospectors, the Gros Ventre and Assiniboine at Fort Belknap were pressured to sell the southern, mountainous part of their reservation in 1895, and that year the Blackfeet were pressured to sell a mountainous section in the western part of their reservation. In 1896 the Northern Arapaho and the Shoshone, who had been sharing a reservation in Wyoming since 1878, agreed to cede a hot springs area in the northeast section of the Shoshone reservation. Congress had its sights on the large Crow reservation as well. In 1882 government officials got tribal consent to grant the railroads right of way through the reservation and cede a large section in the western part. Again in 1891 the Crow were pressured to cede more land. Negotiations with the "**Teton**" began in 1882 to reduce the size of the Great Sioux Reservation. The Teton resisted, and in 1888 Congress determined that their consent was unnecessary. In 1889 North and South Dakota became states and the Great Sioux Reservation was carved into six reservations (Pine Ridge, Rosebud, Cheyenne River, Standing Rock, Crow Creek, and Lower Brule), and the remaining land opened to settlement by non-Indians (see map 7). In Indian Territory, cessions began in 1892 in conjunction with allotment of land to individuals (see **allotments**): in 1891–92 the reservations of the Southern Cheyenne and Arapaho, Pawnee, and Iowa were opened to settlement after tribal members received individual allotments of land. On the Northern Plains, the exception was the case of the Northern Cheyenne. With the assistance of the army officers who had fought alongside Cheyenne scouts, the Northern Cheyenne were assigned to a reservation in Montana created by executive order in 1884; by 1900 this reservation had been increased in size, in large part due to public furor in the East over the Spotted Hawk and Little Whirlwind case. The Indian Rights Association mounted a legal defense for the men and generated publicity that eventually freed them and exposed the racism and slanderous characterizations of the Cheyenne for which settlers were responsible.[3]

The Bureau of Indian Affairs (or Indian Office) began developing regulations governing personal conduct in 1883, and federal officials on the reservations attempted to enforce these rules, although the extent to which they could do so varied from reservation to reservation. Family life was a concern of the Indian Office. **Polygyny** was to be stopped and replaced by monogamy. On Standing Rock reservation one man was prosecuted for joking with a sister-in-law in a suggestive way, a custom that served a useful purpose in Sioux society, where brothers could be called upon to marry a brother's widow and support her children. Men were expected to labor in ways that federal officials considered productive; that is, farming and engaging in other agricultural pursuits (as opposed to doing ceremonial work that benefited the community, for example). Commissioner of Indian Affairs Thomas Morgan (1889–93) even attempted to prevent Indian women from witnessing the butchering of beef; he thought it unsuitably barbaric. Men were ordered to wear short hair and American-style clothing ("citizen's dress"). On the Blackfeet reservation, one agent ordered women to stop beading clothing. The sharing of food and the distribution of property in gift exchange were discouraged and large camps, especially those associated with religious ceremonies and other dances, were banned. The **Sun Dance** in particular and other rituals that involved self-torture were considered barbaric. The Indian Police force and a Court of Indian Offenses were created and implemented on reservations. These native officials, the police and judges, were expected to enforce the regulations. In addition, the local federal agents could imprison violators or withhold food and other supplies, as well as wage work at the agency, from individuals and families who did not conform to the rules.[4]

Schools were an important vehicle in the effort to Americanize native people. Several off-reservation boarding schools, modeled after **Carlisle Industrial Training School** in Pennsylvania, established in 1879, isolated children from their families and taught vocational skills, as well as the reading and writing of English. Carlisle School was established by Lt. Richard Pratt (see **Fort Marion**), who believed that a military regime would instill the discipline necessary to the assimilation process. Students were organized into platoons, wore uniforms, marched to class, and drilled in military formation. Punishments also were influenced by military life: working wearing a ball and chain and marching for long periods of time. Children were "enlisted" at the school and prevented from visiting their families during their enlistment. Youths from Plains reservations attended Carlisle from 1879 to the time of its closing in 1918. Subsequently, a national school system for Indians was organized. Plains reservations also had day schools and government boarding schools. In addition, Catholic and Protestant missionaries operated schools on the reservations. Other off-reservation boarding schools established in 1884 were Chilocco in Indian Territory, Genoa in Nebraska, and Haskell in Kansas. In the 1890s, Pierre, Flandreau, and Rapid City in South Dakota and Fort Shaw in Montana were opened. The goal in all these schools was to eradicate Indian language and customs, usually by harsh punishments for those who seemed to be retaining them. Sometimes reservation leaders sent children to school (particularly to Carlisle) in order to make a favorable impression on the federal officials and thereby attain benefits for their communities. Parents often voluntarily sent children to school, believing they would be fed and clothed. Given the poverty on reservations, orphans generally were placed in boarding schools. Congress began to make cuts in the budget for Indian schools in the 1890s and conditions, already grim due to the high incidence of disease and death, worsened due to inadequate food, clothing, and shelter. At this time medical practitioners did not have the means to cure many of the diseases transmitted in the schools; there were no antibiotics. But doctors did know that tuberculosis was very contagious; still, crowded conditions were tolerated in order to keep enrollments high. One inspection at Blackfeet agency revealed that standing water in school buildings promoted typhoid and conditions were so unsanitary that bath water was changed only once every twenty-four hours and a single towel was used for an entire week. At Carlisle, between 1881 and 1894 eleven out of fifteen children from Wind River Reservation in Wyoming died there or soon after their return home. The curriculum at these schools was referred to as "half-and-half." Children spent up to half of their time in the classroom, where the academic training was very limited and only English was spoken. The remainder of their time they worked to maintain the school—farming, tending stock, repairing facilities, sewing, cooking, and cleaning. Some of the work was dangerous and led to serious injury. The children also furnished cheap labor for nearby settlers under the pretext that they were being "civilized."[5]

Pressure to speed up the pace of assimilation and to open Indian land to settlement led to new legislation in 1887. The General Allotment Act of 1887, or the Dawes Act (see **Henry Dawes**), provided for the assignment of plots of land to individuals and the sale of the remaining "surplus" land on the reservations (see **allotments**). This process was at the president's discretion, and the title to the individual allotments of land was to be held in trust by the federal government for twenty-five years, so that the land was exempt from local taxation and from sale. Allottees constituted a tribal membership roll, which was controlled by federal officials whose concepts of Indian identity did not conform to native ideas, and some allotment rolls included non-Indians. The repercussions of these notions of identity became particularly significant in the twentieth century. Reformers pressed for the 1887 legislation, for they were outraged that Indians were not legally citizens and could not vote (see **Elk v. Wilkins**). Ostensibly allottees could attain American citizenship, but in reality, the doctrine of guardianship precluded that. In other words, Indians were treated as wards of the government, needing protection and therefore not entitled to the ordinary prerogatives of citizenship. In 1891 Congress provided for the leasing of trust land (that which was not allotted or not yet settled by Americans). Thus, the Allotment Act dismantled reservations yet allowed for federal management of individual allotments of land and trust land in general.[6]

The Omaha were the first of the Plains peoples to experience the allotment program. Three years before the passage of the Dawes Act, the Omaha were portrayed as assimilated enough to manage their own lands. Their reservation was divided into allotments assigned to individuals in 1884 and the western section of their reservation sold for settlement by Americans in 1882, while the eastern section was not allotted but held in trust for future allottees. The Omaha experiment became the blueprint for the Dawes Act in 1887. The rationale for the act included the characterization of Omaha allotment as successful. In reality, immediately after allotment, the Omaha experienced problems. Settlers trespassed, allowed their stock to trespass, and leased land from the increasingly impoverished Omaha at below value. The Omaha did not receive all the money they were supposed to receive for the western sector of their reservation, yet they were made responsible for managing the agency. By 1886 some proponents of allotment had to admit that the Omaha were doing worse than before allotment. The Dawes Act passed nonetheless, and the Omaha were made citizens, therefore more vulnerable to the surrounding American society. By the turn of the century, they had to lease most of their land and were in debt to traders who charged usurious interest and encouraged them to spend what little money they had on alcohol. Worse yet, the state authorities in Nebraska set out to tax their lands, despite the federal government's guarantee of their trust status (in trust, the land could not be sold or taxed). By 1894 most of the Omaha were camped along the Missouri River, living in poverty. The Indian Office refused to intervene when Nebraskans stole from them. In 1899 most of the unallotted land that remained in trust was allotted to Omaha born after 1883. After the turn of the century, the Omaha, as well as other Plains peoples, were subject to new legislation that removed trust restrictions and resulted in the sale of allotted lands.[7]

Despite this disaster, allotment proceeded. On the Northern Plains, troops were sent to intimidate the Yankton on their reservation. Despite their vigorous opposition, the Yankton land was allotted in 1894 and about half of their reservation was opened to settlement. The Mandan, Hidatsa, and Arikara reservation was allotted during 1894–95 (although unallotted lands remained in tribal ownership). The Cheyenne-Arapaho reservation in Indian Territory, where settlers waited impatiently on the eastern border, was one of the first to be allotted in 1892. The **Jerome Commission** met with the tribes in 1891 and found them opposed to allotment. The Cheyenne and Arapaho were impoverished, having lost their cattle herds due to Bureau of Indian Affairs incompetence, and the commission threatened them with economic sanctions. Finally, led by the Arapaho chief Left Hand, who as a Ghost Dance devotee was certain that a new world would soon materialize and bring prosperity to Indians, many chiefs agreed to accept allotment. Although the commissioners failed to obtain enough signatures to be in compliance with the **Medicine Lodge Creek Treaty** of 1867 (which required the consent of three fourths of the men for land cession), the reservation was allotted and opened to settlement. Soon the

Cheyenne and Arapaho were outnumbered by settlers ten to one. Settlers trespassed, stole stock and other property, and in some areas terrorized Indian people. The Pawnee, also somewhat comforted by the promises of the new Ghost Dance religion, accepted allotments in 1892. The Iowa land was allotted in 1891. Under protest, allotment took place among the Otoe-Missouria from 1891–99. Horrified by what had happened to the Cheyenne and Arapaho, the Wichita and Caddo, Kiowa, Comanche, and Plains Apache leaders resisted allotment and, although their objections were ignored, managed to postpone it until 1901; in fact, as we shall see, one Kiowa leader took their case to the Supreme Court. Reservations on the Northern upland Plains, where cattle interests had influence and small family farms were less feasible than in Indian Territory, were allotted later during the twentieth century.[8]

The assimilation program of the 1880s and 1890s was not easily implemented. Reservation social and political organization was in many ways a replication of prereservation life, which provided a means of holding societies together, solving social and economic problems, and providing emotional satisfaction. Village peoples rebuilt their villages on the reservations in Indian Territory. The Osage rebuilt their five villages in different sections of their reservation. The Wichita and Caddo occupied different regions on their reservation, and the internal divisions of these tribes were replicated in the settlement pattern as well. Wealthy Caddo and Wichita hereditary chiefs perpetuated traditions of centralized political organization. The four Pawnee bands settled in different areas of their reservation and each farmed cooperatively under the direction of their chiefs. On the Fort Berthold reservation on the Northern Plains, when the Mandan, Hidatsa, and Arikara left Like-a-Fishhook village in the 1880s, they dispersed throughout the reservation, each tribe selecting a different sector. In 1894, the Crow Flies High band of Hidatsa and Mandan returned to the reservation and settled at some distance from the other villages. The bands of nomadic groups, such as the Crow and Blackfeet, dispersed on their reservations. On the reservations where more than one tribe settled (such as Fort Belknap, where Gros Ventres and Assiniboines located, and Wind River, where Arapahos and Shoshones lived), each tribe located in its own region. In this way the prereservation political organizations of the tribes generally were reconstituted.[9]

Further, in the 1880s many of the local agencies, understaffed and poorly funded, were dependent on native leaders for whatever program implementation was accomplished, and even for protection in some cases. Native peoples subverted the assimilation agenda with a wide range of coping mechanisms and tactics designed to adapt new conditions to their own terms. There also was overt resistance to assimilation, legally as well as militarily. Some bands initially refused reservation settlement altogether. About 1872 the Crow Flies High band of Hidatsa with some Mandans left the vicinity of Like-a-Fishhook village and evaded the scrutiny and control of agency officials. They went west near Fort Bu-ford (near the mouth of the Yellowstone River) and camped there, obtaining employment at the post and hunting as long as possible. They did not return to the agency until 1894. On the Crow reservation, where the Crow were resentful of the treatment received from their American allies in the 1880s, some young men were still raiding for horses and attempting to live up to Crow ideals of a warrior's life. One of these men had a vision in which he was promised super-natural aid in his efforts to achieve great things. He carried a sword symbolic of his bond with a spirit helper and defied the agent's prohibition on horse-stealing expeditions. The agent enlisted the help of nearby troops to hunt down Sword Bearer (known as Wraps His Tail before his vision) and his companions. On the Northern Cheyenne reservation, desperate to obtain food for their starving fam-ilies, Head Chief and Young Mule killed a cow illegally grazing on the reserva-tion and, surprised by a cowboy, killed him. When officials insisted they surren-der, they demanded to face the troops in battle and, while the entire tribe assembled to watch, made a suicide charge rather than give up. Other leaders met the challenges of federal domination by resorting to public tour and legal action. When he heard of plans for the Allotment Act, the Hunkpapa Sioux chief **Sitting Bull** visited reservations on the Northern Plains and urged resist-ance. Chief Jake of the Caddo tribe and Lone Wolf, a Kiowa chief, tried to trav-el to Washington to meet with Congress, but their agent had them arrested. Lone Wolf escaped but arrived too late to meet with Congress. The foster son and namesake of one of the Kiowa warriors imprisoned at Fort Marion, he tried to prevent the allotment of the Kiowa–Comanche–Plains Apache reservation by standing on treaty rights and enlisting the support of lobbyists and attorneys. The 1867 Medicine Lodge Treaty had provided that no land cessions could occur without the consent of three fourths of the males. Lone Wolf and his legal team demonstrated that the signatures obtained by the Jerome Commission were fraudulent as well as insufficient to meet the three-fourths test. But in 1903 the Supreme Court decided that Congress could disregard treaties with Indian groups and allot reservations without Indian consent.[10]

Most leaders worked to adapt to assimilation policies by making use of reser-vation economic and political institutions to reinforce their authority. The most successful chiefs convinced the federal officials that they were cooperative and, at the same time, persuaded their people that they were generous providers who could successfully navigate the new reservation conditions. The federal agents on the reservations distributed provisions and manufactured goods that fulfilled treaty obligations or in extreme circumstances were issued to relieve suffering. In the early reservation period, the goods were delivered to the leaders, who distrib-uted them and reserved some for their own use in supporting followers or meet-ing other responsibilities. Cattle were issued in small herds; these leaders directed their men to kill the cattle, as in buffalo-hunting days, and then supervised the distribution of the meat. Indians were hired at the agency, and often the agents relied on native leaders to select these employees. Freight wagons were issued to leaders. In the case of the Southern Cheyenne and Arapaho chiefs, they supervised the freight trains, which brought income to their bands. The Indian Police were particularly important, and it was not unusual for these men to be under the control of native leaders, as in the case of the Northern and Southern Arapaho and the Blackfeet; in this way, repressive federal policies could be subverted. Leaders of bands often agreed to open farms; these large plots were cooperatively cultivated and the leaders distributed the produce, reserving sufficient stores to meet their responsibilities. Cattle were issued to prominent leaders, who also usually levied tolls in the form of cattle from trespassing cattle ranchers. Thus native leaders had herds of beef that they used to support their followers. The ceremonial life on reservations was a vehicle for them to distribute goods and food. Crow chiefs sponsored celebrations on national holidays. Cheyenne and Arapaho chiefs also took responsibility for hosting dances and celebrations. The Osage, wealthier than other tribes on the Southern Plains, had big celebrations where they gave away large amounts of property to other tribes. Chiefs validated their positions by such displays of generosity.[11]

The leaders who served as intermediaries between their people and federal officials in negotiations and dispute settlement made a point of stating their commitment to farming, schools, and other kinds of "civilized" behavior. In reality, their commitment was mitigated by the ways that they made use of the new activities. Chiefs used the results of their agricultural activity to reinforce cooperative labor and chiefly authority. They sent children to Carlisle school, where they became literate and returned to help their fathers in negotiations with the federal government. Northern Arapaho chiefs manipulated their agents' fears about a threat from the Sioux, reassuring the agents that they would protect them in return for supplies. Southern Arapahos actually stood guard over their agent during hostilities on the Southern Plains in the 1870s. Southern Cheyenne and Arapaho chiefs asked for houses, then used them for storage while they continued living in tepees. On many reservations, leaders played off different Christian denominations against each other. The Northern Arapaho had Catholic and Episcopal missionaries competing to provide economic support. The Gros Ventre demonstrated loyalty to the Catholic missionaries who they thought could help them, through the **Bureau of Catholic Indian Missions,** to lobby for their secure placement on their reservation in Montana. Many chiefs realized that they had very little leverage with the federal government but used councils and delegations to Washington as opportunities to lobby for what their people needed. In cession councils, the Northern Arapaho managed to get legal rights to remain on the Shoshone reservation in

Wyoming. The Crow managed to obtain day schools, better prices at the trad-er's store, and resolution of cattle issues. The Comanche and some Kiowa lead-ers were successful in persuading officials that leasing grazing land to cattlemen would facilitate their assimilation; they used the lease money to support their followers and the ceremonies that the federal government was attempting to repress. Native leaders realized that if they could present a unified front in deal-ings with the federal government, they had a better chance of success. In the Northern Arapaho case, the chiefs and the elderly ritual leaders mutually rein-forced one another's authority and the ritual leaders used supernatural sanction to motivate cooperation and unity. When the federal government authorized the leasing of trust land in 1891, agents were instructed to establish "business committees" on reservations to transact the leases. Northern Arapaho chiefs were installed as committeemen in ceremonies supervised by the ritual au-thorities; in this way the authority of the business committee was legitimized. On other reservations, native leaders struggled to use these business commit-tees to improve conditions for their people, despite the limited objectives Con-gress anticipated. Before the organization of a business committee, Southern Arapaho chiefs coped with allotment by insisting on the assignment of their band members' allotments in clusters, where stock would be cared for in com-mon. The Southern Arapaho chiefs' council's decisions were enforced by Ara-paho men's societies in the late nineteenth century. The Osage established a national government to counter federal domination in 1879; the Grand and Lit-tle Osage bands accepted a government in common. They sent a delegation to Washington and succeeded in getting their **annuity payments** in cash rather than goods, thereby obtaining adequate income for their people to buy what they needed and avoiding loss in the value of the annuity due to graft. The Teton Sioux chiefs were viewed as obstacles by the commission charged with getting land cessions in 1889. Based on the 1868 treaty requirement that land cessions be approved by three fourths of the men of the tribes, this commission took the position that the decision should be made by the male tribal members at large. Subsequently, the Teton transformed the three-fourths concept into a new reservation institution, a tribal council (referred to as the "three-fourths council") that sent representatives (the chiefs of the reservation bands or allied bands) to deal with federal officials, who gradually became accustomed to transacting agency business with this group. With the 1868 treaty as a charter, the Teton political ideology in the reservation era included the conviction that rations were guaranteed by the treaty as compensation for land cession. At the turn of the century, the Crow also began to take steps to organize a centralized government that could be effective in dealings with the federal government.[12]

Indian parents often tried to subvert educational policy by refusing to send children to school as long as possible (perhaps by feigning the child's illness) and sheltering runaways. In the boarding schools, children resisted forced assimilation in the ways open to them. For example, they might arrive late for drill or work assignments. Some ran away. Some left as soon as they could and began to live among their people in customary ways. Others learned to read and write and returned to help the older generation counter federal policy. Children tried to form supportive groups in the schools to resist the demoralization that harsh treatment, unsanitary conditions that led to death and disease, and separation from family produced. **Francis La Flesche** attended a mission-supported school near the Omaha agency in the mid-1860s, several years before the Carlisle school and subsequent institutions were established. Here harsh corporal punishments also were used. He tells of how he tried to help a friend who was about to be beaten by a school disciplinarian after he confessed to an infraction in order to spare a smaller child punishment. Ordered to bring a switch, La Flesche made small cuts in the wood so that the switch would fall apart when it was used and spare his friend a vicious beating.[13]

The federal agents' sanctions against polygyny gradually eliminated that form of marriage. But agents were not able to obliterate native ideas about kinship and proper behavior of kinsmen. Nomadic groups had a kinship system that expanded the group of people who could be counted on as relatives. Thus children of one's parents and children of one's parents' brothers and sisters were considered to be equally close in relationship. "Brothers" helped each other in economic and other activities. Similarly, "sisters" cooperated. The warm and supportive feelings between an individual and his or her grandparents were expanded to include the brothers and sisters of grandparents. In short, individuals had a large group of people whom they viewed as kin and from whom they received support of various sorts. "Brothers" farmed together, herded stock together, freighted together, pooled equipment, and contributed to one another's ceremonial obligations. "Sisters" worked together and supported their "brothers" and one another in ceremonial obligations. The value on sharing among kinsmen helped native people cope with the deprivation of reservation life. The village peoples, who generally had **matrilineal** and **patrilineal clans** (and distinguished between fathers' and mothers' relatives in significant ways), and the nomadic Crow, who retained some of the features of Hidatsa village social organization, continued to rely on the principle of clan identity to order social relations. The Crow persisted in retaining the ideal of clan exogamy, and the relationship between a son and his father's clan remained central to Crow ceremonial life. The Osage retained the clan system after moving to Indian Territory; clan prayers and a ban on marriage between members of a clan were central to tribal ceremonies. Due to population loss, some of the clans became extinct, and the Osage focused on ceremonies that could be performed by moiety representatives (see **moieties**) rather than clan representatives. One such ceremony was the mourning ritual, which required a scalp; the Osage substituted hair purchased from a Pawnee.[14]

In their religious life, native people (as people everywhere) sought an explanation for their circumstances, psychological comfort, the social support of others, and affirmation of their values. In trying to secure supernatural assistance during the difficult reservation times, Plains peoples discarded some rituals and modified others. For example, the Sun Dance was either discarded or stripped of its body sacrifice (often described as self-torture) features. The Crow, for example, no longer found a ritual that focused on warfare useful and discontinued the Sun Dance. The Gros Ventre were desperately trying to convince federal officials and Catholic missionaries, who they believed could lobby for them, that, as progressives, they should be allowed to remain in Montana. They ceased holding the Sun Dance under these conditions. The Blackfeet and Northern Arapaho gave emphasis to healing; an individual vowed to sponsor the Sun Dance ceremony in return for the restoration of someone's health. And they retained the element of property sacrifice while eliminating body sacrifice from the ceremony. The Sun Dance began to be held during Fourth of July festivities when it could be disguised as part of a patriotic celebration. Private ceremonies, such as when an individual completed a vow to bring offerings to a tribal **medicine bundle** (the Arapaho Flat Pipe or one of the two Gros Ventre pipes, for example) could be hidden from the agent and adapted to the kinds of difficulties petitioners faced in reservation times.[15]

New ceremonies passed from tribe to tribe, offering new opportunities for religious fulfillment; the most important on the Northern Plains in the 1870s and 1880s was the **Grass Dance** (also known as the Omaha Dance). A men's society ritual among the Teton, the Grass Dance was purchased by the Assiniboine in the late 1870s; the Gros Ventre and Blackfeet purchased the ceremony from the Assiniboine. At the same time, the Crow purchased the ceremony from their Hidatsa relatives. It was adapted to be appropriate to the different tribal traditions. Among the Gros Ventre, sponsoring the dance amounted to a religious vow, and participants gave away property and provided a feast. Among the Crow the regalia of the dance was transferred from ceremonial father to son (from father's clan to father's son), and men with regalia or offices competed in the generous distribution of property, as the two main men's warrior societies in prereservation days had done. Members also cooperated in the economic activities of reservation life (such as cutting hay). The Grass Dance also spread from tribe to tribe in Indian Territory.[16]

In the terrible conditions of reservation life in the 1890s, where often there was insufficient food, high mortality, and a seemingly endless round of reversals of fortune, as well as rumors of more land cessions to come, a new religion developed and spread among many Plains tribes. Word came of a holy man with a new ceremony, the Ghost Dance, that promised to reverse the desperate circumstances of Indian people. Some tribes sent emissaries to visit **Wovoka** (also known as Jack Wilson) in Nevada, where they heard about how his visions in 1889 revealed a new religion and a code of conduct that stressed peaceful relations. Faithful adherents who danced frequently would attain good health, and eventually a new world would materialize where Indians would once again prosper. As a result of exposure to the prophet, several tribes took up the Ghost Dance. Tribes near Wovoka's people brought news of the new religion to the reservation of the Shoshone and Northern Arapaho in Wyoming. A Gros Ventre visiting Northern Arapaho relatives took the news to the Gros Ventre in Montana, and Teton Sioux and Northern Cheyenne visited the Arapaho and took word of the Ghost Dance to their people. The Teton took Wovoka's message to the Sioux, Yanktonai, and Assiniboine at Fort Peck, as well as to the Sioux reservations in North and South Dakota. Boarding school alumni among the Northern and Southern Arapaho wrote letters to each other, so the Southern Arapaho learned about the Ghost Dance. In 1890 there were Ghost Dance followers among the Southern Arapaho and Cheyenne. **Sitting Bull**, an Arapaho in Wyoming whose brothers were in Indian Territory, came to Indian Territory and began to hold huge intertribal Ghost Dances, where he helped people go into trance to see visions of their deceased relatives living amid prosperity. In these ceremonies, Sitting Bull converted Caddos, Wichitas, Kiowas, and Plains Apaches. Only a few Comanches who lived near the northern border of their reservation were converted, for their main chief **Quanah** (also known as Quanah Parker) opposed the Ghost Dance. Pawnees came to the Wichita Ghost Dances and were converted. The prosperous Osage were disinterested in the Ghost Dance, but the Southern Arapaho took it to the Ponca, Otoe-Missouria, Kaw, and Iowa. The Northern Arapaho passed the Ghost Dance to the Gros Ventre, who transferred it to the Assiniboine. The Arapaho version of the Ghost Dance stressed that change would come nonviolently. For the Teton Sioux in South Dakota, the Ghost Dance took on an adaptation that was to have tragic results. Although the Sioux apparently accepted the idea that the new world would materialize through supernatural means, Kicking Bear had a vision in 1890 that a special Ghost Dance shirt could repel bullets. Word leaked to settlers and army officials at the same time that Sioux resentment was building over the breakup of the Great Sioux Reservation and the reduction of rations. To try to suppress the Ghost Dance, the federal agent at Pine Ridge sent for troops, and elsewhere the agents attempted to arrest Sioux participants. The former leader of Sioux resistance, also named **Sitting Bull**, was a Ghost Dance devotee. He was killed on the Standing Rock reservation. Big Foot, a Minneconjou, was asked by federal officials to help negotiate a resolution of the conflict. Troops intercepted him and escorted his band to Wounded Knee Creek, where subsequently a fight between men in his camp and troops broke out. More than 150 men, women, and children in Big Foot's camp, as well as 39 soldiers, were killed at Wounded Knee. Not all Northern Plains peoples embraced the Ghost Dance. For example, the Mandan, Hidatsa, and Arikara did not convert. Generally the dance was gradually abandoned as the new world failed to materialize; often it was replaced by the Ghost Dance Hand Game.[17]

In their Ghost Dance visions, Arapaho saw their deceased relatives in camp with ample provisions, carrying on ceremonial and technological activities, and playing games, including hand games. These involved one team watching another team and guessing in which hand an object was hidden. The Ghost Dance visions inspired revivals of these activities; as people replicated what they saw, their vision provided supernatural validation for the replication and for innovations that developed during the course of revival. In the Ghost Dance Hand Game, an Arapaho seeking supernatural aid would vow to sponsor the hand game ceremony, which involved providing a feast for the participants. One of the two teams would represent the votive and, if the prayers were sincere, win the game, thereby ensuring supernatural aid for the participants. No material gain fell to the winning team, as in the secular, gambling form of the hand game. The Ghost Dance Hand Game spread to the Wichita and the Pawnee. In the Pawnee Ghost Dance, village bundle ceremonies and society dances were revived. A Pawnee, John White, converted to the Ghost Dance religion. He experienced visions that validated his being a leader in the Ghost Dance Hand Game. He introduced this ceremony to his people. In the Pawnee Ghost Dance Hand Game, elements of Pawnee ceremonies (such as a corn offering) and Christian symbolism were incorporated. Other Pawnees had visions that sanctioned their ownership of hand game bundles, and these ceremonies became the focus of Pawnee religious ritual into the early twentieth century. These ceremonies offered hope in desperate times. Just prior to 1892 the threat of allotment and land loss was ever present. Pawnees were dying in shockingly large numbers; in 1876 the population was 2,026 and in 1892, 759. Participation was broad-based as women owned bundles as well as men; it brought prestige and social support and reinforced Pawnee values while promising a reversal of fortune. The Ghost Dance Hand Game spread by way of the Southern Arapaho to the Cheyenne, Wichita, Pawnee, and Otoe. The Northern Arapaho transferred it to the Gros Ventre, who gave it to the Assiniboine.[18]

The diffusion of peyote ritual also was in large part a product of the Ghost Dance movement. Peyote is a cactus with psychedelic properties that grows in northern Mexico and southern Texas. Participants in peyote ritual do not become addicted or physically harmed by its use. The **Lipan** Apache and others lived in the area where peyote grew, and they developed rituals for its use in the eighteenth and early nineteenth centuries. In the late eighteenth century the Lipan had contacts with Comanche, Kiowa, and Plains Apache raiders, and in this way the latter became familiar with peyote rituals. During the Indian wars of the nineteenth century, Comanche, Kiowa, and Plains Apache access to peyote was curtailed, but after the development of railroads and a better transportation system, peyote was readily shipped to Indian Territory in the 1880s. Lipans married to Comanches taught a particular variant of peyote ritual to several Comanches, Kiowas, and Plains Apaches. The ceremony was used as a cure for illness and a ritual to help individuals reorient their lives. It gave expression to native understanding of the supernatural and native social values. During the course of the ritual a group prayed through song throughout the night and experienced visions as they consumed small quantities of peyote. The visions reinforced the tenets of their religion, which stressed cooperation and temperance and integrated Christian ideals to varying degrees, depending on the views of the leader of the ritual. The Ghost Dance ceremonies brought together people from different tribes, so often individuals embraced both the Ghost Dance and peyote. In the 1890s boarding school students from different tribes, communicating in English, informed each other about peyote ritual; thus, a high percentage of leaders of the ritual were boarding school alumni. Traditional doctors, Ghost Dance devotees, and young people who had learned about Christianity became converts. The two most important peyote leaders in Indian Territory were Quanah Parker, the most important Comanche chief, and John Wilson, a Caddo. These two men converted many others. In Indian Territory in the 1880s and 1890s peyote ritual was incorporated into Osage, Wichita, Southern Cheyenne, Southern Arapaho, Ponca, Kaw, Otoe, Pawnee, and Iowa life. From there, missionaries, including John Wilson, took peyote ritual to the Northern Plains, where by the early twentieth century it had converts among Northern Arapaho, Northern Cheyenne, Omaha, Iowa (in Kansas), Ponca (in Nebraska), Crow, Yankton, and to a lesser degree, Arikara, Teton Sioux on several reservations, and some Santee. Elsewhere there was minimal interest or no conversions to the peyote religion.[19]

Where Christianity took hold, it usually was indigenized. Missionaries trained Sioux, particularly Santee and Yankton, for leadership positions in the early reservation period. Sioux missionaries, using religious writings translated into the Sioux language, traveled to Sioux reservations in South Dakota, started congregations, and used native ministers, deacons, and catechists. On Pine Ridge reservation in 1875, Episcopalians established a mission and appointed lay leaders, who preached in the Teton Sioux dialect. The Catholics, who arrived in 1888, also translated scriptures into Sioux. They sponsored church societies of catechists who conducted the church rituals in the Oglala communities on Pine Ridge. Congregations were identified with the local bands and Christianity became associated with band identity. In Indian Territory, the Caddo were receptive to **Seminole** and **Creek** Baptist missionaries. Native people, exposed to some of the ideas and symbols of Christianity, often had visions in which they were offered help and guidance by Christian figures, such as Jesus. Conversions usually did not result in exclusive commitment to Christianity; rather, different religious traditions were viewed as compatible so that individuals might participate in native ceremonies, such as the Sun Dance, **yuwipi** rituals, and peyote ceremonies. Christian symbolism was integrated into peyote ritual and, particularly in Catholic missions, native symbolism might be incorporated into rituals.[20]

COPING WITH LAND LOSS, 1903–33

After the turn of the century, Western politicians dominated Congress, and the states that they represented pressed for the opening of more Indian land and the transfer of Indian-owned resources to the use and control of the growing non-Indian population. Indians were portrayed as hopelessly backward, unworthy of special assistance or protection. Appropriating the language of assimilation, Westerners worked to accelerate the pace of cessions, allotment, and the leasing of Indian land. In 1903 Congress passed the Dead Indian Land Act, which allowed for the sale of allotments of deceased allottees. The land of the tribes allotted in the 1890s began to slip out of Indian ownership. In 1906 Congress passed the Burke Act, which eliminated the twenty-five-year trust period (see **allotments**) and allowed the Secretary of the Interior to change the trust title of an allotment to a fee-simple title if he deemed the allottee competent to manage his or her own property. Unlike an allotment held in trust, an allotment in patent-in-fee status (that is, one with a fee-simple title) could be taxed and sold; and most patent-in-fee allotments were sold soon after their issue. In 1907 Congress granted permission for the sale of the allotments of "noncompetent" allottees. The federal government also made long-term leases of tribally owned (unallotted) land, generally at below-market prices, to business interests, and built irrigation systems using tribal income, systems that largely benefited non-Indian farmers. During the second decade of the twentieth century, "competency commissions" organized by the Indian Office went to reservations and categorized as many Indians as possible "competent" so that their land could be put into patent-in-fee status. Fee patenting was liberalized by Commissioner Cato Sells, whose criteria for fee-simple title was "race" (those described as less than half Indian "**blood**") and years of schooling, without regard to how capable individuals were of managing their property or whether they consented to the change in status. Congress also passed legislation to allow for the per capita distribution of the income of tribal funds (from land sales, for example). The Indian Office empowered the local agent to control the distribution of in-

dividuals' income from trust property (money from the lease or sale of allotments). The local superintendent decided how much of the individual's income would be released to him or her and for what purposes the money could
be spent. At the same time, federal appropriations for Indian education were reduced and the academic curriculum made less rigorous. Thus, the American
West continued to develop economically at the expense of native communities,
and Plains peoples were marginalized in American society and denied opportunities to compete with other Americans in the struggle to build economically successful communities in the West. As Joseph Jorgensen has written, they
were assimilated into poverty.[21]

Congress pressed for more cessions after the turn of the century. On the
Northern Plains there was less pressure for land for family farms, and the tribes
there often avoided ceding large amounts of land. The Crow ceded sections of
their reservation in 1904 and 1908. Some Crow settled on allotments beginning
in 1905, but the reservation was not completely allotted until 1920, when Crow
leaders succeeded in preventing any land from being declared surplus and
opened to settlement. The Gros Ventre and Assiniboine land at Fort Belknap
was not allotted until 1921, and the tribes succeeded in preventing the opening
of "surplus lands." The Blackfeet struggled to prevent the loss of land as well;
they were forced to allot their reservation and cede some of the land in 1918 but
retained the mineral rights to some of their reservation land in common. Allotment was resisted by an elected business council led by **Robert Hamilton**
and not completed until the 1920s. The Northern Arapaho and the Shoshone
on the Wind River reservation had their land allotted in 1900, and in 1905 they
ceded the northern half of the reservation. However, the land was too poor to
attract farmers and eventually was returned to the tribes, including the mineral rights. Farmers did covet the land on the Sioux reservations, which were allotted between 1898 and 1911. Pine Ridge was opened to settlement in 1910;
Rosebud in 1904, 1907, and 1910; Cheyenne River in 1908; Standing Rock in
1913; and Lower Brule in 1906. Fort Peck was allotted between 1909 and 1913
and surplus lands opened in 1917. The Fort Berthold peoples' land was gradually allotted over the years between 1907 and 1928, but unallotted lands ceded
only in 1910. In Indian Territory, the Kiowa, Comanche, and Plains Apache
land was allotted in 1901, but the tribes retained some grazing land in common,
which was finally allotted in 1906. The Wichita and Caddo lands also were allotted in 1901. The Kaw had purchased their reservation and, although they
were pressured to allot it in 1902, the process resulted in no "surplus." The
Osage were forced to allot in 1906–09 but retained mineral rights in common.
Finally, the Ponca resisted allotment until 1907. Allottees on these reservations
faced years of struggle to protect their title to their land and to prevent settlers
from exploiting their resources.[22]

Congress also continued to cut the budget for Indian education. This resulted in competition among the schools to obtain students and resulted in increased flexibility toward parents and children. The Rapid City school, which housed mostly Sioux children from Pine Ridge, Rosebud, and Cheyenne River, tried to actively recruit students whose parents had been given the right to choose their children's schools by the Indian Office after 1905. The school sent catalogs advertising "a good time the first week" and offering a wide range of activities, including social events, music, and athletics. Lieutenant Pratt had started a football team at Carlisle school, which was extremely successful against the best college teams and which Pratt hoped to use to demonstrate that Indians could compete with Euro-Americans. Other boarding schools followed suit, particularly Haskell. Rapid City had basketball teams for boys and girls, and for boys, football and track. Parents demanded that their children be sent home for summer vacation and the school complied. The school also responded to parents' complaints about food. Children were allowed to wear their own clothing. Still, health conditions remained poor and children continued to run away.[23]

Given the escalating poverty in Indian communities in the early twentieth century, how did they cope? There was a range of strategies depending on local circumstances. Generally, though, native leaders tried to organize political resistance through delegations and legal action. They concentrated on obtaining an extension on the trust patents on allotments, more control over money from trust lands, pursuit of legal claims against the federal government for treaty violation, and religious freedom. The experiences of several tribes serve to illustrate the range of circumstances and strategies associated with native Plains societies.

In Oklahoma, native peoples fared worse than on reservations on the Northern Plains because the land loss was more extensive. To a large extent, the response of Oklahoma Indians was an intense ceremonial revitalization and elaboration. A consideration of the plight of the Southern Cheyenne and Arapaho will illustrate the social repercussions of land loss. By 1928 the Cheyenne and Arapaho had lost 63 percent of their allotted lands through heirship sales, other forced sales, and sales that followed the issuance of fee patents. After the passage of the Burke Act, Cheyenne and Arapaho who were declared "competent" were targeted by land speculators, sometimes in collusion with agency employees. The Indians sold their lands for less than market value and, since funds from leasing and sales were released by the agent only in small amounts, families went into debt to merchants. They had to mortgage property as collateral and, unable to repay their debts, lost property worth far more than what they owed. They mortgaged farm equipment and stock, which undermined their ability to make a living on their allotments. As the land base shrunk, cooperative labor became less feasible and most families leased their land; these leases were arranged by the agency superintendent, who leased land for less than market value. Families lived for most of the year in large camps on the allotment of a leader's family, where food was shared. In 1917 a competency commission sent by the Indian Office visited all Cheyenne and Arapaho families and declared almost all the young men competent; fee patents were issued despite the protests of the individuals involved and the tribal government. Women generally were declared "noncompetent," so wives retained an allotment where the family could live. Part of the allotment usually was leased. At the same time the Cheyennes and Arapahos were being stripped of their resources, their value system was being challenged. The sharing of food and other cooperation were portrayed as indicative of their backwardness as a people; this presumption of inferiority was used as justification for removing their resources from their control. The social support inherent in the kinship system was undermined by the heirship regulations, which directed that the spouse rather than siblings would inherit and that biological ties were to take precedence over supportive social relationships in matters of inheritance. Federal authorities also tried to ban the camps in which ceremonies took place throughout the year.[24]

Cheyenne and Arapaho leaders tried to offset the disastrous policies by dissemblance and by steadfastly supporting the ceremonies that held the society together. Chiefs confronted federal authorities in meetings in Washington, and some religious leaders took legal action to protect their right to practice their religion. Dances and property exchanges (see **giveaways**) were held on American holidays, including Thanksgiving, Christmas, Easter, and the Fourth of July, when there was less chance that federal officials would intervene. In their requests for permits for their Sun Dances, leaders described them as Willow or Sage Dances. During World War I, the Sun Dances were portrayed as patriotic fetes where money was raised for the war effort. Dances and giveaways were held at the same time as the camp meetings sponsored by Baptist and Mennonite missionaries. Leaders took responsibility for organizing and contributing to the expenses of these gatherings, and assumed much of the expense of the construction of dance halls or community centers where ceremonies could be held in the winter. The Cheyenne and Arapaho continued to hold their Sun Dances, men's society dances, the Cheyenne Arrow ceremony (in which Cheyennes made offerings to the tribal medicine bundle), Ghost Dance Hand Games, and peyote camps. Gifts of food and property at these events served as sacrifices that brought supernatural attention and support. The Grass or Omaha Dance often was a feature, and dances were held at local fairs where townspeople encouraged Indian participation to attract larger crowds and more profits. These ceremonies helped to relieve the suffering of people with little land and income, for those families with the means carried most of the burden of supporting the camps. The ceremonies also publicly validated ideals of cooperation and generosity, gave the participants emotional support, and offered hope through the religious components of the rituals.[25]

Cheyenne and Arapaho chieftainship, now dependent on recognition for personal qualities such as generosity, was perpetuated, and these chiefs took responsibility for serving as liaisons between their communities and the federal government. Their approach was to stress the sacred nature of their treaties and to try to convince federal officials to protect their lands and continue supporting educational facilities and other services promised in the treaty agreements. They also stressed that tribal government support of farming and education was in compliance with assimilation goals of federal officials. Leaders succeeded in getting the trust status of their lands extended to 1928 (although individuals still faced the possibility of receiving a fee patent on their lands) and they pursued a claim against the government for treaty violation, obtaining legal representation in 1923. Delegates continued to receive presidential medals. These activities, in addition to their ceremonial activity, helped mobilize support from their constituents. Chiefs and other Cheyennes and Arapahos were aware of the kind of negative characterizations that were used to rationalize economic exploitation and they confronted and refuted them, pointing out the discrepancy between the ideology of assimilation and the reality of power differentials in Oklahoma. Much resistance focused on the federal campaign against the peyote ritual. The territory of Oklahoma passed a law in 1899 against the use of the "mescal bean," and several Cheyennes were arrested at a peyote meeting in 1907. In a court case, they proved that peyote was not the same as mescal and the case was dismissed. When Oklahoma applied for statehood, a law against peyote was proposed and leading peyotists from several Oklahoma tribes, including a group of Southern Cheyenne and Arapaho, lobbied against it successfully. They intervened with their congressional representatives to forestall a national law against the ritual in 1918. Helping to defeat the legislation were anthropologist **James Mooney** and others. In 1918 Cheyenne peyote leaders led the way in the incorporation of their religion as the Native American Church, so that it would have equivalence to Christian churches. Once the peyote religion became legal in Oklahoma, peyotists in other states began to incorporate their own churches (the Sioux in South Dakota and the Northern Cheyenne and Crow in Montana, for example).[26]

To the southwest of the Cheyenne and Arapaho, the Kiowa also had to cope with land loss and, additionally, with a series of superintendents more repressive than those at the Cheyenne and Arapaho agency. The Sun Dance was suppressed by 1890 through the threat of attack by U.S. troops. Subsequently, the Ghost Dance took the place of the Sun Dance as a ritual that drew the Kiowa together. With modifications including the addition of several Christian elements, it remained important until 1917. At the same time, Kiowas responded to repression by stubbornly refusing to give up military society dances. They tried to hide these from the superintendents' view by holding the four-day ceremonies on allotments, where they ostensibly were independent landowners. Three societies, largely associated with particular communities or districts, thrived after the turn of the century. The Grass Dance or Omaha Dance had been adopted in 1883. The other two, the Black Legs and Gourd societies, had older origins among the Kiowa but had been dormant until they were revived in 1912. The society dances gave expression to Kiowa values, offered individuals a means of gaining prestige, and helped to offset poverty. Giveaways were held in conjunction with the dances, so that food and property were distributed to those in need. Members of the societies were no longer required to be warriors; in fact, membership was broadened and was completely compatible with peyotism. Members primarily were people from prominent families who had the means to be generous. In fact, the Kiowa families had been ranked in prereservation times, reflecting marked distinctions in wealth and ancestry (captives formed the lowest of the ranked groups). These dances celebrated ancestors' achievements as well as the Kiowa past and offered resistance to the superintendents' repressive policies and the idea that such ceremonies had no relevance in the twentieth century. Society members tried to subvert repressive policies by incorporating their dances into Fourth of July "picnics" and honoring ceremonies for World War I veterans (fourteen Kiowas were in the armed services during the war) and, when the superintendents threatened to withhold dancers' payments from land sales, members first collected the money, then went to the dances. Lyrics of one song of the Grass Dance society were "Go ahead and be arrested/jailed!" Through the dances and songs of these societies, much Kiowa tradition was passed on to the younger generation to be used for new purposes in later years. Traditions also were perpetuated by Kiowa artists who made articles of clothing and other items, told stories associated with the Kiowa past, and painted. In the latter category were the **Kiowa Five**, young Kiowas who were encouraged by their **field matron**, Susan Peters, an agency employee, to paint, then in 1917 sent to the University of Oklahoma, where they received training in modern painting. Instructors had in mind that Kiowa painters gave expression to a primitive style that could be contrasted with styles of superior races; yet, these artists developed a style that drew on Kiowa traditions of painting (see **art**) and focused on representations of the nineteenth century and of dancing activities in the twentieth century. They also were instrumental in popularizing "Indian art" in Oklahoma and elsewhere, helping to create a market for Indian art that helped relieve poverty.[27]

Because of the vast deposits of oil on their reservation, the Osage probably fared better than other Plains peoples in Oklahoma; still, they faced exploitation and serious challenges to their community. The wealth precipitated a struggle between the Osage and a group of people who had been allotted reservation land by the federal government but who were non-Indians or people who, although they had some Osage ancestry, were alienated from the Osage community. These groups competed for control of the elected tribal council that made decisions about Osage resources. By 1912 the elected council was dominated by hereditary chiefs who tried to counter Bureau of Indian Affairs policies that allowed Americans to use Osage resources for less than market value. The council managed to establish a policy of bidding on oil leases, which dramatically increased Osage income and resulted in prosperity for all Osage allottees whether they had sold their land or not. It was difficult to protect the Osage from the problems that accompanied their wealth. Opportunists and criminals flocked to the area and preyed on Osages, robbing them after they collected their lease money and overcharging them for purchases. Some even married Osage women with the intent of murdering them in order to inherit. The scandal convinced Congress to pass a law in 1925 to prevent murderers from inheriting from their victims. However, it was difficult to convict non-Indians of crimes against Indians in Oklahoma. Their wealth also provided the Osage with a cushion against some of the repression and discrimination faced by other Indians. Parents concerned about their children in the agency boarding school insisted that tribal funds be used to hire enough workers so that their children would not have to do the heavy labor and menial tasks at the school. The Osage were able to have lavish giveaways for other tribes and they held gatherings on their reservation and traveled throughout the Plains, even to the Sioux and Crow, where they distributed property and paid for feasts. The Osage did not live in the large houses they built; they camped in their communities, which were oriented to peyote congregations. They built special structures where the peyote rituals took place. The Osage version of the peyote religion incorporated elements of Catholicism, remnants of the missionization experienced by their ancestors, including people of French descent who were incorporated into the Osage communities. During World War I the Osage were able to use their wealth to obtain recognition for the Indian contributions to the state and the nation. Despite the Indian Office's discouragement, 120 Osage joined the military. Many served in the Oklahoma National Guard as members of Company E, known as the "Millionaires Company." In 1919 Congress rewarded veterans with citizenship, and the Osage tribe received a certificate of appreciation for their efforts. In 1924 President Calvin Coolidge commended their valor and their contribution to the Red Cross and the bond drives during the war.[28]

The Northern Plains reservations generally were in less populous states than Oklahoma and considerably more isolated from centers of American settlement. The twentieth-century adaptations made are similar to those in Oklahoma, but there are regional differences and variations even among the Northern Plains groups. For example, the Blackfeet and Gros Ventre faced similar problems but developed different kinds of political responses. A significant difference between the two tribes was the extent to which American men married Indian women. Fort Benton, an American Fur Company post, became the site of the Blackfeet agency. When the trading company declined and went out of business, a large group of former employees, as well as army scouts, whisky traders, guides, ranchers, and cowboys remained in the area. They generally married Blackfeet women and settled on the northern sector of the reservation. Their wives' relatives maintained good relations with them, for the Blackfeet bands were mostly interested in raising horses, while the intermarried Americans were interested in raising cattle and grazing them free of charge on the reservation. Indians traded some of the cattle they received from the federal government for horses and provisions. Gradually, two economic interest groups formed, with the intermarried Americans and their families engaging in entrepreneurial ventures. The federal government leased much of the reservation to outside cattlemen who, as mandated by Congress, had to involve a "business council" in the transactions. (Thus, on the Northern Plains, business councils did tribal business, while in Oklahoma chiefs continued to act for their tribes because the grazing land had been sold.) At first, the traditional chiefs served on the business council, but soon after the turn of the century younger, bilingual men educated at Carlisle and Fort Shaw attained positions on the council. Some of these leaders were from the northern sector of the reservation. They tried to prevent the federal government from charging the Blackfeet tribe and the allottees for the construction and operation of irrigation ditches that were of dubious use, and they worked to postpone allotment and to prevent any surplus land from being sold once allotments were made. A conflict developed between the descendants of the bands from the southern part of the reservation and the individuals whose families were raising cattle on the northern section. Congress forced allotment and sold some of the reservation land in 1918, but the business committee succeeded in getting more reservation land allotted rather than sold, and the mineral rights for these lands were reserved to the tribe. Fee patents began to be issued after 1918 and most of the allotments eventually were lost. The business committee succeeded in getting an attorney and filing suit in the **Court of Claims** for the violation of the 1855 treaty. By the 1920s the interest group that favored cattle raising and individual economic enterprise constituted the majority of the population.[29]

In contrast, the Gros Ventre agency was not near a major trade center and did not attract large numbers of American men. Few Gros Ventre women had American husbands, and these families largely were integrated into Gros Ventre society, participating in ceremonial life and giveaways. All Gros Ventre men had ambitions of raising stock, horses and cattle. The largest operators were prominent Gros Ventre men. A business council was organized here also, and was comprised of middle-aged, bilingual men who were responsible to the Gros Ventre elders who initiated them into council positions. They tried to prevent trespassing and cattle rustling on the reservation, fought irrigation charges, worked to convince the federal government that none of their land should be leased to outside stockmen, and pursued a claim against the United States for the violation of the 1855 treaty. The federal authorities ignored the Gros Ventre success at stockraising and destroyed their livestock in order to lease reservation grazing land to American stockmen at low fees. At this point the Gros Ventre consensus was that allotment would be in their best interest if they could allot the entire reservation and not sell "surplus" land. They also knew that Montanans were demanding land cessions. The Gros Ventre leaders obtained the help of lobbyists in Washington, including the Indian Rights Association, and when the reservation was allotted in 1922 none of it was opened to settlement. The political unity of the Gros Ventre was facilitated by the unity among tribal members, who were not separated by different cultural adaptations or marriage patterns.[30]

The Crow faced similar problems—irrigation charges, forced sale of heirship land, and leases that hurt their efforts to raise stock. Crow leaders were especially determined to prevent any sale of surplus land after they were pressured to begin allotment. Young, bilingual men working in cooperation with the older chiefs organized a new government that was based on district representation. They organized as a business council in 1910 and lobbied Congress, obtained legal assistance, and asked for help from the "friends of the Indian" to divide the entire reservation into allotments with no surplus available for sale. In addition to Chief **Plenty Coups**, **Robert Yellowtail** was a prominent spokesman in the effort. When Congress allotted the reservation in 1920, the Crow delegations had succeeded—no surplus land was identified. Crow unity was facilitated by ceremonial activity. While the Gros Ventre rituals that promoted unity and generated support for leaders were secular in nature, Crow religion was central. The most important ceremony, conducted by the Tobacco Society, was a dramatization of creation and of the Crow's sacred charter to migrate to Montana. In return for planting and harvesting sacred tobacco (given them by a **culture hero**), they received supernatural blessing. The members of the society reenacted the transfer of the ceremony from the culture hero to their Crow ancestors by "adopting" new initiates into the society. There was gift exchange during the adoption in which the amount of property distributed brought prestige; in fact, there were many local chapters of the society that competed to recruit new members through generosity. The Tobacco Society had a very broad membership among the Crow; in 1910 most Crow were mem-

bers and the membership cut across clans and districts. The society was an out-
let for the ambitions of individuals, for a person could start a new chapter upon
receiving instructions in a vision. The relationship between the initiates and
their sponsors symbolized the relationship between individuals and their clan
uncles and aunts (father's clan).[31]

The Gros Ventre made a commitment to Catholicism in large part because
they felt they needed the help of the Catholic lobby to retain their reservation.
The Crow felt their reservation to be secure. Also, while Crows were able to
play off the Catholic and Protestant missionaries against each other, the
Catholics had sole possession of the missionary field at Fort Belknap. Though
secular rituals, the Gros Ventre moiety dances also unified the community and
served to channel food and property to the needy. At the turn of the century,
the men's society moiety dances were transformed into a communitywide moiety system. North of the dance hall was one moiety and south of the hall was
the other. The moieties competed in feasting and distributing gifts at a Christmas–New Year dance for which they raised money throughout the year by a series of smaller dances. The prominent people, including the Gros Ventre leaders, carried most of the responsibility. Individuals could introduce innovations
if they donated generously. At the dances, individuals (men and women, old
and young) held offices for which they "paid" by generosity. Thus, members of
the moieties had to work together and prominent people had to motivate everyone to contribute and participate.[32]

The Northern Arapaho may have emerged with their resource base most in-
tact. They developed a business committee that mobilized support from its
constituents and was buttressed by Arapaho ceremonial organization. The business committee sent delegations to Washington to protest the same policies that
business committees from other reservations were protesting. The water
charges for irrigation systems were unfair, the forced sales and below-market
prices for leases had impoverished Indians, and the per capita payments from
leases on tribal land were too small and resulted in Arapahos going into debt.
The injustices, such as the case of a woman who received $5 for land appraised
at $1,550, did not move federal officials. Another problem on all the reservations
was that the original allotments had been inherited by many descendants, resulting in individuals owning a small share in a parcel of land rather than a plot
of land they could farm or build a house on (fractionated heirship). Arapaho
business committees retained the support of their constituents because of their
traditional relationship with the older ritual leaders. The religious leaders, who
actually selected the committeemen and then informed federal authorities of
the results of the "election," legitimized business committee authority through
a ceremony of installation that reinforced the committeemen's awareness of
their social obligations and their subordination to elderly priests. These priests

perpetuated Arapaho religious ceremonies in part through flexibility. When their Sun Dance was banned between 1913 and 1923, Northern Arapahos participated in the Southern Arapaho Sun Dance. All the Arapaho religious ceremonies (including the Sacred Flat Pipe and Sun Dance) were adapted to the level of knowledge and training of those selected to preside over them. Youths were recruited into a new ceremony, the Crow Dance (a version of the Grass Dance), originated and supervised by an elder. This new ceremony allowed individuals to hold ritual office and make vows of sponsorship to support their prayers. Business committees also were helped to retain influence because until the 1920s they received extra quantities of rations, served as supervisors on work details on agency projects, and collected tolls from people who leased tribal land—all of which allowed them to distribute generously to others. The reservation superintendent had to work through established leaders, for their authority was strong enough to discourage individuals from deviating from the leaders' consensus about reservation affairs. In 1912 President Taft returned the northern section of the reservation to the Arapaho and Shoshone, for this ceded portion had not attracted farmers. The return of this huge territory, which eventually was to be a region of oil development, validated for the Arapaho the wisdom of their leaders. Tribal unity also was buttressed by the fact that Arapahos on the reservation had not married Americans and there was no interest group committed to entrepreneurial activity, as in the Blackfeet case.[33]

In Canada, the Plains peoples were settled on reservations by 1884. Funds for supplies were cut and the lack of food drove some to raid government storehouses. Councils were held at Sun Dance camps to generate unity in leaders' efforts to influence federal government policy. But officials did not see the need to negotiate with peoples they viewed as inferior. Robberies of storehouses continued and became an excuse for the government to arrest leaders. In confrontations on the reservations, some government employees were killed despite the urging of leaders that protest be nonviolent. In 1885 the Métis in Saskatchewan took up arms to defend their homeland and recruited some Plains Cree and Plains Ojibwa in their effort to obtain fair treatment from Canada. Despite attacks from troops, Cree, Assiniboine, and Métis leaders restrained their warriors from annihilating the soldiers; yet, the government arrested Cree and Métis leaders and imprisoned them in order to force their people to desist from demanding that treaty promises be kept. The Canadian troops crushed the movement (see **Northwest Rebellion**). Several Plains Cree, Assiniboine, and Métis were convicted of treason and imprisoned or executed. Big Bear, the Cree leader, was not involved in the rebellion but was jailed anyway. Soon after, some of the Plains Cree fled to the United States, and in 1916 Rocky Boy reservation was created for them and some Plains Ojibwa. Others settled at Fort Belknap and Fort Peck reservations, where they had kinsmen. In Canada after the rebellion, Plains Cree, Assiniboine, and Stoney were dispersed and isolated on more than forty small reservations in Saskatchewan and Alberta. The Blackfeet groups did not participate in the fighting. One of the most important chiefs in the confederacy was Crowfoot, a kinsman of the Cree leader **Poundmaker,** who was a leader in the rebellion. Nonetheless, Crowfoot refused to take up arms and, as a result of his loyalty, rations were increased for the malnourished Blackfeet. Their struggles to survive after the disappearance of the buffalo were similar to the experiences of the Blackfeet in Montana. They worked at cattle ranching but were dependent on rations. Their children were sent to boarding schools. The Northern Piegan and Blackfeet groups were pressured to cede part of their reservations between 1909 and 1918; the Bloods successfully resisted. A few allotments were made but Canada never allowed these to be sold and continued to require tribal consent for land cessions. Thus, in Canada the land base was more secure, and there was less intervention in religion and social custom.[34]

In 1928 conditions on reservations in the United States prompted an investigation. The **Meriam Report** affirmed what representatives of Plains communities had been saying all along—that allotment was an economic disaster, that federal intervention had institutionalized poverty, that the federal education program had damaged Indian children, and that Indians should be allowed freedom of expression. Despite the mistakes of the federal government, Plains peoples had maintained distinct social identities and reorganized and revitalized their ceremonial and religious life, creating in the process intertribal ties of various kinds as well as social bonds among the members of Plains Indian communities.[35]

NOTES

1. Orlan J. Svingen, *The Northern Cheyenne Indian Reservation, 1877–1900* (Niwot: University Press of Colorado, 1993), 113–25.
2. Francis Paul Prucha, *The Great Father: The United States Government and the American Indians*, 2 vols. (Lincoln: University of Nebraska Press, 1984), 609–10, 621–22, 631; Frederick E. Hoxie, *A Final Promise: The Campaign to Assimilate the Indians, 1880–1920* (Lincoln: University of Nebraska Press, 1984), 2, 3, 5, 10, 15, 39, 41, 43; Arrell M. Gibson, *The American Indian: Prehistory to the Present* (Lexington, MA: D. C. Heath, 1980), 491–95.
3. Hoxie, *Final Promise*, 43–44; Prucha, *Great Father*, 631–38; Roy W. Meyer, *The Village Indians of the Upper Missouri: The Mandans, Hidatsas, and Arikaras* (Lincoln: University of Nebraska Press, 1977), 136–37; John C. Ewers, *The Blackfeet: Raiders on the Northwestern Plains* (Norman: University of Oklahoma Press, 1958), 304, 313; Hana Samek, *The Blackfoot Confederacy, 1880–1920: A Comparative Study of Canadian and United States Indian Policy* (Albuquerque: University of New Mexico Press, 1987), 108; Loretta Fowler, *Shared Symbols, Contested Meanings: Gros Ventre Culture and History*,

1778–1984 (Ithaca: Cornell University Press, 1987), 57; Loretta Fowler, *Arapahoe Politics, 1851–1978: Symbols in Crises of Authority* (Lincoln: University of Nebraska Press, 1982), 94; Frederick E. Hoxie, *Parading Through History: The Making of the Crow Nation in America, 1805–1935* (Cambridge: Cambridge University Press, 1995), 119–20, 150, 229; Raymond J. DeMallie, "The Sioux in Montana and Dakota Territories: Cultural and Historical Background of the Ogden B. Read Collection," in *Vestiges of a Proud Nation: The Ogden B. Read Northern Plains Indian Collection* (Burlington, VT: Robert Hull Fleming Museum, 1986), 62–63; Muriel H. Wright, *A Guide to the Indian Tribes of Oklahoma* (Norman: University of Oklahoma Press, 1951), 46, 82, 159, 206; Svingen, 44, 65, 144–45.

4. Prucha, 646; DeMallie, 61; Ewers, 310–11.

5. Hoxie, *Final Promise*, 53–54, 58–60, 66, 68; Samek, 144; William E. Farr, *The Reservation Blackfeet, 1882–1945: A Photographic History of Cultural Survival* (Seattle and London: University of Washington Press, 1984), 53; Scott Riney, *The Rapid City Indian School, 1898–1933* (Norman: University of Oklahoma Press, 1999), 8–10, 18, 28, 62–64, 76, 88, 95, 140, 150, 210.

6. Hoxie, *Final Promise*, 70, 72, 75, 152–61, 213.

7. Judith A. Boughter, *Betraying the Omaha Nation, 1790–1916* (Norman: University of Oklahoma Press, 1998), 96, 102–4, 107, 109, 115, 134, 136, 138–40, 148, 154–55.

8. Gibson, 496–98, 501; Loretta Fowler, *Tribal Sovereignty and the Historical Imagination: Cheyenne-Arapaho Politics* (Lincoln: University of Nebraska Press, 2002), 28–30; Meyer, 137; Alexander Lesser, *The Pawnee Ghost Dance Hand Game: Ghost Dance Revival and Ethnic Identity* (Madison: University of Wisconsin Press, 1978 [1933]), 33; Wright, 159; Blue Clark, *Lone Wolf vs. Hitchcock: Treaty Rights and Indian Law at the End of the Nineteenth Century* (Lincoln: University of Nebraska Press, 1994), 50.

9. Garrick A. Bailey, "Changes in Osage Social Organization, 1673–1906," *University of Oregon Anthropological Papers* 5 (1973): 78; F. Todd Smith, *The Caddo, the Wichita and the United States, 1846–1901* (College Station: Texas A & M Press, 1996), 117–22; Lesser, 34–35; Meyer, 134–35, 138, 142, 146; Hoxie, *Parading*, 175, 184; Ewers, 284–86, 298–99.

10. Meyer, 142; Hoxie, *Parading*, 148–99; Gibson, 496; Svingen, 86; Clark, 36, 39–50.

11. Fowler, *Arapahoe Politics*, 81, 84–85, 91, 97; Fowler, *Tribal Sovereignty*, 6, 8, 10, 13–14, 18–19, 36; Hoxie, *Parading*, 124, 164–65, 176, 210, 273–85; Fowler, *Shared Symbols*, 62–63, 65–66; Samek, 157; Farr, 33; William T. Hagan, *United States-Comanche Relations: The Reservation Years* (New Haven: Yale University Press, 1976), 143, 148, 150–53; John Joseph Mathews, *The Osages: Children of the Middle Waters* (Norman: University of Oklahoma Press, 1961), 727.

12. Fowler, *Arapahoe Politics*, 68–70, 73, 77, 79, 86, 91, 98–99, 107–11; Hoxie, *Parading*, 120, 231; Fowler, *Shared Symbols*, 55, 57, 60, 67–68, 71; Fowler, *Tribal Sovereignty*, 10–12, 20–25, 30, 34–36, 40, 45; Hagan, 176; Terry P. Wilson, *The Underground Reservation: Osage Oil* (Lincoln: University of Nebraska Press, 1985), 25–26, 30, 35, 82; Bailey, 78, 83, 89–90; Thomas Biolsi, *Organizing the Lakota: The Political Economy of the New Deal on the Pine Ridge and Rosebud Reservations* (Tucson: University of Arizona Press, 1992), 32, 34, 41, 43–45.

13. Riney, 16, 18; Francis La Flesche, *The Middle Five: Indian Schoolboys of the Omaha Tribe* (Lincoln and London: University of Nebraska Press, 1963 [1900]), 120–22.

14. Robert H. Lowie, *The Crow Indians* (New York: Farrar and Rinehart, 1935), 46–47; Hoxie, *Parading*, 225; Bailey, 78, 85–88, 93.

15. Ewers, 310–11; Samek, 130–31; Fowler, *Arapahoe Politics*, 114; Fowler, *Shared Symbols*, 56; Hoxie, *Parading*, 209.

16. Lowie, 193, 206–13; Fowler, *Shared Symbols*, 267n57; Ewers, 311.

17. James Mooney, *The Ghost-dance Religion and the Sioux Outbreak of 1890*, Fourteenth Annual Report of the Bureau of American Ethnology for 1892–93 (Washington, DC: Smithsonian Institution, 1896); Alice B. Kehoe, *The Ghost Dance: Ethnohistory and Revitalization* (New York: Holt, Rinehart and Winston, 1989), 6–8, 13–29; Meyer, 152; Lesser, 53–62; Fowler, *Shared Symbols*, 56, 59; Fowler, *Arapahoe Politics*, 102, 123; Svingen, 79–80; Raymond J. DeMallie, "The Lakota Ghost Dance: An Ethnohistorical Account," *Pacific Historical Review* 51 (4) (1982): 385–405.

18. Lesser, 40, 72–73, 75, 78–79, 81, 85, 155–56, 323–24.

19. Omer C. Stewart, *The Peyote Religion: A History* (Norman: University of Oklahoma Press, 1987), 3, 34, 38, 45, 50, 51, 58, 60–61, 64–65, 68–69, 84, 86, 93, 105–6, 110, 116–23, 127, 148, 180–82, 194–95; Wesley R. Hurt, "Factors in the Persistence of Peyote in the Northern Plains," *Plains Anthropologist* 5 (9) (1960): 16–27, 17, 19–23.

20. William R. Powers, *Oglala Religion* (Lincoln: University of Nebraska Press, 1977), 108–9, 113–14; Raymond J. DeMallie and Douglas R. Parks, "Introduction," in *Sioux Indian Religion: Traditions and Innovations*, eds. Raymond J. DeMallie and Douglas R. Parks (Norman: University of Oklahoma Press, 1987), 9–12, 14; Smith, 134; Fowler, *Shared Symbols*, 146–48.

21. Hoxie, *Final Promise*, 85, 108, 113, 115, 148, 150, 161–86, 191, 213; Joseph G. Jorgensen, "Indians and the Metropolis," in *The American Indian in Urban Society*, ed. Jack O. Waddell and O. Michael Watson (Boston: Little, Brown, 1971), 84.

22. Wright, 46, 82, 159, 163, 206, 213; Lesser, 33; Fowler, *Tribal Sovereignty*, 29; Clark, 50, 68, 80–83; Smith, 149–51; Wilson, 45–49, 86, 90, 92; Fowler, *Arapahoe Politics*, 91, 94, 95; Samek, 119–21; Malcolm Mc Fee, *Modern Blackfeet: Montanans on a Reservation* (New York: Holt, Rinehart, Winston, 1972), 52, 54; Paul S. Rosier, *Rebirth of the Blackfeet Nation, 1912–1954* (Lincoln: University of Nebraska Press, 2001), 14, 18, 20, 24, 27, 31–32; Hoxie, *Parading*, 261–62; Meyer, 137, 138, 164–67; Fowler, *Shared Symbols*, 91–92; Biolsi, 6; Frederick E. Hoxie, "From Prison to Homeland: The Cheyenne River Reservation Before World War I," pp. 55–75 in *The Plains Indians of the Twentieth Century*, ed. Peter Iverson (Norman and London: University of Oklahoma Press, 1985), 60, 64, 67; Ernest L. Schusky, *The Forgotten Sioux: An Ethnohistory of the Lower Brule Reservation* (Chicago: Nelson-Hall, 1975), 182–86.

23. Riney, 13–14, 30–31, 36, 45, 49, 55, 57, 113, 120, 125, 132–33, 220.

24. Fowler, *Tribal Sovereignty*, 48–50, 52, 59, 62; Donald J. Berthrong, "Legacies of the Dawes Act: Bureaucrats and Land Thieves at the Cheyenne-Arapaho Agencies of Oklahoma," in *The Plains Indians of the Twentieth Century*, ed. Peter Iverson (Norman and London: University of Oklahoma Press, 1985), 31–53.

25. Fowler, *Tribal Sovereignty*, 63–68.

26. Ibid., 69–74, 76–91; Stewart, 131, 135, 136, 138, 214–15, 217–19, 222, 224, 226, 227, 230–31.

27. William C. Meadows, *Kiowa, Apache, and Comanche Military Societies: Enduring Veterans, 1800 to the Present* (Austin: University of Texas Press, 1999), 98, 100, 104–11, 116, 118, 120–22; Jacob J. Brody, *Indian Painters and White Patrons* (Albuquerque: University of New Mexico Press, 1971), 120–26.

28. Wilson, 117, 119–20, 129–32, 138, 142, 145–47.

29. Thomas R. Wessel, "Political Assimilation on the Blackfoot Indian Reservation, 1887–1934: A Study in Survival," in *Plains Indian Studies: A Collection of Essays in Honor of John C. Ewers and Waldo R. Wedel*, ed. Douglas H. Ubelaker and Herman J. Viola, Smithsonian Contributions to Anthropology 30 (Washington, DC: Smithsonian Institution Press, 1982), 59–72; Ewers, 326; Farr, 26–28, 104–5; Samek, 81, 119–21; Mc Fee, 52–53.

30. Fowler, *Shared Symbols*, 73, 80, 82–85, 90, 91, 93.

31. Hoxie, *Parading*, 202–3, 248–62, 269, 279; Lowie, 12, 19, 274–96; Fred W. Voget, *The Shoshoni–Crow Sun Dance* (Norman: University of Oklahoma Press, 1984), 19–23.

32. Fowler, *Shared Symbols*, 78–79, 84, 86–88, 94.

33. Fowler, *Arapahoe Politics*, 130, 133–34, 139, 141, 148–49, 151, 154, 159–60, 163–64.

34. Loretta Fowler, "The Great Plains from the Arrival of the Horse to 1885," in *The Cambridge History of the Native Peoples of the Americas*, vol. 1: North America, part 2, ed. Bruce G. Trigger and Wilcomb E. Washburn (Cambridge: Cambridge University Press, 1996), 46–48; Samek, 38–41, 46, 49, 58–59, 65–67, 76–78, 82–84, 110–12, 117–19, 172.

35. Lawrence C. Kelly, "United States Indian Policies, 1900–1980," in *History of Indian–White Relations*, ed. Wilcomb E. Washburn, *Handbook of North American Indians*, vol. 4, ed. William C. Sturtevant (Washington, DC: Smithsonian Institution Press, 1988), 72.

CHAPTER 5

The Self-Determination Era

Upon the election of Franklin Roosevelt to the presidency in 1932, there was an abrupt change in Indian policy. The assimilation program was abandoned and, instead, the new director of the Indian Office or the **Bureau of Indian Affairs** (hereafter, BIA), John Collier, attempted to rebuild the economies of Indian communities and to encourage the perpetuation of Indian customs and values. Collier, one of the reformers of the 1920s who criticized the Bureau of Indian Affairs, served as director from 1933 to 1945. He hoped to use federal funds to purchase heirship, fee patent, and ceded lands and restore them to tribal ownership. He and his staff worked with Congress to draft legislation known as the Indian Reorganization Act (hereafter, the IRA). Indians from the affected communities were not involved, although some BIA employees were of Indian descent. The bill became law in June 1934. It provided for an end to allotment and an indefinite extension of the trust status of allotments, restoration of land, credit programs, new criteria for employment in the BIA, and the establishment of tribal governments that would have the power to protect tribal resources and preserve traditional customs. Collier did not succeed in including a provision for a federal court that could deal with problems in tribal government and was unable to keep other promises made on his visits with Indian leaders, namely that they could design their governments themselves and that thirty-year no-interest loans would be available. Referendums were to be held in Indian communities, and a majority of those voting had to agree to accept the provisions of the IRA for the law to take effect. Thus, for the first time Indian communities would be able to vote on whether to accept federal Indian policy. The Indian communities in Oklahoma were excluded from the act, which led Collier to tour them with Oklahoma politicians and develop additional legislation satisfactory to them. The Oklahoma Indian Welfare Act provided for the establishment of tribal governments and credit programs and an end to allotment, but allowed the state to tax oil and gas on Indian land. It passed in June 1936.[1]

Referendums were held and most Plains tribes accepted the IRA: on the Northern Plains, the Blackfeet; Fort Belknap Gros Ventre and Assiniboine; Rocky Boy Cree and Ojibwa; Tongue River Cheyenne; Omaha; Northern Ponca; Fort Berthold Mandan, Hidatsa, and Arikara; Standing Rock Sioux; Cheyenne River Sioux; Lower Brule Sioux; Yankton Sioux; Rosebud and Pine Ridge Sioux; and Santee Sioux. The IRA was rejected by the Crow; Wind River Northern Arapaho; Fort Peck Assiniboine and Sioux; Crow Creek Sioux; and Sisseton Sioux (see map 7). On the Northern Plains, 66 percent of the eligible voters participated, compared to a 60 percent participation rate in the United States during the 1932 presidential election. In Oklahoma, the Osage and Kaw were excluded from participating, but the Cheyenne and Arapaho, Caddo, Pawnee, Iowa, and consolidated Kiowa, Comanche, and Plains Apache voted to accept the new program. The Wichita and Otoe-Missouria opted not to participate. The next step was to prepare constitutions for the tribal governments that were to be organized to participate in the implementation of the new policy. A "model" constitution was prepared by the BIA, which the tribes were pressed to accept, with some modifications permitted in certain instances. Collier did not expect the level of dissent that materialized in Indian communities over his reforms. Where there was perceived economic disparity, for example between allottees and landless Indians, there was conflict over who would be most helped by the changes. There also was conflict where there was not a well-developed tradition of centralized authority. Where this tradition existed, as with Crow, Arapaho, Cheyenne, and Gros Ventre, the vote, pro or con, carried with a large majority. Among the Rosebud and Pine Ridge Sioux, dissension was aggravated by the federal government's refusal to consider institutionalizing tribal councils already in place that had a means of reaching community-wide decisions. Where economic conditions were especially desperate, as with the Yankton, who had lost over half of their trust land, and the Gros Ventre (see below), there was a large vote for IRA reorganization. But Indian communities soon became disillusioned and, therefore, approval of constitutions was more difficult. One of the problems was that the constitutions made most of the "powers" of the tribal council subject to review by the Secretary of the Interior.

Constitutions were accepted by a lower percentage of voters than had approved the IRA. Some communities that had voted to reorganize under the act refused to accept a constitution (Yankton, Lower Brule, Standing Rock); others lived with constitutions that undermined the effectiveness of tribal government. A few examples will illustrate.[2]

On the Pine Ridge and Rosebud reservations, tribal councils had been operating since the 1920s. These councils had elected representatives from districts that formed in natural geographical areas and that dealt with federal officials through chiefs. Some members of the councils were chiefs in their districts, so they were broadly representative of a political tradition based on the treaty relationship between the Sioux and the United States. The tribal government proposed by the BIA called for secret ballots cast by individuals, which made it difficult for district leaders to mobilize support in public meetings. Also, the district organization was to be replaced by "community" representation—communities based on kinship rather than the political organization represented by the three-fourths council (see chapter 4). When Collier's representatives refused to allow constitutions to be written in the traditional tribal council tradition, many Sioux were alienated and stood in opposition to the IRA council for generations to come. Given the proposed responsibilities of these councils, the large numbers of landless people had opportunities to acquire more land and economic help than those with land, which contributed to the controversy. Collier had promised the Sioux more control, but they realized that the constitutions actually gave the Secretary of the Interior the right to review most of the tribal council's actions. As one tribal council leader at Rosebud complained in 1939, "There is too much Secretary of the Interior and not enough Indian." Thus, Thomas Biolsi in *Organizing the Lakota* concluded that the vote for the IRA and the constitutions reflected the expectation of some economic gain, while suspicions of and grievances against the federal government remained unaddressed. In fact, Collier was able to provide relief during the Depression when drought conditions made gardens fail, wild fruits unavailable, and leasees unable to pay allottees. The BIA arranged for rations and federal surplus commodities, and the Indian division of the Civilian Conservation Corps, a **New Deal** program started in 1933, offered Sioux men jobs. They built dams, roads, and fences; dug wells; made firebreaks, corrals, and telephone lines. Women did craft work. Credit was extended to many individuals, but not all who applied. Some communities received special development funds that established settlements with houses, stock, and irrigated fields. Six livestock cooperatives were established at Rosebud and seventeen at Pine Ridge. Economic conditions did improve and there was a moderate reversal of land loss for a few years.[3]

The situation among the Gros Ventre was not that there was conflict over accepting the IRA but that the promises of reorganization were not realized. In

1934, when they met with Collier, the Gros Ventre's stock enterprises had been largely destroyed through drought, the Depression, and forest fires. Half the families were on welfare, a departure from earlier years when the Gros Ventre had been relatively prosperous. In their meeting with Collier they understood that he guaranteed them that they could organize as a tribe separate from the Assiniboine, who also occupied Fort Belknap reservation, and determine their own membership. They also were promised extensive financial aid. On the basis of these understandings the Gros Ventre voted overwhelmingly for the IRA. When an official arrived from Washington to write their constitution, their ideas were ignored and to their shock, he insisted that they would have to organize a joint Gros Ventre–Assiniboine business committee. Believing that financial aid depended on their acceptance of the constitution, they voted to accept it. But when they were told they could not incorporate to manage their own economic enterprises because a "tribe" was not an appropriate organization to manage a corporation (despite the fact that other tribes obtained charters of incorporation), the Gros Ventre refused to accept a charter. By 1937, they were disillusioned with the political reforms of the IRA. They were shocked that the BIA had insisted that tribal membership be defined by "**blood**" descent from Gros Ventres—specifically, a "one-fourth Gros Ventre–Assiniboine blood" rule was required. To the federal government, association with the Gros Ventre community and its values was irrelevant. Because the Gros Ventre were about to receive money from their claim against the federal government for treaty violations, they wanted to exclude people who had never associated with them. One business committee member remarked in 1939, "The Interior Department goes on with its arbitrary rule the same as ever." In fact, the joint council's opinions on hiring, leasing, expenditure of tribal funds, and the credit program were ignored.

Some economic help was provided, but the extent of rehabilitation was less than the Gros Ventre had hoped for or been led to expect. Several economic cooperatives were established that provided some employment: a bull pool, a hay farm, a tribal cattle herd, and a timber operation. The loan program was inadequate to finance mechanized agriculture or to rebuild the cattle herds of individuals and the land base remained inadequate for building up Gros Ventre cattle ranches. Some land (30,000 acres) was purchased for the Gros Ventre, but it was not good grazing land and the BIA would not allow the business council to buy allotments from individuals. Cattle were issued to individuals, but they were "drought cattle," sickly animals purchased from non-Indians by the federal government and sold for higher prices to the Gros Ventre. Gros Ventre families had to lease much of their land and the BIA continued to withhold the lease money and deduct irrigation fees even though the Gros Ventre were unable to work the land. The number of cattle owned by the Gros Ventre actually declined from 1941 to 1951. Relief work was another problem because the federal government hired non-Indian people and allowed them to build a town on the reservation, which put a strain on reservation resources and caused social dissension in the Gros Ventre community. The business council pursued oil leases to raise income, but the BIA delayed approving them during the 1930s and 1940s. When the Gros Ventre received their claim (see **Court of Claims**) money in 1937 it was distributed per capita, not used for communitywide economic development. In an effort to support business committee authority, the superintendent of the reservation interfered with Gros Ventre ceremonial life by insisting that the committee take over the dances organized by moieties (see chapter 4). Thus the cooperative economic customs that promoted unity among the Gros Ventre were weakened. From the Gros Ventre perspective, reorganization was largely disastrous.[4]

Among the Blackfeet, both "full-" and "mixed-bloods" accepted the IRA (see "**blood**"). By the late 1920s, each group was determined to gain control over reservation economic development due to BIA mismanagement. As Paul Rosier explained in *Rebirth of the Blackfeet Nation*, competing economic interests rather than cultural heritage or ancestry had given shape to political conflict. An elite (2 percent of the population) owned 85 percent of the stock. Most Blackfeet were poor and came to the realization that their problems were caused by BIA mismanagement. Working together, Blackfeet leaders in 1933 succeeded in obtaining the right to lease land for oil production on the reservation. In so doing, bands once politically autonomous began to coalesce into one polity. In a council meeting in 1929, Peter Oscar told the crowd, "There is one nation on this reservation what you call Blackfeet, mixed bloods and full-blooded Indians. Help each other. . . . We must all work together if we are to accomplish something for our own benefit." In 1931, elderly chief Mountain Chief advised people in his community, "Now, I am asking you full-bloods—I want you to be friendly with the mixed-bloods. . . . They are of the same blood as we are. . . . They are our tribe. . . . We all belong on the reservation and we should try to get along together as a tribe." An emergent class consciousness remained a political force in the years after the Blackfeet, in repudiating BIA dominance, overwhelmingly accepted an IRA constitution and centralized government. Although the "mixed-blood" leaders outnumbered the "full-bloods," the business committee responded to their advocacy by providing for the needs of impoverished "full-" and "mixed-blood" people. The committee distributed a large part of tribal income from oil and the claim settlement in per capita payments and supported community centers, women's craft cooperatives, loans to needy families who lacked collateral, relief payments (including health care and funeral expenses), funds for celebrations, and beef rations. They prevented the sale of land bordering Glacier National Park and they included unelected "full-blood" representatives in council deliberations, even delegating to them the decision on how to apply "blood" criteria for enrollment in the Blackfeet Nation. In addition to providing for the poorest sector of the population, the committee gave aid to stockmen (a minority of their constitutents), expanding the cattle and sheep businesses on the reservation with IRA funding.[5]

The Cheyenne and Arapaho in Oklahoma also desperately needed economic aid and, for that reason, accepted the Oklahoma Indian Welfare Act. They did succeed in preparing a constitution that reflected their political tradition at the time of the New Deal. But they realized that they had little choice in the matter. The Depression and the drought of 1934–36 drove leasees out of business, resulting in a drastic decline in lease income for the Cheyenne and Arapaho. Indians could not farm their lands themselves, for they could not borrow money on trust land (which could not be used for collateral) to purchase the heavy equipment they needed to be competitive. Collier met with Oklahoma tribal representatives in Oklahoma City in 1934 and promoted his reorganization program. As on the Northern Plains, the representatives were suspicious. The Cheyenne and Arapaho feared that the program to increase the tribally owned land was another way of taking land out of individual Indian ownership. They insisted that their claims should be settled if the Collier regime was truly a "new deal." The promises of land for those without it and of rehabilitation funds were well received, however. The Cheyenne and Arapaho were under considerable pressure to accept the OIWA because its sponsor, Senator Elmer Thomas, was chair of the Indian Affairs Committee in Congress and instrumental to their effort to file a claim for the violation of the 1851 treaty. The bill offered loans, land acquisition, the extension of the trust status of allotments, and employment for Indians in BIA positions. Further, Collier warned them there would be no economic assistance if they rejected reorganization. The preparation of a constitution, which was accepted in 1937, was a stumbling block here as elsewhere. The Cheyenne and Arapaho had a business committee (since 1928) that was broadly representative and that incorporated elderly chiefs from all of the communities. Local communities met and sent resolutions and petitions through their representatives to the business committee. Chiefs and religious leaders were influential, regular participants. The BIA wanted to reduce the size of this committee and eliminate a formal role for chiefs. The Cheyenne and Arapaho prevailed in that on the reorganized business committee each Cheyenne district would send a chief (chosen by other chiefs); the Arapaho would elect representatives, but in practice, where chiefs were able to serve, they were elected. The BIA's flexibility on this issue probably reflected the acceptance of chieftainship in Oklahoma, where in the eastern part of the state, leaders had held the title of chief for generations. The Pawnee constitution also provided for a chiefs' council with authority over the elected council. Among the elected Cheyenne and Arapaho representatives in 1938 were several bilingual men who viewed their role to be that of assisting the older chiefs in dealings with the federal government. The tribes had equal representation on the business committee and tried to work together toward consensus, although they had different viewpoints on some issues. Both viewed their treaty history as a sacred sanction for the partnership between chiefs and bilingual, younger men. They viewed their relationship with the federal government to be rightly based on treaties. Reorganization brought the Cheyenne and Arapaho an expanded land base, but they remained poor. Insufficient funds undermined the credit program and the BIA continued to withhold lease money from Indians. Acreage used by the federal government in administering the agency was returned to the tribes and rehabilitation communities were established for several families (similar, though less developed than on Rosebud and Pine Ridge reservations). But farming was a risky business in western Oklahoma and the families struggled with little success. Land loss continued because the state of Oklahoma required that allotments be sold before Indians received welfare payments. By 1939, 68 percent of the allotted lands had been sold. The committee members also were disillusioned with the self-determination aspects of Collier's program. They complained that their views on hiring and leasing were ignored. Over time, the level of participation in business committee elections declined as the people's expectations went unrealized.[6]

Collier was unable to overcome the Northern Arapaho's suspicions of reorganization. They rejected both the IRA and a constitution, insisting on retaining the business committee organization already in place. The local superintendent on the reservation continued to press them to change, for example, to adopt the secret ballot method of voting; to elect younger, formally educated men for the committee; and to set up electoral districts where residents would vote on one representative. Business committee members insisted on discussing important issues in general councils and continued to be responsive to the concerns of elderly religious leaders. They relied on social pressure rather than formal, constitutional provisions for holding committee members accountable. Elders insisted that representatives had to be elected at large so that they kept the welfare of all the people in mind. Many of the New Deal economic reforms benefited the Wind River reservation even though the tribes there refused to accept the IRA, but the business committee had to fight the BIA in order to realize these gains. Both their assertiveness and their eventual success helped to reinforce leaders' authority roles, that is, the mutually supportive roles of business committee members and religious leaders. A sore point was the fact that the unallotted tribally owned lands on the northern sector of the reservation had oil wells that had been capped; the business committee wanted oil production in order to relieve poverty. Once the wells succeeded in bringing substantial income to the tribes, the BIA withheld the income from this mineral production from tribal members. The business committee worked with attorneys to convince Congress to force the BIA to release part of the money in the form of per capita payments. These payments decisively raised the standard of living on the reservation. Another problem was that the BIA pressured the Shoshone to purchase a large cattle ranch with funds from a claim settlement in 1937. This ranch was given to the Arapaho (who eventually repaid the Shoshone) and the federal government lent money to the Arapaho to buy cattle. The ranch became a source of jobs for Arapaho and of an annual dividend for tribe members. But the business committee had to fight the BIA in order to operate the ranch themselves. The successes of the business committee after 1937, and the support they received from religious leaders, helped prevent turnover and serious complaints from constituents.[7]

To encourage Indian arts, in 1935 Collier established the Indian Arts and Crafts Board. He arranged funding for clubs and cooperatives through which work could be marketed. Officials also tried to influence the development of the arts toward "traditional" styles. The Museum of the Plains Indian opened in 1941 among the Blackfeet and a crafts shop in Rapid City featured work of the Sioux. In Oklahoma the Southern Plains Indian Museum opened in Anadarko and a crafts shop was established at the Fort Sill Indian School. Among the Kiowa, federal funding supported a project to make dance costumes. In this way, employment for Indian women was provided.[8]

The extension of religious freedom by the IRA had lasting effects on the Plains. Probably the most dramatic example is the introduction of the Sun Dance on the Crow reservation, a reversal of the federal government's efforts to suppress this ceremony. The Crow had rejected the IRA, but one of the Crow leaders who had supported the reforms was recommended by the tribe to be the reservation superintendent. Collier appointed **Robert Yellowtail**, who spearheaded religious innovations. In 1938, inspired by visions, William Big Day decided to vow to sponsor a Sun Dance, but the Crow ceremony had been discontinued. He apprenticed himself to a **Sun Dance** leader on the Wind River reservation, so it was the Shoshone ceremony, somewhat modified over time, that became incorporated into Crow ceremonial life. Yellowtail used agency resources (trucks to haul poles and brush, a buffalo from the herd recently acquired by the tribe, and tribal police to maintain order) to support the Sun Dance ceremonies in 1941. The Sun Dance ceremony focused on restoration and maintenance of health and, during World War II, the safe return of Crow soldiers.[9]

The United States entered World War II in December 1941, and the government's resources were diverted from the New Deal to the war effort. Progress on Collier's programs slowed as BIA appropriations declined. The pace of land acquisition slowed. Money for loans was less available, yet 95 percent of the loans previously made had been repaid by 1945. The complaints against the BIA's relationship with tribal business committees continued and, as we shall see, contributed to the establishment of both the Indian Claims Commission and the National Congress of American Indians, both of which had a major impact on postwar Indian societies.

Plains Indian communities contributed to the war effort in various ways and the war had significant social repercussions for them. Collier attempted to convince the War Department to organize an all-Indian division administered by the BIA, but, while African-Americans were segregated, Indian servicemen and women were integrated into the armed services' training programs and fighting units. Apparently, Indians were regarded as "naturally" good soldiers. Plains communities gave enthusiastic support to the war effort, purchasing war bonds and sending young people into combat. On Sioux reservations, men volunteered in disproportionate numbers and were killed in disproportionate numbers as well. Elderly Sioux at Pine Ridge complained that men over 35 years of age could not join the military service. Forty percent of Crow men and nearly 50 percent of the Sioux and Assiniboine men at Fort Peck served in the military. Several Comanche soldiers were recruited by the army into the Signal Corps where they served in the European theater sending messages in the Comanche language, which was difficult for the Germans to decode. The Sioux and Cheyenne agreed to drop the pursuit of their claims against the government for the duration of the war. Plains Indians also worked in defense plants and in the airplane industry in cities including Los Angeles, Denver, Tulsa, and Oklahoma City.[10]

Economic consequences accompanied the out-migration to towns near reservations or Indian communities or to more distant places. For example, there were 200 Sioux working at defense plant installations near Pine Ridge. Family income more than tripled. The income of these workers was greater than what they had known before and they gained experience in nonagricultural wage work. Military pay also raised Indians' standard of living. On the other hand, the federal government took land from Indian communities for military purposes and declined to return it after the war. Much of the land acquired under the IRA was lost. The federal government took 400,000 acres from Pine Ridge in 1942 for use as an aerial gunnery range, paying allottees a minimal 75 cents an acre (which included mineral rights) and forcing families off their land. Another 100,000 acres of tribal land was appropriated. Oil and gas leases on Indian land were made on liberal terms as well.[11]

After the war most veterans and workers in the defense industry returned to the reservations, but some stayed in urban areas and began to form communities that were to figure importantly in Indian affairs in the years to come. On the reservations the return of veterans stimulated a resurgence and florescence of ceremonial activity. Activity among the Kiowa is a good illustration. More than 300 Kiowa men and women went to war. Peyote ceremonies were held for men going into battle and they were given protective medicines. One man who was captured and sent to a prisoner-of-war camp attributed his survival to his medicine pouch, which the Germans allowed him to keep. Christian prayer meetings also were held. The men's societies and women's organizations also held ceremonies where the soldiers were given social support and prayers, largely in the form of songs. Although the two women's societies had been discontinued by 1905, the war was the impetus for the establishment of three women's organizations that combined elements of the traditional women's society ceremonies with service club activity. The Kiowa War Mothers, the Carnegie Victory Club, and the Purple Heart Club involved virtually all Kiowa families in ritual life. So the women's martial roles in the recognition of warriors' bravery and the encouragement of valor were revitalized. In the Kiowa view there was a direct link between the ceremonial activity of women and religious leaders and success in battle. The dances sponsored by the women's groups became a vehicle for the expression of local community identity and, as each organization supported the others' events, strengthened tribal unity. When veterans returned they were honored by the few surviving elderly men who were members of men's warrior societies. Veterans were given names that reflected their accomplishments in battle. After the war, women's groups also held dances and supported the men's societies in honoring the veterans. Interestingly, although Kiowas were invited to join the American Legion and Veterans of Foreign Wars groups in nearby towns, they were uncomfortable with the central role that alcohol played in these groups' activities and they felt socially marginalized. Songs composed about battle experiences continued to figure importantly in Kiowa ritual life in the years to come.

Among the neighboring Cheyenne and Arapaho, the battle experiences of veterans stimulated a number of chiefs' initiations, so that the ranks of chiefs swelled. These positions were largely ceremonial at this time, with the chiefs responsible for promoting ceremonial activity, but the war experience was a link symbolically with chieftainship in the prereservation era. Cheyenne men's societies also initiated many of these veterans. On some reservations, for example among the Northern Arapaho at Wind River, American Legion organizations were organized with an Indian membership and assumed new ceremonial duties in the postwar society. Women's auxiliaries assisted them, thus reinforcing the martial role of women in Plains Indian society. The war dance, associated with the old **Grass Dance**, became central to intertribal gatherings that came to be known as **powwows** and brought together peoples from the Northern and Southern Plains. There was a reinvigoration of dancing and songs from the exchange of songs and other ritual customs that followed, and art based on beading, featherwork, and hide decoration flourished.[12]

After the war, veterans began to enter reservation politics, running for election to business committees. Their wartime experiences were regarded favorably on the Plains. On Lower Brule reservation, a nineteen-year-old veteran was elected chair of the business committee as a way of honoring him. At Crow Creek reservation, all the officers on the committee were veterans in 1945. By 1946 more than one third of business committee members were veterans. Veterans also became involved in state and national politics, especially in conjunction with the National Congress of American Indians (NCAI). Having experienced equal treatment in American society away from their home communities, as well as a higher living standard, they became active politically to change laws and policies. They pushed for change—eligibility for social security, veteran's benefits, the lifting of prohibitions against the sale of alcohol to Indians—with the help of the NCAI. This group, founded in 1944, was the first national political organization controlled by Indians. Its philosophy, personnel, and tactics were influenced by the New Deal (for example, the organization's constitution). A small group of BIA employees from several tribes started the organization by sponsoring a convention that drew delegates from reservations and Indian communities throughout the country. Most of the delegates were from the Plains and eastern Oklahoma. The NCAI emphasized tribal revitalization and made use of the contributions of Indian veterans during the war to try to influence federal policy. They worked for the elimination of legal discrimination and the maintenance of special legal status for Indian communities, supporting benefits for Indian veterans and the passage of the Indian Claims Commission Act in 1946. Tribes pursuing claims had had to appeal to Congress for legislation to allow their cases to proceed to the federal Court of Claims. Collier urged the formation of the Indian Claims Commission in order to allow for a speedier resolution of claims (but actually the commission did not finish its work until 1978). Veterans working with the NCAI campaigned for a fair share of the GI Bill and an end to the prohibition of the sale of alcohol to Indians, which was not accomplished until 1953. The income of veterans and their families sharply declined after the war and many resorted to trying to obtain fee patents so they could sell their land. Between 1946 and 1950 requests for patents-in-fee multiplied fourfold. Congress refused to help protect the Indian land base by allowing tribes to purchase the allotments with federal funds. Unable to mortgage trust land to get loans, veterans turned to the Veterans Administration for economic and educational assistance, applying for loans and educational benefits.[13]

The NCAI lobbying activity dovetailed with a shift in Congress away from support of Collier's programs. Collier resigned in 1945, and his successors returned to assimilationist policies. From the 1950s to the mid-1960s, Plains Indians (as well as Indians elsewhere) had to contend with "termination" legislation and with the BIA's policy of relocating Indians to urban areas away from their local, rural communities. During this time, federal policy was to end the federal trust relationship. Funding was withdrawn for BIA schools; instead, public schools received money for Indian students. Responsibility for health care for Indians was transferred from the BIA to the Department of Health, Education and Welfare, where public health programs were developed for Indians. Congress established the Indian Claims Commission to "get out of the Indian business." Applications for fee patents were encouraged and approved in large numbers. In 1953 Congress passed House Concurrent Resolution 108, which established the policy of ending the trust relationship between the United States and the tribes. Tribes were categorized in terms of how ready they were to be "terminated," that is, to assume full responsibility for their resources and their social welfare. Several Plains tribes were threatened with termination, but only the Northern Ponca actually were terminated. The NCAI fought the termination policy and so did tribal governments, insisting on the need for the federal government to obtain the consent of tribes before they were terminated. In fact, business committees found a renewed sense of purpose and were able to mobilize their constituents around the filing of claims with the Indian Claims Commission and the contestation of termination efforts on the part of Congress. On the other hand, when the tribes won a claim, the judgment generally was distributed per capita rather than used for economic development. Business committees were not able to invest the money in the future development of their communities. The tribes had to prepare rolls of members qualified to receive the claim payment, and the blood degree requirement (see **"blood"**) and other federal interventions limited the tribes' ability to decide their own membership.[14]

In addition to termination, the BIA vigorously promoted the relocation of Indians, that is, the removal of individuals and families from their home communities and their resettlement in urban areas. The BIA paid transportation expenses and one month's living expenses, and provided counseling. In part relocation was a response to the significant rate of growth of the populations in Indian communities, which reflected improved health conditions. These communities could not support the growing population. Relocation also was intended as a means of assimilation into the wider American society. Many of the relocatees were from Plains societies, but in urban areas they settled into an impoverished existence and after a short period of time many (from 30–75 percent) returned to their home communities. Those who remained participated in the activities of Indian centers.[15]

Termination and relocation had significant repercussions in Indian communities on the Northern and Southern Plains. In the north, in the case of the Gros Ventre on Fort Belknap, tribally owned enterprises were dissolved, the loan program was discontinued, the Gros Ventre and Assiniboine tribes were not allowed to purchase land from allottees, and individuals were encouraged to relocate. As people moved away, the community ceremonies became less important and more difficult to organize. The business committee's constituents lost confidence in the committee. When oil began to be extracted, the committee sought to secure the royalties for the tribes, as had been promised at the time of allotment. But, in keeping with termination policy, the federal government insisted that individuals should receive the income from mineral production, and it was distributed per capita in the 1950s. No funds were available for economic development. In comparison, the business committee on Wind River reservation had been able to convince Congress to allocate part of the income from mineral royalties for per capita payments and reserve part of it for social programs administered by the committee. Thus, the Northern Arapaho business committee continued to have an economic role on Wind River reservation. The per capita payments there were substantially more than at Fort Belknap, and Arapahos built houses, installed electricity, and generally raised their standard of living in the 1950s. The population on Fort Belknap reservation increased dramatically—38.4 percent from 1950 to 1955. With such limited economic opportunity, many left the reservation and obtained training for jobs elsewhere. In the context of the significant out-migration and the decline of community activity, a legal definition of Gros Ventre tribal membership based on Gros Ventre "blood" quantum was accepted by the tribe in 1958.[16]

The Mandan, Hidatsa, and Arikara on Fort Berthold reservation experienced a similar political, economic, and ceremonial transition during the termination era. This reservation was flooded by the Garrison Dam project. After the war the Army Corps of Engineers and the Bureau of Reclamation built dams on the Missouri River and reservoirs on tributaries; Fort Randall Dam took part of the Yankton reservation and flooded part of the Lower Brule and Crow Creek reservations. Another dam flooded the Cheyenne River and Standing Rock reservations. Inadequate compensation and economic deterioration followed. When the Garrison Dam flooded the Fort Berthold reservation, the federal government paid several million dollars in compensation in 1957. With the support of Congress, tribal members voted for the per capita distribution of this money. Subsequently, after the tribes were relocated to less fertile lands, they went into an economic decline from a condition of "moderate affluence," according to Roy Meyer in *The Village Indians of the Upper Missouri*. The proportion of the population that did not migrate to towns was increasingly on welfare. Also contributing to poverty was a very liberal policy of issuing fee patents from 1953 to 1961, when many sold their land. The annual powwow on the reservation became the focal point of ceremonial life.[17]

On the Southern Plains, the Southern Cheyenne and Arapaho also experienced extensive out-migration because of postwar poverty. In 1950 almost half of the members of these tribes were living in cities, probably most in Oklahoma, Kansas, and Texas. This group began to see their relationship to the Cheyenne and Arapaho tribes differently than those still living in the home community. They sought the per capita distribution of tribal assets, rather than the development of the home community. The business committee finally succeeded in pursuing their claim for treaty violation, and the Indian Claims Commission found in their favor in 1955. Thus, tribal members expected a judgment in the amount of millions of dollars to be potentially available for distribution. In 1959 the tribes decided to require that those who sought enrollment be of one fourth Cheyenne and/or Arapaho descent ("blood"); members did not have to live in the home community. The tribal roll increased by one third in anticipation of the payment, and urban members began to participate in tribal politics, challenging the business committee and running for office on a per capita payment platform. Efforts of the business committee to build the land base were often thwarted. With Congress hostile to economic development and land acquisition and reducing support for Indians, the business committee succeeded primarily in getting the return of lands used by the federal government for administration purposes; but the local school was closed. The business committee succeeded in negotiating oil leases but constituents, led by the urban sector, insisted on a per capita distribution of the oil money rather than using it for community development. The counterpoint to the individualism in the political sector was the powwow, which became the focus of the home community's ceremonial life and drew in the urban population as well. Stimulated by the dance activity surrounding veterans from World War II and the Korean War, communities in the 1950s initiated men into Cheyenne and Arapaho chiefs' positions and the Cheyenne military societies. Powwows were organized with the help of "head staff," individuals invited to hold honorary positions during the dances. Urban residents were among those selected and a variant of the giveaway was developed that eliminated economic differentials between urban and rural participants. Families sponsored giveaways in honor of individuals who had achievements in the urban world, and the powwows served as "homecoming" celebrations for urban people as well as a way to express tribal identity.[18]

The threat of termination worked to stimulate the Kiowa's renewal of men's societies, and the return of people from jobs in urban areas helped change the social organization of the Kiowa community. World War II and the Korean War, which stimulated the "sendoff" and "homecoming" of veterans, led to a formal revival of the Gourd Society in 1957 and the Black Legs Society in 1958. The Gourd Society changed its organization and ceremonial activity to incorporate a broad membership. This society evolved into the Kiowa Gourd Clan, which worked to strengthen Kiowa traditions by not requiring that members be veterans and by allowing people from other tribes (primarily in-marrying spouses) to join. The Gourd Clan incorporated Kiowa warrior tradition, feasting, and giveaways that drew members' families into the dances. The Black Legs Society integrated the Kiowa Veterans Association and warrior society traditions. Members had to be veterans and enrolled in the Kiowa tribe, and women's groups assisted the society in their dances and activities. A uniform dress code reinforced Kiowa tradition, synthesizing the symbolism of Kiowa military societies and the U.S. military: members carried a lance with military decorations. The leader of the revived society, Gus Palmer Sr., had twenty-one eagle feathers on his lance to represent twenty-one bombing missions made in World War II. Members wore a red cape in memory of one of Palmer's ancestors who captured a red cape from a Mexican officer. A society tepee was decorated in military symbols and served as a memorial to those killed in battle. News of the termination policy and a move to separate the Kiowa, Comanche, and Apache business committee into three autonomous governments suggested to some that the federal government intended to cease recognition of the Kiowa tribe. As one man put it, "We have to show that we were still Indians. . . . So that's one reason why I think that this culture and dancing all came back." The membership of the Kiowa Gourd Clan and Black Legs Society dramatically increased until virtually all Kiowa participated. As the powwow became the focus of Kiowa ceremonial life, the military society activity there was the most important element. Families worked together to support feasts and giveaways associated with powwows. Prior to World War II the business committee was dominated by elite families (the prereservation high-ranking families), who were prominent in the society. As the ability to speak English and deal with American bureaucracy became more important, lower-ranking families were elected. They also were incorporated into the Gourd Clan and Black Legs Society and participated in powwows, so this ceremonial activity promoted pan-Kiowa unity and identity. Individuals from other tribes also were drawn into Kiowa ceremonialism, and the exchange of powwow songs and dances (especially the Gourd Dance) and other traditions among Plains tribes continued into the 1960s and afterward.[19]

During the termination era, Plains Indian leaders worked together to protect the resources of their communities and the political status of tribes. At the same time there was a florescence of ceremonial activity that involved intertribal gatherings (powwows). In Oklahoma the tribes had been gathering for dances throughout the reservation and postreservation eras. Songs and dances were diffused from tribe to tribe, often with modifications that allowed for culturally appropriate innovations. The Plains groups from northern Oklahoma (formerly the villagers, such as Ponca, Osage, Otoe, and Missouria) had a Grass Dance tradition that became known as the "straight" dance style (where dance outfits were tailored and made of cloth, for example) and the formerly nomadic groups from western Oklahoma had developed a "fancy" dance style of war (or Grass) dance (where outfits featured feathered bustles). Powwows came to include both these traditions, as well as "gourd dances," in which dancers moved in unison shaking gourd rattles. The war dance involved a body of dancers, each dancing freestyle, moving around the center of the dance area in a circle. Women danced in place or moved in a circle. Male singers sang for the dancers in unison around a bass drum and women singers sang with them an octave higher. In the mid-1950s, the Oklahoma traditions diffused northward to South Dakota, where the Grass Dance tradition had been influenced by Canadian Plains and other Northern Plains peoples. There was an exchange of songs and dance styles that in subsequent years shaped the modern Plains powwow. This tradition was adopted by urban Indian centers as well, and eventually the Plains-inspired powwow traditions were diffused throughout the United States. On the Plains this florescence also included revivals of other ceremonies: Ponca and Osage dance societies, the Black Legs men's society among the Kiowa, and a renewed interest in self-torture in the Sun Dance on some Sioux reservations.[20]

Beginning in the 1960s, there was another policy reversal. The Kennedy-Johnson years saw an effort on the part of the federal government to eradicate poverty throughout the United States and the development of a broad-based civil rights movement that affected Indian communities nationwide. The Vietnam War also figured in the transformation of American society at this time. President Johnson initiated the "War on Poverty," which included legislation that gave tribal governments new powers and significantly affected the living standards of Indian people. The director of the BIA from 1961 to 1966 was Phileo Nash, an anthropologist who pressured Congress to make Indians eligible for War on Poverty funds and who referred to the shift in policy as a "New Trail." At first only reservation-based communities were included in the poverty programs, but eventually the Oklahoma tribes were able to participate. Tribes applied for federal funds for housing, educational, and job training programs. They also submitted proposals for economic development. The funding for the programs was given directly to tribal governments, not to the BIA, and tribal officials did the hiring and made policy decisions. Tribal governments expanded and gained experience in administering programs. Probably the most important piece of legislation was the Economic Opportunity Act of 1964, which created the Office of Economic Opportunity that administered the Community Action Program, Project Head Start (a preschool educational program), and Legal Services. The CAP funds were used to hire Indians to work on projects beneficial to their home communities. Legal Services provided assistance to Indians faced with local discrimination. Before 1960 the BIA did not help to build houses and improve the sanitary facilities in Indian communities; in 1965 the Housing and

Urban Development program began working with tribes and with the Indian Health Service branch of Public Health to build houses on allotments and housing developments on tribal land. Richard Nixon was elected in 1968, and he continued the Johnson policy of self-determination. The Office of Economic Opportunity was reorganized and the name changed to the Office of Native American Programs; Nixon's policy was "self-determination without termination." The Indian Civil Rights Act, passed in 1968, required that Indian communities give their consent before state governments could extend control over tribal affairs. The Elementary and Secondary Education Act of 1972 allowed for the establishment of Indian-controlled schools and Native American studies programs in schools near Indian communities. During the Vietnam War, Plains Indian men and women entered the service in large numbers. After the war these veterans qualified for educational benefits, and many took advantage of them to work for college degrees. The civil rights movement had a profound effect on relations between Indians and other Americans. Urban Indians got firsthand experience in protest demonstrations, and this style of activism eventually surfaced in the rural Indian communities. The social changes during the 1960s and 1970s profoundly affected Indian communities.[21]

On Fort Belknap reservation, the War on Poverty brought hundreds of skilled and unskilled jobs and administrative positions in 1964 and 1965. Jobs and new housing drew many Gros Ventre back from the cities. Elderly Gros Ventres came back to the reservation to retire where they got houses and, sometimes, positions in Native American studies programs. The prestige of the business committee grew and the committee positions attracted young, college-educated Gros Ventres, many of whom were veterans who had gone to college with the assistance of veterans' benefits. After the passage of the Self-Determination Act, developed by the Nixon administration and signed into law by President Gerald Ford in 1975, a Gros Ventre became reservation superintendent and the Fort Belknap tribes contracted for health, legal, educational, and other programs. Improvements in living standards were dramatic. Unemployment decreased from 77 percent in 1965 to 44 percent in 1979. In 1966 only 2 percent of tribe members had attended college; in 1981, 18 percent. When the Gros Ventre won their claims against the federal government in 1972 (for the 1888 land cession) and 1983 (for the 1874 cession), they reserved 20 percent of the payment for social programs.[22]

Conditions on Rosebud reservation also improved, but reflected a widespread problem: the programs were not funded well enough to help all those who qualified. Eight thousand Teton Sioux resided on the reservation in 1979 and about 14,000 lived off the reservation. The reservation was divided into 22 districts, and lifestyles varied widely. In the most rural, isolated areas, people lived in substandard housing and relied to a great extent on hunting small game and harvesting wild fruit and vegetables such as turnips and onions. The tribe still owned a cattle ranch (purchased during the New Deal period) and was buying land, including allotments from owners who wanted to sell. New jobs, most of which were poverty program positions, had relieved some of the unemployment, but still the rate was 65 percent (compared to 7 to 12 percent nationally). Many families relied on commodity foods distributed by the Department of Agriculture rather than food stamps, for which they were eligible but which required embarrassing face-to-face encounters with state officials. The benefits and problems of programs are illustrated by the housing projects at Rosebud. HUD offered different types of housing that required different kinds and levels of contributions by homeowners. Some housing was so substandard that the federal government forgave the money due on its purchase, which meant that some families had paid most of the purchase price and others very little. Thus, there was considerable resentment over perceived inequities. Sioux people believed that some families received preferential treatment and often blamed the business committee for these kinds of problems. Moreover, the housing programs could not meet the demand. In 1979 there were 1,000 applicants and funds for 150 homes. For a population of 8,000 there were 2,000 modern houses. Many families lived in log cabins with wood-burning stoves. Many homes, new and old, had no running water or indoor plumbing. Still, housing conditions had improved since the early 1960s.[23]

Nixon's policy of "self-determination without termination" led to the federal government's support for the reversal of termination, that is, the restoration of tribal status. On the Plains, the Northern Ponca tribe was restored. The legislation that became known as the Self-Determination Act, signed into law by President Gerald Ford in 1975, allowed tribes to contract for all the services performed by the BIA as well as apply for grants. Additional legislation passed during Ford's and subsequent presidencies continued the self-determination policy. The Health Care Improvement Act of 1976 strengthened health care services. In 1978 the Indian Child Welfare Act gave tribes jurisdiction over children of tribal members. In 1982 the American Indian Tax Act allowed tribes to tax business activity on Indian land. Federal courts were supportive of self-determination. For example, in 1981 *Merrion v. Jicarilla Apache Tribe* upheld the authority of tribes to collect a severance tax on oil and gas production on tribal land. In 1988 the Indian Gaming Regulatory Act provided for federal regulation of casino and high-stakes bingo enterprises and facilitated the establishment of these enterprises in the face of state opposition. In 1990 the Native American Graves Protection and Repatriation Act made possible the return of Indian remains from museums and other repositories to tribes identified with the remains. In 1993 the Religious Freedom Restoration Act gave federal protections to Indian religious practices.[24]

All this legislation and judicial activity created new opportunities for tribal government but also new challenges. The Cheyenne and Arapaho circumstances illustrate this. Their per capita income in 1990 was two fifths that of the state of Oklahoma, and 64 percent of the Cheyenne and Arapaho population qualified for food stamps. Much of the tribal and individual income came from leases, but the federal government has been shown to have seriously mismanaged these resources, producing lower income than the tribes were due. Contracting resulted in many more jobs and more and better services. In contracting the programs, the tribes received the administrative overhead (that is, indirect costs) in addition to the direct costs of the programs themselves. Administrative departments funded by indirect costs operated the programs for the Cheyenne and Arapaho. The Finance Department maintained financial records. The Public Works Department was responsible for environmental projects in water safety and waste disposal. Other departments were Planning, Personnel, Public Information, and Enrollment. The tribes managed programs and contracts in social services, education, health, and job training that were contracted from the BIA, Department of Labor, Health and Human Services, Department of Agriculture, and Department of Commerce. Social Services operated a general assistance program (which provided less money than state agencies but was easier for tribal members to use) and a youth shelter. This department also was responsible for child welfare and had a child protection worker who tried to unite parents and children or place children with relatives or Cheyenne or Arapaho foster families rather than non-Indians. The child welfare workers adopted a more culturally sensitive approach to their cases, setting standards appropriate to the Cheyenne and Arapaho community rather than the non-Indian one. One of the important programs of the Health Department was an ambulance service; local hospitals in the area could not be relied on to transport Cheyenne and Arapaho. The substance abuse program incorporated Native American ceremonies into the treatment of recovering addicts. The Education Department operated four Head Start Centers that incorporated native language and culture studies and the department managed the tribes' scholarship program. Job training programs, law enforcement (police officers, an attorney general and assistant attorney general, and a public defender), a tribal court (with district and supreme court justices who had jurisdiction over cases involving trust land and disputes between tribal members), home improvement and home building, food distribution, elderly nutrition, and fire suppression (a training program for individuals who fought forest fires)—all were designed to be sensitive to the social and cultural circumstances of the Cheyenne and Arapaho. In addition to their programs, the Cheyenne and Arapaho tribes owned businesses (shops that sold cigarettes and sundries, high-stakes bingo halls, a gambling casino, and a ranch).[25]

Despite the quicker pace of economic development, contracting led to conflict between the business committee and its constituents. According to the 1975 legislation, the programs were supposed to be funded at the same level as when federal agencies had responsibility for them. In fact, funds were siphoned off by the BIA and the Indian Health Service for administrative costs, so the tribes had less money to do basically the same work. There was not enough funding to provide jobs and services to all who qualified; the business committee was accused of favoritism. The Secretary of the Interior had approved a revised version of the tribes' constitution in 1975, but this document made no mention of who was to be responsible for the funds from contracting, tribal businesses, and taxes. The business committee had to assume responsibility for these monies and, as a result, was vulnerable to accusations of abuse of power from constituents. The tribes received overhead costs for administering the programs, the amount of which was determined by the federal government at a flat rate. Some programs did not pay the overhead, and the federal government expected the tribes to make up the difference. Tribe members opposed making up the difference with tribal funds. The federal government considered these shortfalls to be "deficits," and reports in the local media described them as such, although generally the financial problems were not due to overspending or misappropriation of funds. Constituents who did not understand these complicated financial transactions were critical of the business committee's management.[26]

The civil rights movement, as well as the Indian education legislation, stimulated ceremonial revival on several Northern Plains reservations. The American Indian Movement (AIM) played a role in these developments. The movement started in 1968 during a time of social activism, energized by the antiwar movement in the country at large, which raised the visibility and influence of all minority groups. The women's movement had some influence on the entry of Native American women into tribal politics; during the 1960s they began to be elected to business committees. AIM was organized in Minneapolis largely as a protest against police mistreatment of Indians. It was media oriented, seeking to draw public attention to the plight of Indians. In 1972, AIM leaders attending the Rosebud reservation fair organized a caravan of Indian people who traveled east from city to city on the way to Washington, D.C. to protest the violation of treaties and the treatment of Indians. Opposed by the NCAI, they occupied BIA offices and eventually negotiated their departure. President Nixon's attention was somewhat diverted from developing Indian legislation because of the protest activity of AIM and of protestors in general. The following year, invited to the Pine Ridge Sioux reservation by some opponents of recently elected business committee members, AIM members (a few of whom were Sioux) occupied a small settlement at Wounded Knee, which was then fresh in the public mind due to the recent publication of Dee Brown's *Bury My Heart at Wounded Knee*. Surrounded by federal mar-shals and FBI agents, AIM leaders played to the press: Russell Means (a Sioux whose family was originally from Pine Ridge) stated, "You might as well kill me, because I have no reason for living." Shootings of government agents re-sulted in arrests of AIM leaders, and to Indians around the country the move-ment acquired a violent reputation. After the Wounded Knee incident, an AIM member ran for election to the business committee on Pine Ridge but was defeated. At Rosebud in the 1970s, most Brule Sioux were fearful of and hostile to AIM members, whom they viewed as outsiders who had come to the reservation to find their "roots" and were responsible for an escalation of vio-lence there. AIM leaders apprenticed themselves to religious leaders and par-ticipated in the Sun Dance, Native American Church meetings, and other rit-uals. A few Sioux religious leaders acted as their "spiritual advisors," and AIM participation brought attention to native religious rituals. AIM lost national visibility after the end of the Vietnam War in 1973. By the 1980s, there was a reconciliation on the Rosebud and Pine Ridge reservations between AIM and residents, and there was broad-based participation in Sioux rituals, particular-ly in the powwow context. AIM's emphasis on pride in being Indian had a con-siderable influence on young Indian people everywhere.[27]

On Fort Belknap reservation, AIM influenced ceremonial life as well. Sev-eral Gros Ventres living in cities during the late 1960s became involved with AIM and with urban poverty programs and participated in demonstrations and media events. In the cities, ceremonial life was intertribal in focus. When the AIM members returned to Fort Belknap they wanted to participate in native religion. They sought spirit helpers in vision quests and tried to participate in the Sun Dance and peyote meetings on the reservations where these rituals were held. At Fort Belknap they became involved in trying to establish or reestablish these forms of "traditional" ritual in a community where ritual re-vitalization centered on the powwow tradition. They were met with suspicion and hostility at Fort Belknap and avoided the powwows already established there, which they labeled as un-Indian because of the "materialism" exhibit-ed, as expressed in giveaways and dance contests. They opposed veteran sym-bolism because of their hostility to the United States and its treatment of In-dians. AIM members instead organized a new powwow, the Chief **Joseph** Powwow, in 1974. The symbolism recalled the Indian warrior who fought the United States (as Chief Joseph resisted reservation life) and honored martyr-dom. The new powwow was validated by a vision experience of one of its or-ganizers. The giveaway and contest prizes were transformed so that everyone in attendance received gifts.[28]

The civil rights movement also gave impetus to the legislation to facilitate the return to tribes of human remains and other objects from museums and other repositories. For example, the Omaha secured the return of their sacred pole, given to the Peabody Museum in 1888; the pole was brought to the Omaha community in 1989, and later the tribe arranged to have it kept at the University of Nebraska. Human remains were repatriated from the Nebraska State Historical Society. In 1993 and 1994 the Southern Cheyenne and Arapaho repatriated remains from the Smithsonian Institution.[29]

Plains peoples today all have tribal governments that manage tribal economies and social services for their membership, and they all have embraced the ceremonial complex associated with the powwow. Membership rolls have increased due to population growth and, in some cases, changes in the criteria for membership. The tribes have maintained distinct social and cultural identities despite the centuries of hardship and dislocation. Plains peoples also have contributed to American culture, for example, in giving names to rivers, states, and towns, and have helped shape the economic and political history of North America.

NOTES

1. Graham D. Taylor, *The New Deal and American Indian Tribalism* (Lincoln: University of Nebraska Press, 1980), 12, 17–18, 25–28, 30, 33–36.
2. Ibid., 39, 43; Theodore H. Haas, *Ten Years of Tribal Government Under I.R.A.* (Chicago: United States Indian Service, 1947), 17–20, 32, 34; Muriel H. Wright, *A Guide to the Indian Tribes of Oklahoma* (Norman: University of Oklahoma Press, 1951), 46, 52, 82–83, 159, 206; Martha Royce Blaine, *The Ioway Indians* (Norman: University of Oklahoma Press, 1979), 298; Thomas Biolsi, *Organizing the Lakota: The Political Economy of the New Deal on the Pine Ridge and Rosebud Reservations* (Tucson: University of Arizona Press, 1992), 61, 70, 77, 84–87, 92–97; F. Todd Smith, *The Caddo, the Wichita and the United States, 1846–1901* (College Station: Texas A & M Press, 1996), 154; Terry P. Wilson, *The Underground Reservation: Osage Oil* (Lincoln: University of Nebraska Press, 1985), 167; R. David Edmunds, *The Otoe-Missouria People* (Phoenix: Indian Tribal Series, 1976), 82.
3. Taylor, 18, 119, 121; Biolsi, 62, 109, 111–14, 117, 120, 123–24, 140, 147, 155, 157.
4. Loretta Fowler, *Shared Symbols, Contested Meanings: Gros Ventre Culture and History, 1778–1984* (Ithaca: Cornell University Press, 1987), 95–109, 114 (quote on 104); Loretta Fowler, "Political Middlemen and the Headman Tradition Among the Twentieth-Century Gros Ventres of Fort Belknap Reservation," *Journal of the West* 23 (3) (1984): 54–63, 60.
5. Paul C. Rosier, *Rebirth of the Blackfeet Nation, 1912–1954* (Lincoln and London: University of Nebraska Press, 2001), 20–21, 31, 38, 40–41, 49, 52–53, 58, 71, 86, 95–97, 102, 107, 109, 114, 120, 139, 147, 153, 166, 168, 172, 174, 178–79, 184–85, 189, 192–93, 195, 198, 202–3, 207, 210, 212, 214 (quotes on pp. 56, 65).
6. Loretta Fowler, *Tribal Sovereignty and the Historical Imagination: Cheyenne-Arapaho Politics* (Lincoln: University of Nebraska Press, 2002), 93, 101, 105, 107, 109–11, 113–14, 116–17,

121–22; Alexander Lesser, *The Pawnee Ghost Dance Hand Game: Ghost Dance Revival and Ethnic Identity* (Madison: University of Wisconsin Press, 1978 [1933]), xii.

7. Loretta Fowler, *Arapahoe Politics, 1851–1978: Symbols in Crises of Authority* (Lincoln: University of Nebraska Press, 1982), 173–75, 177–79, 181, 183, 187–88, 193–98, 201–2, 204, 216.

8. William C. Meadows, *Kiowa, Apache, and Comanche Military Societies: Enduring Veterans, 1800 to the Present* (Austin: University of Texas Press, 1999), 176.

9. Fred W. Voget, *The Shoshoni-Crow Sun Dance* (Norman: University of Oklahoma Press, 1984), 24, 129, 131, 134, 139, 142–46.

10. Alison R. Bernstein, *American Indians and World War II: Toward a New Era in Indian Affairs* (Norman and London: University of Oklahoma Press, 1991), 22–24, 26, 41, 44, 46, 59–61, 64–65, 67, 68, 70–71, 73, 76, 79; Kenneth William Townsend, *World War II and the American Indian* (Albuquerque: University of New Mexico Press, 2000), 62, 72, 172, 186.

11. Bernstein, 64, 65, 67, 68, 71, 73, 76, 81, 85–86.

12. Meadows, 126–33; Townsend, 141; Fowler, *Tribal Sovereignty*, 94–98; Fowler, *Arapahoe Politics*, 193.

13. Bernstein, 112–14, 116–18, 121, 123, 127, 128, 132–37, 141–42, 146; Taylor, 94, 108, 139–40, 144–50.

14. Donald L. Fixico, *Termination and Relocation: Federal Indian Policy, 1945–1960* (Albuquerque: University of New Mexico Press, 1986), 14–15, 18–19, 22, 26–27, 31, 33, 35–36, 40, 73, 75, 92, 97, 100, 162, 175, 207.

15. Ibid., 135–36, 138–39, 141, 149.

16. Fowler, *Shared Symbols*, 99, 102, 103, 105–10, 114; Fowler, *Arapahoe Politics*, 206–8.

17. Roy W. Meyer, *The Village Indians of the Upper Missouri: The Mandans, Hidatsas, and Arikaras* (Lincoln: University of Nebraska Press, 1977), 230–31, 235, 238, 240–41.

18. Fowler, *Tribal Sovereignty*, 94–96, 119–20, 123–27, 131–32.

19. Meadows, 133–41.

20. William K. Powers, *War Dance: Plains Indian Musical Performance* (Tucson: University of Arizona Press, 1990), 10, 11, 14, 24–25, 29–31, 41, 56, 58.

21. George Pierre Castile, *To Show Heart: Native American Self-Determination and Federal Indian Policy, 1960–1975* (Tucson: University of Arizona Press, 1998), 10, 13–14, 19–20, 24–29, 32, 35, 72, 81, 91, 107.

22. Fowler, *Shared Symbols*, 115–21.

23. Elizabeth S. Grobsmith, *Lakota of the Rosebud: A Contemporary Ethnography* (New York: Holt, Rinehart and Winston, 1981), 18–34, 109.

24. Castile, 148, 153, 157, 168–69, 171–72, 178–79; Charles F. Wilkinson, *American Indians, Time, and the Law* (New Haven and London: Yale University Press, 1987), 130; Elizabeth S. Grobsmith and Beth R. Ritter, "The Ponca Tribe of Nebraska: The Process of Restoration of a Federally-Terminated Tribe," *Human Organization* 51 (1) (1992): 1–16.

25. Fowler, *Tribal Sovereignty*, 156–73.

26. Ibid., 172–83.

27. Castile, 111, 115–18, 124, 129, 132–33, 138, 140, 144–45; Grobsmith, 51–53, 69, 81, 107–8.

28. Fowler, *Shared Symbols*, 145–47, 154–56, 163–75.

29. Fowler, *Tribal Sovereignty*, 197; Robin Ridington and Dennis Hastings, *Blessing for a Long Time: The Sacred Pole of the Omaha Tribe* (Lincoln: University of Nebraska Press, 1997), xvii, xix, xxiii, 189, 201, 212–13, 218.

Aerial view of three square Upper Republican house floors (left center, top center, and lower right) on Medicine Creek, southwestern Nebraska, dated ca. 1400. These houses were in a village of the Central Plains tradition. (NAA–Smithsonian Institution, RBS 25FT17-123)

House floor at the Dodd site on the west bank of the Missouri River in Stanley County, South Dakota (six miles above Pierre), ca. 1000–1500. The later circular house has been partly removed by excavation of the earlier rectangular house with entrance ramp in foreground. This house was in a village of the Middle Missouri tradition. (NAA–Smithsonian Institution, RBS 39ST30-89)

Wichita grass lodge; photo taken in Oklahoma, ca. 1900. (University of Oklahoma, Western History Collection, Campbell coll. 434)

Wichita woman with braided squash mat.
Photo by Edward Curtis 1927
(NAA–Smithsonian Institution, 89,16392)

Pawnee earth lodge, Loup Fork, 1871. Photo by William H. Jackson (University of Oklahoma, Western History Collection, Phillips coll. 1718)

Pawnee women building earth lodge at St. Louis Exposition, 1904. (University of Oklahoma, Western History Collection, Campbell coll. 2165)

Mandan woman paddling bull boat. The boat was made of buffalo hide stretched on a pole frame. Photo by Edward Curtis, 1908 (University of Oklahoma, Western History Collection, Campbell coll. 2016)

Wife of Black Horse with dog travois, Northern Cheyenne, 1921. Photo by T. M. Galey (University of Oklahoma, Western History Collection, Campbell coll. 26)

Indian camp (probably Arapaho), 1870, on the Southern Plains. Shows buffalo meat drying, buffalo hide tepees, and hides staked out to dry. PHOTO BY WILLIAM SOULE (ARCHIVES AND MANUSCRIPT DIVISION OF THE OKLAHOMA HISTORICAL SOCIETY, 14597)

Comanche village: women dressing robes and drying meat. Oil-on-canvas painting by George Catlin, 1834. Also shows tepees painted with men's battle exploits. (SMITHSONIAN AMERICAN ART MUSEUM, GIFT OF MRS. JOSEPH HARRISON, JR.)

Bull Dance, Mandan O-kee-pa (or Okipa) Ceremony. Oil-on-canvas painting by George Catlin, 1832. This ceremony was an enactment of events in Mandan origin stories. The sponsor of the ceremony is praying, leaning against the barrel-shaped altar (with a cedar tree, representing the culture hero, inside) in the center of the plaza. The four poles contain prayer offerings, three of cloth and one of a white buffalo skin. There are twelve dancers representing Buffalo beings, eight in buffalo skins with willows tied on their back, two painted white representing Day, and two painted black representing Night. In the center are singers. At the left is a black-painted figure representing chaos and sacrilege. In the ceremony, he is defeated and driven out of the village. The ritual is performed for the renewal of all life. (SMITHSONIAN AMERICAN ART MUSEUM, GIFT OF MRS. JOSEPH HARRISON JR.)

Cheyenne military society riding to meet army scouts, bringing a flag of truce. Drawing by Making Medicine (Cheyenne), Fort Marion ledger art. The leader of the society is at the far left.

Fort Union on the Missouri in 1833. Engraving with aquatint, after Karl Bodmer. Assiniboine Indians are moving toward the fort where they trade buffalo robes that the American Fur Company ships by boat down the river.

Mato-Tope (Four Bears), Mandan chief. Watercolor by Karl Bodmer, 1834. Four Bears is painted stripped for battle. He has his exploits symbolized on his body; this indicates his high status and intimidates enemies. The wooden knife symbolizes a knife he took from a Cheyenne in hand-to-hand combat. The six sticks in his headdress represent gunshot wounds from which he recovered (demonstrating the efficacy of his medicine power). The yellow hand on his chest symbolizes that he has taken captives. The yellow stripes on his arms represent specific battle exploits. (JOSLYN ART MUSEUM, GIFT OF ENRON ART FOUNDATION)

Members of Sioux Delegation of 1875. Seated, left to right: Sitting Bull, Oglala (not the Hunkpapa leader); Swift Bear, Brule; Spotted Tail, Brule chief. Standing: Julius Meyer, merchant; Red Cloud, Oglala chief. In this delegation there were thirteen Sioux from Red Cloud agency and six from Spotted Tail agency. Federal officials unsuccessfully attempted to convince them to cede the Black Hills.

Photo by Frank F. Currier, Omaha, Nebraska. (NAA–Smithsonian Institution 3684-d)

White Bull's coup: stealing horses from General Terry's advancing column on the Little Big Horn River, Montana, June 26, 1876. This is a ledger drawing by White Bull, nephew of Sitting Bull, Hunkpapa Sioux. The drawing is dated April 9, 1932. White Bull wrote: "This made my name known, taking from those coming below. Soldiers and Crows were camped there." White Bull stole horses from the camp represented by tepees on the right. He was twenty-six years old at the time. His "medicine" is worn around his shoulder. (UNIVERSITY OF OKLAHOMA, WESTERN HISTORY COLLECTION, WHITE BULL COLL. 23)

Buffalo hide yard, 1878, Dodge City, Kansas; owned by Robert M. Wright and Rath. Shows 40,000 hides. Bob Wright is sitting on the stack of hides. (UNIVERSITY OF OKLAHOMA, WESTERN HISTORY COLLECTION, CAMPBELL COLL. 736)

Crow captives from Sword Bearer's uprising, Crow reservation, November 1887. (UNIVERSITY OF OKLAHOMA, WESTERN HISTORY COLLECTION, CAMPBELL COLL. 1603)

Issue day at Camp Supply, 1869. Arapahos receiving supplies. PHOTO BY WILLIAM SOULE (ARCHIVES AND MANUSCRIPT DIVISION OF THE OKLAHOMA HISTORICAL SOCIETY, 2785)

Horse travois on burro and woman's saddle on riding horse, Crow reservation, ca. 1890. The burro is dragging tepee poles. PHOTO BY P. P. PRANDO (UNIVERSITY OF OKLAHOMA, WESTERN HISTORY COLLECTION, CAMPBELL COLL. 114)

Ghost Dance, Southern Arapaho, 1891. The man in the foreground is in trance. PHOTO BY JAMES MOONEY (NAA–SMITHSONIAN INSTITUTION 91-20182)

Cheyenne girls playing with miniature tepees, 1895. Girls learned adult skills by mimicking women's activities. (Archives and Manuscript Division of the Oklahoma Historical Society, Hickox coll. 9496)

Laundry day at Riverside School, Anadarko, Oklahoma, 1901. Boys are washing clothes as well as girls, a departure from Wichita and Caddo custom. Photo by Annette Ross Hume. Albert Lamar, Wichita, second from left; Patrick Miller, Caddo, cranking machine, fourth from left; Sam Oliver, Wichita, extreme right; Bertha Wallace, Wichita, extreme left. (University of Oklahoma, Western History Collection, Phillips coll. 348)

Osage Peyote house, 1910–21.
(NAA–Smithsonian Institution 90–7259)

Osage girls with car, February 1928, at Grayhorse Indian Camp, Fairfax, Oklahoma. Anna Morton, Florine McCullen (Shawnee), Helen Morton Bear. (University of Oklahoma, Western History Collection, Cunningham-Dillon coll. 536)

Kiowa Five with Professor Jacobson, 1929. Left to right: Tsa-to-ke, Hokech, Mopopo, Professor O. B. Jacobson, Asah, Auchiah. They began studying with Jacobson in 1927. (UNIVERSITY OF OKLAHOMA, WESTERN HISTORY COLLECTION, OU COLL. 1170)

Giveway at Cheyenne powwow in Watonga, Oklahoma, August 1947. Horses were given away as well as other goods. PHOTO BY PIERRE TARTOUE (ARCHIVES AND MANUSCRIPT DIVISION OF THE OKLAHOMA HISTORICAL SOCIETY, TARTOUE NEG. 20912.5.88)

Kiowa Black Legs Society members, Anadarko, Oklahoma, May 17, 1998. Left to right: Parker Emhoolah Jr., John Emhoolah Jr., Bucky Emhoolah. Note the beaded war insignia and the capes. The tepee is family-owned; half is painted in black, white, and yellow stripes after the tepee of a well-known Kiowa warrior and the other half has symbols of war exploits from the twentieth century. Photo by C. R. Cohen (Archives and Manuscript Division of the Oklahoma Historical Society, C. R. Cowen coll. 19687.IN.KIO.BL.5.25)

World War II code talker, Charles Chibitty (Comanche), Fort Sill, Oklahoma, March 7, 1996. Photo by C. R. Cohen (Archives and Manuscript Division of the Oklahoma Historical Society, C. R. Cowen coll. 19687.IN.CO.4.7.A)

Comanche license plate, Anadarko, Oklahoma, August 5, 1998. The tribe issues the plates and collects a tax on them. The tribal plates can be used in lieu of state plates. Photo by C. R. Cohen (Archives and Manuscript Division of the Oklahoma Historical Society, C. R. Cowen coll. 19687.IT.AIE.98.13.9)

Part II

———∞∞∞———

People, Places, and Events

age-graded societies A few Plains peoples had groups that undertook ceremonial and/or martial activities whose members were approximately the same
age. Teenage youths were drawn from all the families and bands and initiated
at the same time into the lowest ranking society. As they aged they moved up
the series of societies, gaining more important ceremonial knowledge and social responsibility. By the time they were elderly they would have progressed
through the entire series. At any one time, ideally, all the men in a community would belong to one of the age-graded societies and the older societies would
have authority over the junior ones. The Arapaho, Gros Ventre, Blackfeet,
Mandan, and Hidatsa had age-graded societies. The latter two peoples also had
a system of stratification based on hereditary status; high-ranking people could
afford to "pay" for membership or key positions in the society immediately
above theirs more readily than low-ranking people. On the other hand, for the
Arapaho and Gros Ventre, purchase of membership was not required; rather,
gifts were given in the amount an individual could afford and the senior society gave gifts to the initiates in return. The ceremonies of the societies were in
many ways similar, but each of the five peoples mentioned adapted the age-
grade system to their own circumstances. Most Plains peoples did not have age-
graded societies (see **military societies**).

allotments   When reservations were allotted, individuals were assigned parcels of land (allotments). The title to the land was held in trust by the federal government so that it could not be sold or leased without federal approval and it could not be taxed. On some reservations allotments were 360 acres, on others less. Often families and bands took their allotments in clusters along wooded streams where they had access to water and firewood. These allotments could be inherited; the heirs received a share in the allotment rather than an actual piece of land. This is referred to as fractionated heirship.

American Fur Company   This trading company was organized in 1808 by the financier John Jacob Astor with the assistance of President Thomas Jefferson. Astor wanted to establish posts along the route of Lewis and Clark. The company began to compete in the upper Missouri River area in 1822 and by 1827 had succeeded in buying or driving out competitors. Furs were shipped to Europe and, after 1930, buffalo robes were purchased from Indians with manufactured goods expressly made for Indians, according to their tastes. The company stayed in business until the 1860s, and its employees were extremely influential in dealings between the U.S. government and Indian peoples.

annuity payments   The federal government agreed in the context of peace councils and treaties to provide tribes with an annual payment, usually in the form of manufactured goods. These were considered compensation for damages or a guarantee of federal protection in return for loyalty. The goods included blankets, clothing, metal pots, glass beads, paints, knives, and axes. At first the annuities were considered luxuries, but gradually Plains peoples came to depend on them because they lost the ability to obtain furs and robes to trade for these goods.

"Apache"   Apachean-speaking people moved into the Southwest before the sixteenth century and separated into seven groups, most of whom remained in the Southwest. The **"Plains Apache"** (sometimes referred to as Kiowa-Apache because of their early alliance with the Kiowa) probably consisted of autonomous bands hunting bison on foot east of the Rocky Mountains in the mid-sixteenth century. In the eighteenth century they formed an alliance with the Kiowa. They signed the **Medicine Lodge Creek Treaty** in 1867 and settled on a reservation in Indian Territory with the Kiowa and Comanche.

The **Lipan**, another of the Apache divisions, lived south of the Plains Apache and farmed as well as hunted buffalo. The Comanche pushed them farther south into southern Texas in the eighteenth century. In the nineteenth century, most settled on Apache reservations in New Mexico. Both the Plains Apache and the Lipan were organized into bands by means of **bilateral descent** and led by successful men who could attract a following. While Lipan ritual focused on the use of peyote, the Plains Apache had two men's and one women's societies and four tribal **medicine bundles**. Men joined the society of their choice, and men from the societies sometimes policed the camp.

The Plains Apache population always was small compared to other peoples: in 1867 it was about 500; in 1951, when an official roll was maintained, there were 400 enrolled members. In 1992 there were more than 1,300 members on the roll due to a "**blood**" requirement of one eighth Plains Apache ancestry. Their name for themselves was not "Apache"; rather the native term of self-designation meant "people." Today they are known as the Apache Tribe of Oklahoma and are headquartered at Anadarko, Oklahoma. The term "Apache" was used by the Spanish; it is of unknown origin (Raymond DeMallie, ed., *Handbook of North American Indians: Plains*, vol. 13, general editor William C. Sturtevant [Washington, DC: Smithsonian Institution Press, 2001], 937–38).

"**Arapaho**"   In the early eighteenth century there were five groups speaking different dialects (variations that were mutually intelligible) of the Arapaho language. For most of the time they were probably politically autonomous. The **Gros Ventre** settled in the Saskatchewan River country. By the early nineteenth century, the others had formed into Northern and Southern Plains divisions, and each had a political system that allowed for centralization of authority.

Arapahos lived in bands, the membership of which was based on **bilateral descent**, led by successful men who could attract a following. Men's societies were organized into an age-grade system. Boys entered at the lowest grade or rank and, by vowing to enter a higher grade and making a prayer-sacrifice, they rose in the system, gaining greater ritual knowledge as they aged. Governmental tasks were associated with the grades. Women supported the activities of the men and wives acquired ritual status along with their husbands. An elderly group of male and female priests supervised the age-grade system and the **Sun Dance**; thus, the religious leaders used the power of their offices to support the overarching political system. Arapahos believed in a pervasive life force that they could tap into for aid by prayer-thought and prayer-sacrifice, including prayer with the tribal **medicine bundle** (the Flat Pipe), and the Sun Dance. Religion supported values of group harmony. The Sun Dance was a reenactment of events in the creation of the world and human life, as well as a prayer for world renewal. It was also an opportunity for individuals to make prayer-sacrifices, as were the age-grade ceremonies. Acquisition of personal medicine bundles was of secondary importance. Northern and Southern Arapahos, recognized as different tribes in the late nineteenth century, settled on reservations in Wyoming and Oklahoma, respectively.

The population of both divisions was about 3,600 in 1835. In 1874 the northern division numbered 1,092 and the southern division, 1,644. In 1988 they each had a one-fourth degree Arapaho "**blood**" requirement and the Northern Arapaho totaled about 3,700 and the Southern Arapaho, about 3,000. By the year 2000 the Northern Arapaho Tribe had 6,500 members and the Southern Arapaho had about 4,000. The Arapaho name for themselves means "our people." The name "Arapaho" probably was derived from a Crow term meaning "tattooed," which was borrowed by American trappers in the early nineteenth century. Arapaho at that time had a standardized tattoo for males (on the chest) and for females (on the forehead) (DeMallie, 857–60).

"Arikara"   Arikara lived in politically autonomous villages until the United States began to treat them as one tribe in the late nineteenth century. Some villages were allied. The villages had a winter and a summer location where they farmed for subsistence and traded. They also went on two annual buffalo hunts in summer and fall. Each village had an hereditary chief, and after the villages consolidated there was a head chief. Each village also had a medicine bundle that represented the village's history and relationship with the all-pervasive life force. Arikara society was stratified, with the highest ranking families providing chiefs and priests for the bundle ceremonies. Warriors and members of the curing societies ranked below them, and the remainder of the population were "commoners." Individuals might improve their position through, for example, war exploits. Men's military societies drew members from all the villages and served as police. There also were women's societies. The curing societies had sacred bundles, and individuals could obtain supernatural help through a vision experience or obtaining someone else's power. The main ceremonies were the village bundle ritual, primarily for agricultural success, and the curing society ritual, where doctors displayed their considerable powers.

The population was about 2,500 in 1804; 1,500 in 1850; 379 in 1905; and 682 in 1950. The name "Arikara" was apparently a Pawnee term for an Arikara band or village; the term was adopted by the Spanish. Its meaning is obscure but possibly refers to an animal with horns or a horn headdress (DeMallie, 387–88).

art   Plains peoples have a long tradition of painting on hide, as well as embroidery work with quills and beads, and featherwork. The modern painting tradition began when Plains Indians were given training in painting during the **New Deal** (see **Kiowa Five**). Artists have built on this tradition to develop personal styles. Richard West Sr. (Cheyenne) and other artists taught at Bacone College in Muskogee, Oklahoma, where many Plains artists studied. Among the early artists to achieve prominence were Oscar Howe (Crow Creek Sioux), Blackbear Bosin (Kiowa-Comanche), Doc Tate Nevaquaya (Comanche), and

Amiotte (Oglala Sioux). Song making also was a well-developed art form. In the twentieth century, native singers began to make commercial records.

Ashley, William   Ashley (1778–1826) was a fur trader and politician in the St. Louis area. He moved to St. Louis in 1819 and invested in real estate. In 1822 he partnered with another man to organize a trading venture to the upper Missouri. Because of the difficulties of trading in that region, he developed the Rocky Mountain System wherein trappers were established in the mountains to trap all winter and to bring furs to a rendezvous on Green River in the spring. The furs then were carried overland along the Platte River to St. Louis. In 1826 he sold his interests in the trading company.

"Assiniboine"   The Assiniboine lived in politically autonomous bands for which there was no overarching structure; treaty making with the "Assiniboine" tribe or nation was an uncertain matter for the United States. Bands were comprised of kinsmen (see **bilateral descent**) and led by persuasive and generous men. Prominent men and the band leader appointed warriors to police the camp; several men's societies helped to inspire bravery. Assiniboines believed in Wakan Tanka, an all-pervasive life force (see **Wakonta**); they made prayer-sacrifices to gain the attention of spirit representations of the life force, and individuals who gained spirit helpers had personal **medicine bundles**. Some became shamans, or specialists who were particularly skillful in communicating with the spirit world and could help others, for example, by curing illness. Prayer-sacrifices were made by individuals who vowed to participate in the **Sun Dance**. There were also societies for men with medicine power to obtain and doctor horses and to hunt.

The population was about 4,508 in 1794; 4,800 in 1850; 1,421 in 1926; and 4,129 in 1998. Today the Assiniboine live on Fort Belknap and Fort Peck reservations in Montana and several in Canada. Their self-designation was "Nakota" or "people." The French borrowed the Ojibwa name for them, Assiniboine, meaning "stone enemy" (DeMallie, 590–91).

Atkinson–O'Fallon expedition   Colonel Henry Atkinson and Benjamin O'-Fallon, an Indian agent, met with representatives from several tribes along the Missouri River in 1825 in order to make peace and increase American influence with the Plains peoples. They made a show of military force, firing cannons. Nine treaties of peace and friendship were made in which "tribes" (as designated in the treaties) agreed to trade exclusively with American licensed traders and to return stolen property (seized from traders). The participants included Ponca, Yankton, Cheyenne, Crow, Arikara, Teton, Yanktonai, Mandan, Hidatsa, Otoe and Missouria, Pawnee, and Omaha.

Battle of the Little Bighorn   On June 25, 1876, U.S. troops launched a military expedition against "hostile" Sioux and Cheyenne. Not expecting such a large concentration of Indians and poorly coordinating a combined attack, Lt. Colonel Custer and his troops were surprised by warriors who greatly outnumbered them. All 200-plus of Custer's soldiers were killed. Public outcry energized the army and they continued to relentlessly pursue the Sioux and Cheyenne.

Bent, William   Bent (1809–69) was born in St. Louis and began trapping furs on the upper Arkansas River at the age of fifteen, working for his older brother Charles. Charles started Bent, St. Vrain and Company, which was a competitor of the American Fur Company. With his brother, William opened a post (Bent's Fort) on the Arkansas River in 1834 to trade primarily with the Southern Arapaho and Cheyenne and other tribes on the Southern Plains. He was married to a Cheyenne woman, Owl Woman, from a prominent family (her father was Arrow Keeper), and his children were raised among the Cheyenne and lived their lives in the Cheyenne community. After Owl Woman died, he married her sister. William served as a guide for General S. W. Kearny in the Mexican War of 1846–48 and became the principal owner of the trading company in 1849 after the death of his brother. He was the Indian agent for the Cheyenne and Arapaho during the 1860s. Bent retired to Westport, Kansas.

Big Bear   Born in 1825, he rose to a leadership position among his band of Plains Cree (actually a band comprised of Cree and Ojibwa) and, during negotiations with the Canadian government for reservation settlement, he gained influence among many other Plains Cree. He tried to negotiate the best terms he could and hold the government to its promises. Canadian officials regarded him as a troublemaker, and when violence occurred between a few Plains Cree and Canadians during the Riel or **Northwest Rebellion** in 1885, the Canadian government held Big Bear responsible. He was arrested and put on trial. Convicted, he served three years in prison; he died in 1888.

bilateral descent   In a bilateral descent system, individuals trace their descent equally from their mother's and father's lines and consider the relatives from both sides to be equally close in relationship; they view themselves to be in relationships of mutual responsibility with these relatives. Individuals do not belong to clans.

bison   Plains peoples relied on the bison or buffalo for food, clothing, shelter, containers, and tools. Buffalo hunting was by stalking (particularly in winter), driving into corrals or over cliffs, and impounding until acquisition of the horse allowed collective hunting by means of the chase and surround. Much of the meat was preserved as pemmican (sun-dried strips of meat pounded together with buffalo fat and marrow and fruit paste). The hide was used for lining cooking pits and making tepee covers, shields, cord and rope, and clothing. Robes were made from the buffalo hide, and deer hide was tanned (for use in making clothing) using a mixture of buffalo fat and brains. The buffalo robe also was used as bedding. Women sewed with buffalo sinew, and the horn was used for spoons, bows, and other items. Tools, such as hoes and scrapers, were made from bone. Dried dung was used for fuel and absorbent packing in baby cradles; hooves made good glue. Rawhide containers for meat, ritual objects, and clothing also were used. Decorative art included painting on buffalo robes, tepees, and rawhide containers.

Black Hawk War   Black Hawk was a Sauk warrior. The **Sauk** prospered in the fur trade, dealing with both the Spanish and the English. When the Americans assumed control of the trade, the Sauk were bypassed in favor of groups farther west. They began to decline economically and joined with the English against the Americans in the **War of 1812**, in which Black Hawk fought prominently for the English. Some Sauk land had been ceded in 1804 without the full consent of all the villages. Black Hawk was one of the leaders who opposed this. Subsequent treaties were ignored by settlers who trespassed on Sauk lands. When the Sauk were ordered to move west in 1832, Black Hawk was among those who resisted. He was defeated and died in 1838.

Black Kettle   He was the leader of the Half-Sioux band of Southern Cheyenne and was the most prominent peace chief during the 1860s. In Colorado the Cheyenne were threatened with attack by settlers who were trespassing on land assigned to the Cheyenne and Arapaho by treaty. The Indians were instructed by federal officials to camp on Sand Creek in the fall of 1864, where they were guaranteed protection. However, the camp of the peace chiefs was attacked by local militia led by Colonel Chivington, and many Cheyenne and some Arapaho were massacred there. Black Kettle and his wife escaped, and he continued to work for peace and for a reservation where the Cheyenne could live without fear of attack. Subsequently, he signed the **Medicine Lodge Creek Treaty** of 1867, agreeing to accept a reservation in Indian Territory. While still working for peace, he was camped with his followers on Washita River in November 1868 when troops led by Custer attacked. He and his wife and many other Cheyenne were killed. Nearby camps of Cheyenne, Arapaho, and Kiowa rushed to aid Black Kettle's people and Custer withdrew, taking several captive women and children with him.

Blackbird   A powerful Omaha chief who controlled trade above his village on the Missouri River by establishing a relationship with traders in which they gave him lavish gifts and he facilitated their business. He was born in 1750 and captured by Teton Sioux as a youth. After he returned to the Omaha, he became a skilled shaman (an individual who could harness supernatural power and use it for or against others) and a warrior. He was not from an elite family but used his abilities and his ties with traders to claim chieftainship. He died from smallpox in 1801.

Blackfeet   The Blackfeet were a division of the Blackfeet Confederacy, which also included the **Blood** and the **Piegan**. They resided mostly in Canada and obtained a reservation there, where the name is spelled Blackfoot. The group known as the Blackfeet in Montana are actually mostly Piegan. All three Blackfeet groups were organized into bands by **bilateral descent** and led by men with reputations for bravery and generosity. Blackfeet families with many horses had considerably more prestige than those with only a few, and their members could afford to make prayer-sacrifices to obtain **medicine bundles** as well as attract followers; wealthy families were morally obligated to help others. The larger bands had councils where prominent men deliberated on matters affecting the band. The men's societies were **age-graded**; they were important in war and had other duties in policing the camps. Medicine bundle priests formed a society and performed rituals on behalf of all the people. Women made a vow or prayer-sacrifice to sponsor the **Sun Dance**; men then participated, making their own prayer-sacrifices.

The population of all divisions was about 8,000 in 1814; 8,300 in 1885; 19,865 in 1987; and 31,186 in 1997. Their self-designation meant "persons having black feet"; possibly it refers to black moccasins. This term was borrowed by the Cree and translated into English as "Blackfeet" (DeMallie, 622–23).

Blackfeet Confederacy   The Blackfeet, Blood, and Piegan allied with the Gros Ventre and the Sarcee in the eighteenth century to become a powerful confederacy against other tribes, particularly the Cree, Assiniboine, and Shoshone. The Gros Ventre withdrew from the confederacy by the 1870s. In the confederacy's heyday, after members acquired horses and guns, it drove the Shoshone from northern Montana. The Blackfeet, Blood, and Piegan bands spoke the Blackfoot language, designated themselves as "prairie people," and referred to the confederacy as "brave people." Each of the three divisions also had a self-designation (DeMallie, 622–23, 664–67).

"blood"   Prior to federal intervention, Plains peoples viewed identity in cultural terms, often adopting captives and visitors who learned to follow the customs of their relatives. Euro-Americans viewed identity in racial, biological terms, so that individuals who were descended from parents of different heritage were viewed as "mixed blood," particularly if at least one parent were of Euro-American as well as Indian descent. From the Indian perspective, genetic heritage did not define cultural identity; behavior did. Tribal rolls prepared under federal supervision in the twentieth century often listed individuals in terms of "blood" quantum (full, half, one-fourth, for example). Some tribes adopted this approach and applied "blood" criteria in their enrollment process. In this case, legal and cultural identity do not correspond directly. Individuals may be accepted as culturally Indian (as culturally Crow, for example) yet not qualify for enrollment because of their blood quantum; individuals may qualify for enrollment (for example, in the Crow Tribe) yet not be considered culturally Indian (Crow, for example).

Blood   (See **Blackfeet Confederacy**). They reside on a reservation in Canada. Their self-designation means "many chiefs." The Cree term for them means "blood people"; it was borrowed by the English and French (DeMallie, 624).

Buffalo Hump   Buffalo Hump was a Comanche warrior who was a prominent leader in battle. His name was Potsanaquahip or Male Buffalo, and he was from the southern division of Comanche. He led revenge raids after a peace party of Comanches was murdered in the Council House massacre. He became an important intermediary chief from about 1845 to 1862, meeting with Texan and U.S. officials.

Bureau of Catholic Indian Missions   President Grant began encouraging missionaries to work on reservations in the late 1860s (see **Grant's Peace Policy**), but the Protestant missions were favored. In 1874 the Bureau of Catholic Indian Missions was created to oversee the Catholic missions and schools on Indian reservations. The bureau lobbied for support and also lobbied on behalf of Indians affiliated with its missions.

Bureau of Indian Affairs   In order to centralize the administration of Indian affairs, the Bureau of Indian Affairs or Office of Indian Affairs (also known as the Indian Office or Indian Bureau) was created in 1824 within the War Department, and was transferred to the Department of the Interior in 1849. In 1832 Congress authorized the president to appoint a commissioner of Indian affairs to manage the office. Employees are charged with implementing congressional legislation and federal Indian policy, including overseeing trust land.

"Caddo"   "Caddo" is the shortened version of the name of one of the major divisions of these people, who were organized into many villages at the time of

European contact. The native term meant "the real chiefs." Centralized political structures held villages together in alliances; there were three major confederacies throughout most of the contact period. Leaders were known as *caddi*. The Caddo lived in the Red River Valley and northeast Texas until forced to remove to central Texas and the Indian Territory (Wichita Agency). The 1994 population was 3,200 enrolled members. Today the Caddo Tribe has its headquarters in Binger, Oklahoma.

Cahokia   Cahokia was the largest urban center north of Mexico. Located across the river from what is now St. Louis, it reached its peak between 1000 and 1150 A.D. Part of the Mississippian tradition, the center was occupied from 700 to 1250 and covered about 200 acres surrounded by a palisade. There were 100 mounds (the largest with a base of 16 acres), which supported elite residences, public buildings, and elite burials. Cahokia was important in long-distance trade and was supported by a farming community of 30,000 to 40,000 people that stretched for 100 miles along the Mississippi River.

calumet ceremony   The calumet ceremony was used to establish trading relationships. The custom spread from one Plains people to another, and when Europeans arrived they participated. When a stranger (the trader coming to a village) arrived, he was carried to the village leader, who adopted him ceremonially, thereby offering protection and initiating gift exchange. Europeans introduced liquor into the ceremony. The term "calumet" comes from Norman French *chalumet*, a shepherd's pipe. The shaft of the ceremonial pipe smoked by the "kinsmen" was the calumet, but later the entire pipe might be referred to as a calumet. In Indian trade the social ties created were as important as the economic transaction; the calumet ceremony symbolically reinforced social ties.

Carlisle Industrial Training School   The school, opened in 1879 and closed in 1918, was the first nonreservation boarding school for Indians and was directed by Richard Pratt, an army officer who was fresh from running the Union prisoner-of-war camp in St. Augustine, Florida (see **Fort Marion**). The school operated in military fashion, with uniforms and drills, and stressed vocational training. Children from all the Plains reservations were sent there.

Cherokee   The Cherokee lived in the Southeast Woodlands area in what is now Virginia, Kentucky, the Carolinas, Tennessee, Georgia, and Alabama at the time of European arrival. They farmed intensively and hunted forest game. The British forced land cessions in the eighteenth century and the United States insisted on more cessions, so by the nineteenth century, the Cherokee were largely confined to the mountainous areas of their territory. Some groups of Cherokees began moving west in the late eighteenth century, intruding on Osage territory. In 1833 they ceded their lands east of the Mississippi; they were removed by the United States in 1838 to Indian Territory in the exodus known as the Trail of Tears.

"Cheyenne"   The Cheyenne were organized into bands and had an overarching political structure, which was complicated by the fact that some of the bands were non-Cheyenne or were comprised of Cheyennes and families from other tribes. The division between the peace chiefs who tried to negotiate a peaceful settlement with the United States and the Dog Soldiers who organized military resistance as long as possible also complicated the U.S. government's efforts to deal with a "Cheyenne Tribe." The Cheyenne live on a reservation in Montana and in western Oklahoma, where they once had a reservation.

Before the Cheyenne moved onto the Plains as nomadic buffalo hunters, they were likely organized into **matrilineal clans**; subsequent to the move to the Plains, they developed a **bilateral descent** system. The Cheyenne had several men's military societies (including the Dog Society); membership was voluntary, but often a man joined the society of his father or another relative. There also was a society of chiefs chosen from all the main bands; their role was to promote peace internally and consult with the military societies on external matters. The chiefs' society appointed military societies to police the camps. Band leaders influenced people by persuasion and generosity. The Cheyenne believed in an all-pervasive life force that humans could tap into during tribal rituals such as the **Sun Dance**, as well as rituals involving the two tribal medicine bundles (the Arrow bundle, kept by the Southern Cheyenne, and the Buffalo Hat bundle, kept by the Sutaio people among the Northern Cheyenne). Individuals undertook vision quests and had personal **medicine bundles**. The Sun Dance was a reenactment of creation stories and a prayer for world renewal as well as a vehicle for personal prayer-sacrifice.

The population was about 3,200 in 1837; 3,887 in 1880; 4,000 in 1950; and 15,000 in 2000. The Cheyenne self-designation is "those of this group" (*Tsistsistas*). The term "Cheyenne" is a French borrowing of a Sioux term of unknown meaning (DeMallie, 880–81).

Chickasaw   The Chickasaw lived in the Southeast Woodlands in what is now northern Mississippi and northeast Arkansas and ranged into Kentucky and Tennessee before Europeans arrived. They farmed intensively and hunted forest game. The United States pressured them to cede land in the early nineteenth century and, after the Indian Removal Act, they began to send representatives to Indian Territory to look for a good place to settle. Visits between

1834 and 1837 did not result in a selection, but they were pressured to remove in 1838 and settled just west of the Choctaw.

Chipewyan   Athapaskan-speaking groups living in the Subarctic, they hunted caribou and other forest animals. They lived in the northernmost part of Saskatchewan and Manitoba until they started moving south toward the trading posts. They gradually entered southeastern Alberta and southeastern Saskatchewan.

Choctaw   The Choctaw lived in the Southeast Woodlands in northwestern Alabama and Mississippi before the arrival of Europeans. They farmed intensively and hunted forest animals, primarily deer. The entry of French and English trading interests produced political disputes among the Choctaw, as did the emergence of the United States as the main rival of British interests. Some Choctaw traveled west to hunt and avoid the troubles, some as far west as the Arkansas River, where they intruded on Osage and Caddo. The Americans introduced the Choctaw to European types of agriculture. The United States pressured the Choctaw to cede land in the early nineteenth century. In 1820 they ceded land in Mississippi in exchange for land in Indian Territory. In 1831 they started removing to Indian Territory, where they faced hostility from the nomadic peoples.

Chouteau, Auguste   Auguste Chouteau (1749–1829) was one of the first traders to work out of St. Louis. In 1794 he got exclusive rights from Spain to trade with the Osage. He formed the Missouri River Fur Company with his son Auguste and Manuel Lisa. His brother Jean Pierre (1758–1849) also was a trader and became Indian agent for the tribes west of the Missouri in 1804. Auguste's sons, Auguste Pierre (1786–1838) and Pierre Jr. (1789–1865), followed their father into the fur trade.

Claremore   Claremore or Clermont was principal chief of the Arkansas River village of Osage. In 1802 he led his followers away from Osage villages near the Missouri and went west along the Arkansas River to northeastern Oklahoma and southeastern Kansas. This band had a trading relationship with the Chouteau family and Manuel Lisa. Claremore opposed the use of liquor and emphasized the buffalo hunt for subsistence. Other Osage leaders used the name Claremore after his death.

"Comanche"   The Comanche were organized into bands. Usually politically autonomous, they formed alliances based on regions of the Plains and sometimes selected spokesmen for these divisions in order to deal with Spanish, Mexican, and American authorities. A "Comanche Tribe" was a problematic category, for the northern and southern divisions often had different views when it came to dealings with the United States. Comanche bands were based on **bilateral descent** and led by men who attracted followers by generosity and success in raiding generally. The band leader had authority in matters of camp movements and hunting. Comanche believed in an all-pervasive life force that could manifest itself in natural forms in dreams and visions; men and women took responsibility for tapping into that force to obtain supernatural help. They could obtain supernatural assistance or "power" from other individuals who had it or undertake prayer-sacrifice for a vision (an encounter with a spirit representative of the life force). With this power individuals could be successful in raiding, curing, and other aspects of life. Those with impressive powers could attract followers on war parties or in building polities. The Comanche borrowed the **Sun Dance** from the Kiowa, but their religious life mostly focused on medicine societies of people who had power from the same source and conducted ceremonies attended by large numbers of Comanches seeking cures or other assistance. The Comanche had three main **military societies** that had some policing duties.

The population was about 12,000 in 1851; 1,656 in 1875; 7,200 in 1979; and 10,000 in 1999. Their self-designation meant "person." The term "Comanche" was derived from a Ute term meaning "stranger," which was borrowed by the Spanish (DeMallie, 900–2).

Coronado, Francisco Vásquez de   Coronado (1510–54) was born in Spain and came to Mexico in 1535. Tales of gold north of Mexico prompted him to lead an expedition north. In April 1540 he started for southeastern Arizona, where he attacked the Zuni. He continued on and intimidated the Hopi, Acoma, and Rio Grand Pueblos. By 1541 he was marching through Texas and western Oklahoma on the Southern Plains. There he encountered Indians hunting buffalo on foot. He reached a Wichita village and, disappointed not to find gold, killed his Indian guide. He returned to Mexico by 1542 and lived out his days as a minor colonial official.

Court of Claims   This is a federal court empowered to hear claims brought against the federal government. Indians sought to press suits against the federal government for treaty violations. They had to get permission from Congress in the form of legislation in order to file their cases. The court's docket was so overbooked with Indian claims cases that the suggestion of an Indian Claims Commission established to hear them was regarded favorably by Congress; the commission was instituted in 1946.

Crazy Horse   Crazy Horse was an Oglala Sioux warrior who resisted reservation settlement. Born about 1840 in the Black Hills, he was the child of an Oglala father and a Minneconjou mother. He participated in the attacks on forts during the war over the Bozeman Trail and was a leader in the fight against General Crook on the Rosebud River in 1876. He fought in the **Battle of the Little Bighorn** and stayed away from the agencies for the most part. He came in to Fort Robinson to negotiate a peace in 1877 and when he tried to leave, he was arrested and killed.

"Cree"   The Cree were a large group of people living in the eastern Subarctic region in many small, politically autonomous groups. They lived by hunting forest animals and fishing. After they began to trade fur pelts to European traders, game became scarcer in their region and they tried to expand westward, where they could act as middlemen in the trade with groups to the west. Some bands became dependent on the European traders and remained near the trading posts. Some Cree peoples gradually began to rely more on game in the grasslands or Plains to the south and southwest of the Subarctic and became known as **Plains Cree**.

Creek   The Creek lived in the Southeast Woodlands in Georgia and Alabama when the Europeans arrived. They farmed and hunted forest animals. Creek towns had residents from diverse cultural and linguistic backgrounds, and these people tried to work together in the eighteenth century to resist colonial domination. In 1832 they were forced to start removing to Indian Territory.

Cross Timbers   In north central Texas, central Oklahoma, and eastern Kansas, this transition zone delineates the break between the grassland Plains and the prairies. It is a thick oak forest twenty miles wide running from north to south.

"Crow"   The Crow were organized into three politically autonomous divisions, not all of which were always represented at treaty councils. Once on the reservation in Montana, they worked at building a political structure that could represent all the Crow. Crow groups originated as groups of families that left the **Hidatsa** villages and moved west to hunt the bison as full-time nomadic hunters, possibly in the late seventeenth century. The Crow retained a **matrilineal clan** organization (twelve or thirteen clans). Crow society was less hierarchical than the rank-conscious Hidatsa. An individual's mother's and father's clans both had important obligations to him, and he to them. Men relied on favorable blessings obtained in dreams of the spirit world by the men of their father's clan; they reciprocated by feasting and giving gifts to their benefactor. Boys joined a youth's military society to prepare for a career as a warrior, accompanying war parties as errand boys. Later they would be invited to join one of the military societies. As in military societies among Plains tribes generally, members policed the hunt and the camp and settled disputes. The highest ranking warriors were those who did four prescribed acts of bravery: took a weapon from an enemy, struck the first blow on an enemy, captured a picketed horse from an enemy, and led a successful war party. Men sought help from the spirit world throughout their military careers; by means of a vision quest (see **medicine bundle**) or petition to a bundle owner in his father's clan, a man acquired supernatural aid. Bundle owners also belonged to societies that had periodic ceremonies attended by all Crow where prayers for good fortune were made. Individuals might also pledge to sponsor a **Sun Dance** to aid a revenge expedition against an enemy tribe. The Crow settled on their reservation in Montana in the 1880s.

The population was about 9,000 in 1780; 3,500 in 1881; 1,679 in 1930; and 2,781 in 1950; in 1998 the enrolled population was 9,814. The self-designation comes from a particular band and has reference to a bird. "Crow" is the English translation of the native term used by many tribes to refer to these people (DeMallie, 714–15).

cultural traditions   Anthropologists use the term "cultural" to refer to the ideas a people have about the world and their place in it and the values that they hold. Cultural traditions are represented through social activity, including religious rituals and oration.

culture hero   Culture heroes figure importantly in origin stories. They are supernatural beings or part-human, part supernatural persons, and they play a key role in the creation of the natural world or the instruction of humans in how to prosper and live well. Sometimes they combine supernatural abilities with reprehensible actions (for example, trickster behavior).

Dawes, Henry   Henry Dawes (1816–1903) was a Republican senator from Massachusetts with a background in reform issues and abolition. He served as a representative before being elected to the Senate. In his reelection campaign in 1879 he seized on the issue of Indian policy reform to energize the electorate. The **Standing Bear** tour had moved public opinion in favor of reform, and Dawes capitalized on it. Reelected, he became chair of the Indian Affairs Committee and presided over the passage of the General Allotment Act (also known as the Dawes Act). He and the other reformers (opposed by Western senators) thought that the allotment system would ensure the Indians would not be pushed off their lands. Dawes was reelected in 1880 and 1886. He also expedited increased appropriations for Indian education.

De Soto, Hernando   De Soto (1496–1542) was born in Spain and came to the Americas in 1514. He joined in the conquest of Central America and Peru and became the Governor of Cuba in 1536. Approval for the conquest of Florida launched De Soto's expedition in 1539. He landed on the west coast of Florida and marched north through Georgia, the Carolinas, Tennessee, and Alabama. He had conflicts with Choctaw and Chickasaw, and crossed the Mississippi in June 1541. Moving on into Arkansas and Oklahoma, he did not find gold, and he turned back east toward Louisiana. In May 1542 he died of fever near the Mississippi River. The survivors of the expedition continued on, led by Luis de Moscoso.

Dehahuit   Dehahuit was a Kadohadacho who became the most important *caddi* among the Caddo between 1800 and 1833. He worked to negotiate favorable treatment from both the Spanish and the Americans, playing them off against each other. He died in 1833.

Delaware   The Delaware (or Lenape) were speakers of an Algonkian language. Until the early eighteenth century, they lived in the Delaware River valley in the Eastern Woodlands, where they farmed and hunted forest animals. They ceded land to the English in the seventeenth century and moved west to Pennsylvania, then Ohio. They arrived in Indiana between 1800 and 1820, still trying to avoid war. They were in Missouri from 1821 to 1829 and went to Kansas between 1830 and 1867. These migrations put them in competition with the Plains tribes. Many moved to a reservation in Indian Territory in 1867. Some groups chose not to go. The Delaware who settled with the Caddo have federal recognition as a tribe.

Dog Soldiers   The Southern Cheyenne had four men's military societies. Individuals joined whatever society they wanted, although often sons joined their father's society. During the Indian wars of the 1860s and 1870s, the young warriors resisted the advice of the peace chiefs to accommodate the United States when they were asked to renegotiate treaties or ignore treaty violations on the part of settlers. These warriors tried to remain in buffalo country and to keep settlers out. Gradually, they began to travel together as a band, bringing their families with them. Sioux and some Northern Cheyenne joined this band under the leadership of the Dog Society, and the group became known as the Dog Soldier band. Men from the other three military societies functioned within the Southern Cheyenne camps that were trying to maintain peaceful relations with the United States. The Dog Soldiers were the last of the Southern Cheyennes to settle on the reservation in Indian Territory.

Du Tisné, Claude-Charles   Du Tisné (or Dutisné) made two trips from the Illinois country, in 1718 and 1719, to explore the Missouri River and make alliances with Indian groups that could serve as middlemen in the trade. He met with Pawnee, Osage, and Wichita. He gave the Pawnee favored-nation status and made a trading alliance with them.

Dull Knife   Dull Knife (or Morning Star) (1810–83) was a prominent Northern Cheyenne warrior. He fought in the Indian war of 1864–65, the war over the Bozeman Trail, and the war over the Black Hills in 1876–77. He signed the Fort Laramie Treaty of 1868. During the Black Hills war, his village was attacked on the Powder River by Colonel Ranald Mackenzie in November 1876. The camp's provisions were destroyed. The Indians barely survived the winter, and by spring they surrendered. Dull Knife thought he and his people could stay on the Northern Plains, but instead they were sent to Indian Territory. They suffered in the unfamiliar climate and had inadequate food. In September 1878 Dull Knife and another leader, **Little Wolf**, escaped to the north with 300 people. Over six weeks, they traveled 1,500 miles, evading their pursuers. At the North Platte River, the two groups split and took different routes north. Dull Knife's group went toward Red Cloud's agency at Pine Ridge but they were captured and held prisoner. Fearing that the soldiers would murder them, they broke for freedom in January 1879 and many were killed. Dull Knife and several members of his family arrived at Pine Ridge and were allowed to stay. Eventually he was allowed to move to Montana.

Eastern Woodlands   "Eastern Woodlands" refers to that part of North America east of the Plains. It can be subdivided into the Northeast and Southeast Woodlands. Native people here lived in relatively permanent villages and farmed and hunted forest game. Some groups on the coast also fished and collected shellfish. Wild plants were important for food and medicine. The fur and slave trades significantly affected these societies after the arrival of Europeans.

Elk v. Wilkins   This was an 1884 Supreme Court case. John Elk was a "**Santee**" who had left the Santee reservation and lived in Omaha, Nebraska. He was denied the right to vote on the grounds that he was not a citizen. The Supreme Court agreed: he was not born within the United States, and Congress had not established a naturalization process for Indians in this situation. This case influenced the writing of the Dawes Act, which provided for Indian citizenship.

factory   A factory was a trading establishment licensed by the federal government. The United States tried to compel Indians to trade exclusively at the government factory (for example, the Osage Factory). The system was established in 1796 and abolished in 1822.

field matron   Indian agencies were staffed at first with just an "agent" to handle Indian affairs. Then as the Bureau of Indian Affairs bureaucracy grew, more employees were added: blacksmiths, government farmers (to instruct Indians), interpreters, clerks, school personnel, and (beginning in 1890) field matrons. These women were hired to visit Indian homes and instruct women on child care and the principles of sanitation.

first fruit ceremonies   Farming was a religious act; the earth produced when humans maintained proper relations with the powers of creation. One way to do this was to show thanks for fertility and abundance by offering food to those creative forces before partaking of it. When crops or wild plants (fruits) were ready to harvest, some of this food was offered in prayer.

Fletcher, Alice   Fletcher (1838–1923) worked for Indian rights organizations before she became involved in professional anthropology. She did research among the Omaha, Sioux, and Pawnee, and also sought to help them. In the belief that allotment would allow the Omaha to keep their land in the face of settler expansion, she drafted a plan for allotment and served as the allotting agent for the tribe. She worked closely in her studies of Indian life with Francis La Flesche, whom she adopted as a son. In 1886 she joined the staff of the Peabody Museum. Fletcher was the first anthropologist to make a formal study of Plains music.

Fort Marion   After the **Red River War** (1874–75), in which Southern Cheyennes, Comanches, and Kiowas engaged the U.S. Army, the United States decided to imprison many of the warriors involved. Richard Pratt (1840–1924) had served in the army during the Civil War, and in Indian Territory he was the commander of Indian scouts at Fort Sill in 1875. He was assigned to convey the prisoners of war to prison. Seventy-two Indians were selected (some were innocent) and taken to Fort Marion Military Prison at St. Augustine, Florida. They were held there three years, and Pratt developed an educational program for them that stressed literacy and vocational education using the services of local teachers and craftspeople. He encouraged artwork (among the more famous artists were Cohoe and Howling Wolf, Cheyennes). In 1878 the prisoners were released. Some went to Hampton Institute (established in Virginia in 1868 for the education of African Americans) to continue their education. Eleven prisoners went with Pratt to a new boarding school he started in 1879, **Carlisle Industrial Training School**.

Four Bears   Four Bears was a Hidatsa war chief famous for his war exploits, the symbols of which were painted or otherwise symbolized on clothing (shown in the paintings of Karl Bodmer). His martial career was aided by visions in which spirit helpers advised him. He rose to prominence as war chief after 1837 and helped lead the relocation of the Hidatsa to Like-a-Fishhook village in 1845. He signed the Fort Laramie Treaty of 1851 on behalf of the Hidatsa. He also was a bundle owner, but his influence was based on his military prowess. (A Mandan chief named Four Bears also was painted by Bodmer.)

giveaways   Property was given to guests for religious and social reasons at ceremonies. A property sacrifice would help a person's prayer. Property given in appreciation for the support and assistance of others worked to perpetuate that assistance. Property also could be given in expectation of a return gift at some time in the future; the exchange would reinforce the social ties between the parties. Today, giveaways at **powwows** express these ideas and values, usually about the social purpose of giving property to others. At powwows, a family typically gives away dress goods, blankets, groceries, and shawls.

Grant's Peace Policy   Ulysses S. Grant came under pressure from Eastern reformers who were appalled by the army's attacks on Indians. President Grant started a peace initiative in 1869 known as his "Peace Policy." A series of laws and executive acts influenced by reformers, particularly Quakers who criticized Indian Office corruption, resulted in agents being nominated by church officials, the establishment of a Bureau of Indian Commissioners to oversee expenditures of appropriations designated for Indians, and assimilation policy and legislation. Grant's policy was opposed by the Department of War.

Grass Dance   Originally a warrior's society, the Grass Dance (known by different names among Plains tribes) spread from tribe to tribe. The regalia of the dance mimicked warfare and honored brave warriors. Modern powwow dancing has borrowed many elements from the Grass Dance.

Grattan Massacre   Lieutenant John Grattan (1830–54) was a graduate of West Point who was assigned to Fort Laramie along the Oregon Trail. In 1854 the Brule and Oglala were there to receive their annuity goods. A cow owned by an emigrant was killed by a Minneconjou man, and Grattan used this opportunity to try to get combat experience. He ordered the Brule chief to produce the thief; Conquering Bear said he had no authority to do that but would pay for the cow. Grattan was not satisfied. Shots were fired and in the melee Conquering Bear was killed, whereupon Grattan and all his men but one were killed by the Brule. After this, young warriors retaliated by pillaging settlers and travelers. The Bureau of Indian Affairs blamed Grattan for the incident, but the army sent a punitive expedition in 1855 led by General **William Harney**.

Gros Ventre   From the mid-eighteenth century, Gros Ventres were wealthy in horses, which they used for communal bison hunting, war, and trade. Social inequalities based on horse ownership existed, but these were mitigated by values that associated social prominence and leadership with generosity to the less fortunate. Families who camped together throughout the year formed a band; the Gros Ventre had ten to twelve. Band leaders led by example and persuasion. At least one band joined the Southern Arapaho in the early nineteenth century. Tribal religious ceremonies reinforced values of cooperation. All supernatural power was believed to emanate from a life source; humans could tap into this power through intense thought (in prayer or song). Power also was delegated to beings in nature. Humans obtained power through prayer to the life source directly or to spirit representations of it; power was obtained to cure or harm, assure success (especially in battle), and foretell the future. Acts of sacrifice helped demonstrate the sincerity of an applicant's prayer (thus, property or body sacrifice figured importantly in ceremonies). The two tribal **medicine bundles** represented the Gros Ventre's special relationship with the life force and with events in creation stories. These bundles contained pipes that individuals could use in prayer-sacrifice that benefitted all Gros Ventre as well as the petitioner. A worthy individual could be apprenticed to each of the priests who directed pipe rituals and make property sacrifices in order to acquire the priesthood himself. Individuals who vowed to sacrifice in the **Sun Dance** also established a relationship with an instructor of higher ceremonial rank. The Gros Ventre **age-grade system** also operated by means of individuals (with their families helping) vowing to sacrifice in order to obtain ritual knowledge from the more advanced age grades by prayer to the life force. Supernatural sanctions underlay the avoidance of conflict among men in the same **moiety** and grade. In this way, the Gros Ventre enforced tribal unity and had an overarching political structure. Competition between moieties encouraged bravery in battle and generosity to the needy. The Gros Ventre settled on Fort Belknap reservation in 1878, near their sometime allies the Assiniboine. See **Arapaho**.

Their population was about 2,300 in 1805; 3,000 in 1855; 624 in 1895; and 1,873 in 1964; in 1998 the enrolled population was 3,078. Their self-designation was "white clay people." "Gros Ventre" was a French term of questionable origin, but quite possibly a translation of native terms meaning "begging men." The Plains Cree name for the Gros Ventre meant "falls people" because of the region in which they lived in the Saskatchewan country, and the English in Canada referred to them as Falls Indians (DeMallie, 692).

Hamilton, Robert   Hamilton was born in the 1870s and lived in the house of a trader on the Blackfeet reservation in Montana. He was educated at **Carlisle** school, graduating in 1896. He worked for thirty years on behalf of the Blackfeet, advocating for an elected business committee that would manage reservation resources (especially oil and grazing land) and fighting against allotment. In the early twentieth century he was the most prominent leader on the reservation.

Hancock, General Winfield S. A West Pointer, he served in the Mexican War, the Indian wars of the 1860s, and the Civil War. In 1867 he met Plains Indians in a peace council but did not trust the promises made by the participants and subsequently ordered Colonel George Custer to destroy a Cheyenne village. This led to retaliatory raids in western Kansas. Hancock's lack of success in ending conflict with Indians led to his replacement in 1867 by General Philip Sheridan. Hancock held other commands between 1869 and 1872. He was a Democratic candidate for president in 1880; unsuccessful, he returned to military service.

Harney, General William Harney (1800–89) was a career army officer who served in the Mexican War of 1846–48 and the Indian wars. In 1855 he led a retaliatory expedition against Teton Sioux after the **Grattan Massacre**. Harney forced the surrender of some warriors, including **Spotted Tail**, and forged an agreement with the Teton in 1856 that allowed for travel over the **Oregon Trail**. The United States did not agree to ratify this treaty. Harney retired from active duty in 1863.

"Hidatsa" The Hidatsa tribe is a product of treaty relations in the United States. Actually, Hidatsa villages were politically autonomous, and the residents spoke different dialects and had somewhat different lifeways. Hidatsa villages had winter and summer locations; women farmed and men hunted buffalo. **Matrilineal clans** were organized into **moieties**. A council of elders representing the clans and households governed the village. A war chief was selected, chosen for his military successes, and the priest of the most important **medicine bundle** was the peace chief. In each village the men were organized into **age-grade societies**; the society of middle-aged men was assigned policing duties in the village. Women had age-graded societies, largely borrowed from the **Mandan**, that had acquired supernatural power for farming and hunting. Village and clan bundles were transferred after an individual had a dream in which a supernatural being instructed him to acquire the bundle through prayer-sacrifice (donating property). The transfer ceremony was a major event in the village, and individuals could make vows to sacrifice to the bundle as an aid to prayer. Some individuals sought personal power through the vision quest.

The population was about 4,000 in 1780; 2,700 in 1804; 377 in 1872; and 933 in 1950. "Hidatsa" as a tribe name postdates the amalgamation of three divisions in the mid- to late nineteenth century. "Hidatsa" was formerly the name of the largest division or village; it probably meant "willow village" (DeMallie, 344–45).

Hopewell   Hopewell was a way of life centered in the Midwest. It lasted from 200 B.C. to 500 A.D. and was characterized by a religion that involved elaborate burials, some horticulture, and hunting and gathering. The Hopewell people engaged in long-distance trade and buried their dead in elaborate mounds. The Mississippian tradition of more intensive farming succeeded Hopewell beginning about 800.

Iesh (Jose Maria)   Iesh (or Jose Maria) (1806–62) was the main Caddo *caddi* in the 1840s and 1850s. He was from the Nadaco division of Caddo and played a major role on the Southern Plains in trying to arrange peace councils and discouraging violence. He successfully kept the various divisions of Caddo unified. Iesh signed a peace treaty in 1843 with Texas and tried to encourage peace between the Wichita and Texas. He was a delegate to Washington in 1847, where he became convinced that peaceful relations were the only way the Caddo would survive as a people.

Illinois   The native peoples referred to as "Illinois" were the Peoria, Miami, Cahokia, and others who spoke Algonkian languages and were allied. They lived in what is now Illinois, parts of Wisconsin, Iowa, Missouri, and northeastern Arkansas. This area was part of the **Eastern Woodlands**, and these peoples farmed and hunted. In the seventeenth century the Iroquois tribes to the east began attacking the Illinois in order to displace them; the Iroquois wanted to control their territory to expand their fur-trading activity. The Iroquois launched a war of extermination and terror; for example, captives were tortured to death. The Illinois retreated west into Sioux territory, where they became embroiled in war with the Sioux. Ninety percent of the Illinois population was lost. They supported the Americans in the Revolutionary War, but the United States did not keep the promises of protection made to the Illinois. Instead, they were pressured to cede their lands. They were moved west of the Mississippi River in the early nineteenth century, where they came in conflict with Plains peoples in the Missouri River valley. In the late nineteenth century many settled in Indian Territory (as what is now the Peoria Tribe of Oklahoma).

Indian Removal Act of 1830   Responding to public pressure to open Indian lands to settlement, Congress ignored treaties that guaranteed Indians their land and instead provided for the removal of Indians west of the Mississippi. In being forced to leave, Indians left behind crops, houses, furniture, household goods, clothing, and stock. Their lands and homes were appropriated by U.S. citizens.

Indian Rights Association   Founded in Philadelphia in 1882 by Herbert Walsh and Henry Pancoast, this organization worked on behalf of Indians until it disbanded in 1994. These reformers embraced assimilation in the late nineteenth and early twentieth centuries, working for Indians' protection under the law, education, citizenship, individual land title, and honest and competent administration in the Indian Office. The organization had great public visibility and lobbied on behalf of Indians in Washington. It took an antitermination position in the 1950s and supported self-determination in the 1960s.

Indian Territory   Indian Territory was not a territory in a political sense, as it was not organized with a territorial government. But Congress set it aside for the use of Indians who were being removed from other areas. After 1830 the region that today includes Kansas, Nebraska, and Oklahoma was referred to as "Indian country" or "Indian Territory." It was effectively reduced by the Kansas-Nebraska Act of 1854, which removed the northern sector. By 1885 all the land in Indian Territory was assigned to Indians. There were efforts on the part of Indians to organize as an all-Indian state, but the federal government did not approve.

Iowa   The Iowa probably had politically autonomous villages and became known as the Iowa tribe when the United States began to make treaties with them. The Iowa villages were occupied by **patrilineal clans** that might form an alliance, and the clans were organized into **moieties**. Clans were ranked and had specific responsibilities. There were two hereditary chiefs. Chiefs' families outranked the families of prominent warriors, and both these groups outranked commoner families. The clans owned **medicine bundles** that were used in ceremonies to assure the prosperity of the people. Men belonged to **military societies,** and there was a society of men and women who could cure; individuals could make prayer-sacrifices in curing ceremonies.

Their population was about 800 in 1805; 219 in 1875; and 348 in 1961 (residing on a reservation in Kansas and in northern Oklahoma); in 1996, there were 2,608 (2,147 in Kansas and 461 in Oklahoma). The term "Iowa" derives from a Sioux word, also used by Chippewa and Ottawa Indians, the meaning of which is obscure; the French borrowed it as "Iowa" (DeMallie, 445).

Jerome Commission   By the Springer Amendment to the Indian Bill of 1889, the president had authority to open Oklahoma to settlement and to appoint a commission to negotiate with the tribes there to open reservations to settlement as well, so that the land could be added to the newly created Oklahoma Territory. Also known as the Cherokee Commission, this federally appointed three-man commission was charged with completing allotment agreements with tribes in Indian Territory. They began in 1891 and finished in 1896. Using threats and promises, the commissioners visited the tribes and pressured them to agree by majority vote. The commissioners were David Jerome, former governor of Michigan and chair; Warren Sayre of Indiana; and Alfred Wilson of Arkansas.

Joseph (Chief Joseph)   Joseph (1840–1904) was a Nez Perce born in Oregon. He signed an 1855 treaty giving the Nez Perce rights in the region, but trespassing settlers led to conflicts between them and the Indians. The 1861 gold rush aggravated the situation. In 1871 Joseph became the principal chief of one of the main Nez Perce bands. He tried to negotiate for a reservation for the Nez Perce in their homeland and succeeded, but subsequently the federal government reneged on the agreement and sent troops to remove the Nez Perce in 1877. They decided to resist. The army pursued them all year as this small group of about 650 tried to avoid battle and to find refuge with **Sitting Bull** in Canada. Thirty miles from the Canadian border, the troops led by Colonel Nelson Miles caught them, and many were killed. The survivors were sent to Indian Territory, then in 1883–84 some were returned to Idaho to the Nez Perce reservation; in 1885, the others, including Joseph, were sent to live on the reservation of another tribe in Washington.

Jumanos   The term "Jumano" was used in the eighteenth century by Spaniards in New Mexico to refer to peoples who were tattooed. The term probably designated different groups at different points in time.

Kaw   The Kaw had ranked **patrilineal clans** organized into **moieties**. The clans owned **medicine bundles** and there were two tribal bundles. The three divisions of Kaw had hereditary peace chiefs and ranked warriors who earned their status through battle exploits. The Kaw obtained a warriors' or **military society** ceremony from the Ponca. They believed in an all-pervasive life force (see **Wakonta**).

Also referred to as Kansa, the Kaw numbered 1,375 in 1853 and were largely ignored by the federal government. In 1990 they organized under the Oklahoma Indian Welfare Act and began to enroll members and develop their small land holdings economically. The population was 673 in 1990 and 2,333 in 1998. Their self-designation has an obscure meaning; it was adopted as "Kansa" by Europeans (DeMallie, 472, 474–75).

"Kiowa"   The Kiowa lived in bands that were largely politically autonomous; thus, the United States found treaty making difficult. Kiowa were organized into bands based on **bilateral descent**. Band leaders were high-status men very generous with their wealth, which was based on the ownership of large numbers of horses. The Kiowa classified people according to wealth and accomplishment. The highest ranking families had many horses and provided leaders for bands and tribal **medicine bundle** custodianship. Other families had prominence but less than the highest ranking, and a third group of families had few horses (captives were ranked with this group). Social mobility was possible. Men's **military societies** also varied in their prestige. A women's society had access to supernatural power to aid warriors. The Kiowa believed in a pervasive life force that they tapped into through dreams or vision quests (see **medicine bundle**). There were ten tribal medicine bundles kept by prominent men who could use the bundles to enforce peace within the camps or cure illness. Men and women with access to a great amount of supernatural power also organized into societies that offered aid to others. The Kiowa **Sun Dance** was a ceremony for tribal well-being and prayer-sacrifice by individuals.

The population in 1875 was about 1,000; in 1990, 9,421 self-identified as Kiowa; and by 2000 there were 12,500 enrolled members. Their self-designation is an old band name, the meaning of which is obscure. This term is the source of the name Kiowa (DeMallie, 920–22).

Kiowa Five   Susan Peters, a **field matron** at Anadarko, started art classes as part of a New Deal program to encourage arts and crafts. In 1926 she arranged for her students to take segregated art classes at the University of Oklahoma with Professor Oscar Jacobson. The five male students went on to have careers as artists. Their names were Spencer Asah, Jack Hokeah, Stephen Mopope, James Auchiah, and Monroe Tsatoke. The sixth student was a woman, Lois Smoky. The Kiowa Five helped to influence an Indian style of painting and to create a market for it.

"Kitsai"   The Kitsai were a small tribe (at least after European contact) with a southern division, mostly allied with the Wichita, and a northern division, mostly allied with the Caddo. They spoke a language distinct from the Wichita. They are no longer a separate tribe but have merged into the Wichita. Their population was about 300 in 1849 and 52 in 1893. Their self-designation is of obscure meaning and was borrowed by the French as "Kitsai" (DeMallie, 570).

La Flesche, Francis   His father Joseph was the son of a French trader and his mother was an Omaha or Omaha-Iowa. Born in 1857, Francis accompanied his father in trading expeditions but chose to affiliate with his mother's people. As a child, he attended the mission school on the Omaha reservation, then attended boarding school. In 1881 he was hired as a clerk in the Bureau of Indian Affairs. In 1892 he obtained a degree in law. He worked with anthropologists **Alice Fletcher** and James Dorsey researching the Omaha, the Osage, and other Siouan peoples and in 1910 was hired by the Bureau of American Ethnology. He received an honorary degree of Doctor of Letters from the University of Nebraska in 1926 and retired from the bureau in 1929.

La Flesche, Susette   Susette La Flesche (1854–1903) was a lecturer, writer, reformer, and artist. She was the sister of Francis and of Susan Picotte, who became a physician. As a child she attended the mission school on the Omaha reservation and Elizabeth Institute for Young Ladies in New Jersey and trained to be a teacher. She also studied art at the University of Nebraska. She applied to the Indian Office for a teaching job on the reservation but was rejected as unqualified. She appealed and was hired but paid half the salary of her non-Indian predecessor. She learned of the plight of **Standing Bear**'s Ponca while she was a volunteer nurse in Indian Territory and interpreted for him on his trek back to Nebraska. Calling herself Bright Eyes, she and her brother Francis helped Thomas Tibbles, a social crusader, abolitionist, newspaperman, and retired minister, publicize the problems of the Ponca, touring Eastern cities in 1879 and 1880. In 1882 Susette married Tibbles, and they traveled the world lecturing.

La Harpe, Bénard de (Jean-Baptiste Bénard, Sieur de La Harpe)   La Harpe (1683–1765) was an agent of the Company of the Indies. He was part of the growing colonial society of Louisiana: traders, military men, laborers, African slaves, and Indians. La Harpe established direct French contact with the tribes of the Southern Plains after 1719 and established Nassonite Post among the Caddo. Risking attacks from Apaches, in 1719 he traveled to the Wichita, met with nine villages, and established military and trade agreements that lasted until 1763.

La Salle, Réné-Robert Cavelier, Sieur de   La Salle came from a prominent family in France. He went to French Canada in 1666 and became involved in the fur trade. He explored the region to find a water route to the Pacific Ocean and studied Indian languages to facilitate his explorations. La Salle founded a chain of fur trading posts between the Great Lakes and the Mississippi River in the Lake Ontario region between 1674 and 1677. In 1678 he began to explore south to the Ohio River, and he built Fort Crevecoeur on the Illinois River (near Peoria). In 1681 he explored the upper Mississippi River and followed it south to the Missouri River. He named the region Louisiana in honor of King Louis XIV and claimed it for France. In 1686, while establishing a colony near what is now Houston, he went on an expedition to south central Texas among the Caddo there. On this trip he was murdered by some of his men.

Lewis and Clark expedition   Meriwether Lewis (1774–1809) grew up in Virginia, was a neighbor of Thomas Jefferson, and served in the army, where he met William Clark. Lewis became President Jefferson's private secretary in 1801, and they made plans for an overland expedition to follow the purchase of Louisiana from France. William Clark's career focused on the army and he was an experienced Indian fighter. The expedition's goal was to strengthen the United States's claim to the area west of the Missouri and to find a route to the Pacific Ocean, as well as to promote good will among the Indian tribes of the region, especially the Sioux. There were 27 soldiers, Clark's African American interpreter York, and an interpreter for the Sioux with Lewis and Clark. They left St. Louis in May 1804. In North Dakota they added Charbonneau as interpreter and his consort **Sacajawea** to the group. They returned from the trip in September 1806. In 1808 Lewis became territorial governor of Louisiana. Clark (1770–1838) entered the fur trade on the Missouri and in 1813 became the governor of the newly opened Missouri Territory. He also served as superintendent of Indian Affairs for the upper Missouri and Mississippi tribes and played a role in the removal policy.

Lipan   See "**Apache**."

Lisa, Manuel   Lisa (1772–1820) was a trader and Indian agent on the Missouri River. He was born in New Orleans and went to St. Louis in 1790 to engage in the fur trade. In 1807 he was the first trader to go up the Missouri to Crow and Blackfeet country to trade. In 1809 he organized the St. Louis Missouri Fur Company with partners (it was reorganized in 1812 as the Missouri Fur Company). He established Fort Mandan in 1809 at the mouth of the Knife River and a fort among the Arikara in 1811. In 1812 he built Fort Lisa on the Missouri River, near where the city of Omaha is now. In 1814 he was appointed Indian agent for the upper Missouri tribes north of the mouth of the Kansas River (the Omaha, Otoe, Pawnee, and Ponca).

Little Raven   As a young man, Little Raven (1809–90), a Southern Arapaho, was a warrior. He went through the age-graded societies and became one of the seven highest ritual leaders, directing all the ceremonies. He had a talent for diplomacy and tried to maintain peaceful relations between the Arapaho and the miners and settlers in Colorado in the 1860s. The **Sand Creek Massacre** ended the diplomatic efforts there. Little Raven signed the **Medicine Lodge Creek Treaty** in 1867 and afterward successfully worked to change the location of the Arapaho reservation in Indian Territory. On the reservation he was the main liaison between the federal officials and the Arapaho. Little Raven's leadership position was buttressed not only by his religious authority but also by support from his brother and brother-in-law, who were prominent Arapahos.

Little Wolf   Little Wolf (1820–1904) was a Northern Cheyenne war leader. An officer in the Bowstring military society, he fought in the war over the Bozeman Trail and the Black Hills, including the **Battle of the Little Bighorn**. He signed the Fort Laramie Treaty of 1868. When **Dull Knife**'s village was attacked by troops in November 1876, Little Wolf was wounded. He surrendered and was sent to Indian Territory with most of the Northern Cheyenne. He and Dull Knife led the escape from the Southern Cheyenne and Arapaho agency; when they reached the North Platte, his group continued to elude the pursuers and reached Montana in 1879. He was persuaded by his friend Lieutenant W. P. Clark and Cheyenne scouts attached to Fort Keogh to surrender there. He was enlisted as a scout, and his people were allowed to stay in Montana. In 1880 he killed another Cheyenne in a dispute over the treatment of his daughter. The penalty for murder was exile, and he left with his family to live alone until he died.

Louisiana Purchase   In 1803 President Thomas Jefferson arranged to purchase from Napoleonic France a vaguely delineated territory that was the western half of the Mississippi River basin known as "Louisiana." He wanted to encourage American interests there and eliminate the threat of a European power controlling the region. The total purchase price was $27,267,622, and the total area was 800,000 square miles that stretched from the Mississippi River to the Rocky Mountains and from New Orleans north to the Canadian border.

"Mandan"   Mandan villages were politically and ceremonially autonomous. **Matrilineal clans** were organized into **moieties** (Corn and Buffalo). Women farmed and men were responsible for hunting buffalo. Earth lodges were built around a ceremonial plaza. A sacred cedar post and cottonwood planks were erected as a shrine to the **culture hero** and as a representation of important events in Mandan history; there was also a ceremonial lodge. There were two village **medicine bundles**, and clans owned bundles transferred matrilineally or from father to son. The owners of the most important bundles formed a village council. Men and women were organized into **age-graded societies**; the society of middle-aged men policed the village. The most important society, Okipa, was represented by a medicine bundle and gave access to power for hunting and prosperity. The Okipa ceremony was a dramatization of the Mandan origin story and the exploits of the Mandan culture hero as well as a prayer for earth renewal. An individual sponsored the ceremony as a prayer-sacrifice and young men participated, making their own prayer-sacrifices.

The population was about 9,000 in 1750; 1,500 in 1781; 209 in 1910; 1,200 in 1990. Their self-designation meant "people." The term "Mandan" was borrowed by Europeans from the Sioux name for them, the meaning of which is obscure (DeMallie, 352, 363–64).

matrilineal clans   Matrilineal clans are comprised of individuals who believe they are descended from the same ancestor and that the genealogical connection is through the female line; thus, an individual belongs to the clan of his or her mother. That person's father belongs to another clan, the clan of his mother. The clan owns material and intellectual property that it transfers to its members.

medals   To formalize an alliance between an Indian group and a nation-state, Indian representatives were selected to receive symbols of mutual respect and support. The Spanish gave medals and canes, for example. The United States gave medals, often with the likeness of an American president. In Canada flags served a similar function.

medicine bundle   The term refers to objects that symbolize human relationship or encounter with a supernatural being; the objects are wrapped in rawhide or some other covering. There are bundles that represent a people's connection with the supernatural (tribal medicine bundles or clan bundles), and individuals can own personal medicine bundles that they purchase or obtain on a vision quest. On a vision quest the individual suffers for the attention of supernatural beings and, in a vision, receives powers and instructions that are later represented in the bundle that the person makes.

Medicine Lodge Creek Treaty   A treaty council to end the fighting during 1864–66 between the Southern Plains tribes and the army was held on Medicine Lodge Creek near Fort Learned in southern Kansas. More than 5,000 Cheyenne, Arapaho, Kiowa, Comanche, and Plains Apache attended. The tribes ceded most of their territory and agreed to accept reservations in Indian Territory. The United States agreed to provide annuity goods (see **annuity payments**) and other support. The peace chiefs viewed this council as a necessary peace overture. However, not all the Cheyenne, Kiowa, and Comanche were in favor of the agreement, and sporadic fighting continued until 1875.

Meriam Report   Lewis Meriam (1883–1972) was a statistician who worked at the Brookings Institution. He was hired to direct a survey of conditions on Indian reservations in 1928. The report was published as "The Problem of Indian Administration." Meriam and the rest of the research team (including the Winnebago Indian Henry Roe Cloud) concluded that the Indian Office had failed in its duty: allotment, health programs, and education were disastrous for Indian people. The report helped reformers build support for the **New Deal** programs.

military societies   Plains peoples all had societies comprised of men who encouraged each other in war through various kinds of rituals. These societies also had governmental duties. The number of societies, their roles, and their ceremonies varied. A major distinction was between **age-graded** and ungraded societies. Most Plains peoples had ungraded societies, meaning a man could join the society of his choice. Ungraded societies often competed against each other.

Missouria   The Missouria probably had politically autonomous villages and retained some independence from the **Otoe** after they merged villages in 1794 to bolster their strength against enemies. Their population was about 80 in 1829; after the merger, population figures represent a combined Otoe-Missouria population. Their self-designation was a term the meaning of which is obscure but that may have meant "those who build a town at the mouth of a river." "Missouria" is derived from the Illinois word meaning "people having dugout canoes" (DeMallie, 461).

moieties   The term "moiety" refers to a dual division in a community. The two moieties may be composed of clans or other kinds of groups. There is reciprocal assistance between moieties. Sometimes there is competition channeled toward socially constructive ends. "Moiety exogamy" means that members of a moiety marry outside the moiety, taking spouses from the opposite moiety.

Mooney, James   Mooney (1861–1921) was an Irish American from Indiana. He worked on a newspaper there and in 1885 came to the Bureau of American Ethnology, where he worked for thirty-six years. He made field studies of the Cherokee, the Kiowa, the Cheyenne, the Sioux, and the Ghost Dance of 1890. He also worked on the *Handbook of North American Indians*, published in 1907–10. He was helpful to Indians in the fight to prevent the criminalization of peyote and the effort to obtain a charter for the Native American Church in Oklahoma. The Bureau of American Ethnology disapproved of his political activity and prevented him from doing any more research in Oklahoma.

Moscoso, Luis de Alvarado   After the death of De Soto in 1542, Moscoso led the Spanish expedition. Using Spanish-speaking captive children as guides, he entered the Caddo country and traveled across southwest Arkansas and into the Red River country and northeast Texas. The children could not speak Caddo so could not communicate with the Caddo. He passed through their country noting temple mounds and farms. Kadohadacho warriors ambushed the expedition and, subsequently, Moscoso tried to intimidate the *caddi* by mutilating a captive and sending him as an emissary. The Caddo fled their villages and Moscoso set fire to the houses. He continued on into Hasinai country, robbing and killing the people. He returned to the Mississippi River in 1543.

New Deal   When Franklin D. Roosevelt ran for president, he campaigned on the promise of a "new deal" for the marginal and poor during the economic

slump of 1932. He was elected by a landslide and developed legislation to provide emergency relief and work programs, public works, agricultural recovery,
social security insurance, and other kinds of federal projects. The Indian component of the New Deal was developed by the Commissioner of Indian Affairs
(see **Bureau of Indian Affairs**), John Collier.

Northwest Rebellion   Louis Riel was involved in a resistance movement of
Métis in 1869 and was exiled from Canada because of it. His father was a
Chipewyan and his mother was from the Red River settlement of the Hudson's
Bay Company. He was well educated, and when he left Canada he went to the
United States and became a citizen. He was teaching in a mission school in
Montana when a delegation of Métis came in 1884 and asked him for help. Riel
prepared a Bill of Rights and proclaimed a provisional government for the
Métis. Led by him, in 1885 the Métis rebelled against the treatment they received from Canada. They were in economic decline and were denied the
right to participate as equals in Canadian society. Riel's followers seized a
church at Batoche on the Saskatchewan River and located there. Troops attacked and defeated them, and in November 1885 Riel was hanged for treason.
The Métis finally achieved formal recognition of aboriginal status in 1982 and
the right of self-government in 1994.

Omaha   The Omaha farmed near their villages for most of the year and made
buffalo hunts in the winter and summer. They were organized into **patrilineal
clans**, which were assigned to **moieties** (Sky and Earth). Clan chiefs were
ranked and clans owned **medicine bundles**. The two principal chiefs were selected from each moiety. Men worked their way up the hierarchy by acts of
generosity and sacrifice. Seven chiefs made up a council that, in cooperation
with ritual leaders, exerted authority. Warriors earned prestige but were not as
highly ranked as chiefs. Omaha believed in an all-pervasive power (see **Wakonta**) into which individuals could tap, but the greatest power was made manifest
in the two tribal medicine bundles. Societies of individuals with curing powers
were important, and a Sacred Pole bundle symbolized tribal unity and represented events in Omaha creation stories. The Omaha live on a reservation in
Nebraska.

Their population was about 1,100 in 1796; 984 in 1871; 2,006 in 1950; and approximately 5,000 in 1998. "Omaha" was their term of self-designation; it meant
"upstream" (DeMallie, 413–15).

Oregon (Overland) Trail   Fur traders found an overland route west along the
Platte and Sweetwater rivers. In 1811–12 Wilson Price Hunt led trappers along this
trail, and the next year Robert Stuart's party followed a longer part of it. The trail
stretched 2,000 miles from Independence, Missouri through Kansas, Nebraska,

and Wyoming to the Columbia River country of Oregon. Trappers used the trail regularly in the 1820s and 1830s. But in the 1840s the settlers and adventurers going west to Oregon and California increased the traffic on this road dramatically. Travelers stripped the area of wood and grass. Ecological changes cut off the bison herds from their annual migratory routes, jeopardizing subsistence for Plains Indians.

"Osage"   Osage villages were politically and ceremonially autonomous. Treaty making was difficult for the United States, bent on identifying "tribes" represented by an individual or a few individuals. Osage villages farmed and went on two buffalo hunts annually. The village residents were organized into **patrilineal clans**, which were assigned to **moieties** (Sky and Earth). Each village had two chiefs. Clans owned **medicine bundles** and each moiety provided a chief, whose position was hereditary in a clan. Men were ranked: the chiefs were above warriors, who were above commoners. The chiefs also were ranked, and they tried to raise their positions through generosity. After completing seven prayer-sacrifices, a chief could join the council of chiefs. This council and a group of ceremonial authorities made decisions for the village. Warriors were chosen from the clans to police the villages. There also were curing societies; individuals dreamed or made a vision quest to obtain medicine power. There were two tribal medicine bundles through which the villages sought help from the all-pervasive life force Wakada (see **Wakonta**). There also was a Sacred Pole bundle, representing events in the origin story, that symbolized the unity of all Osages.

The population was about 4,100 in 1842; 1,783 in 1900; and 5,300 in 1952; in 1990, 9,527 identified themselves as Osage. "Osage" is their self-designation, which was the name of a clan and has an obscure meaning. This term was borrowed by the French (DeMallie, 493).

Otoe   The Otoe probably had politically autonomous villages and only became known as the Otoe tribe in treaty making with the United States. The Otoe farmed and went on two buffalo hunts annually. They were organized into **patrilineal clans** (originally seven) and **moieties** (until reservation times). Clans owned **medicine bundles** that symbolized their histories and their relationship with supernatural power. There were two principal chiefs, and the hereditary chiefs formed a council. Both clans and chiefs were ranked and chiefs outranked warriors, who outranked commoners. Police were appointed. The Otoe believed in an all-pervasive life force (see **Wakonta**) and individuals could access power to succeed by vision quests and by dreams. There were curing societies and societies devoted to agriculture.

Their population was about 1,200 in 1829. They combined with the **Missouria** in 1794. The population was about 459 in 1878; 1,009 in 1959; and 1,520 in 1998. "Otoe" was their self-designation, the meaning of which is obscure (DeMallie, 453, 460).

Ottawa   The Ottawa lived in the **Eastern Woodlands** in the Great Lakes area, where they hunted and fished. They were prosperous middlemen in a regional trade before Europeans arrived. In the mid-seventeenth century the Iroquois attacked them from the east, intending to eliminate them from the fur trade and take control of their territory. The Ottawa retreated from Michigan to Wisconsin. Their French allies helped them return to Michigan in the eighteenth century, where they fought against the British at the time of the **Seven Years' War**. Their leader Pontiac tried to defend Ottawa interests against the British but was defeated. The Ottawa accepted lands in Kansas during the removal era. In 1846 they ceded these lands and some moved to Indian Territory; others went back to Michigan and to Ontario.

patrilineal clans   Patrilineal clans are comprised of individuals who believe they are descended from the same ancestor and that the genealogical connection is through the male line; thus, an individual belongs to the clan of his or her father.

Pawhuska   Pawhuska or White Hair (1750–1809) was chief of the Big Osage village. His personal name became a name for hereditary leaders of the village until 1894. He became chief in 1797, met Lewis and Clark, and was a delegate to Washington, where he met with President Jefferson. He signed the first cession treaty in 1808 and died in 1809. His son succeeded him and took the name. The second Pawhuska was an ally of the United States and sided with the Americans in the **War of 1812**, although the Osage did not fight. He moved his people near Auguste Chouteau's post to secure their position in the trade and in 1825 signed the cession treaty. He died in 1833. Four other chiefs took the name thereafter.

"Pawnee"   The Pawnee have been a "tribal" entity since the mid-nineteenth century, when they began to make treaties with the United States. Before that they were organized into four politically autonomous divisions or bands. After acquiring horses, the Pawnee gave equal attention to farming and hunting, making communal hunts in summer and winter. Members of villages were related matrilineally and villages owned **medicine bundles** representing their history and their association with celestial beings that were manifestations of an all-pervasive life force, **Tiratwahat**. Villages had hereditary chiefs, and the chiefs from the villages in a division formed a council. Priests conducted the village bundle rituals to assure village prosperity. The villagers were stratified into elite and commoner groups. Individuals who attained power to cure organized into societies. The village chief appointed warriors to execute his decisions and police the village. Men also were organized into military societies, some more prominent than others.

Their population was about 6,223 in 1806; 8,400 in 1847; 2,447 in 1872; 629 in 1901; 1,149 in 1950; and 2,500 in 1996. There was no native term for the four divisions as a whole. The native terms for the divisions themselves were Skiri ("wolf"), Kitkahahki ("little earth lodge village"), Pitahawipata ("men going downstream"), and Chawi (meaning obscure). The term "Pawnee" is derived from a Siouan term meaning "alien people," which the French borrowed (De-Mallie, 543–45).

Petalesharro   Petalesharro, a young warrior, was the son of the Skiri chief; in 1816, perhaps on his father's orders, he rescued a female captive who was about to be sacrificed in a Pawnee ceremony. The chief was attempting to stay on good terms with the Americans, who then controlled the trade and held the balance of power. Petalesharro went with an 1821 delegation of lower Missouri and Platte River valley chiefs to Washington, D.C., where his portrait was painted. He was the most popular member of the Pawnee delegation on its tour of Eastern cities because of the publicity his action had received. In Washington he received a silver medal from the girls at Miss White's Select Female Seminary; the inscription on it was "To the Bravest of the Brave."

Piegan   (See **Blackfeet Confederacy**.) The northern bands of Piegan settled in Canada and the southern bands on a reservation in Montana. The meaning of their term of self-designation is obscure; it was borrowed by the Cree and then Europeans as "Piegan" (DeMallie, 627).

Plains Apache   See "**Apache**."

Plains Cree   The Plains Cree are small groups that once were part of the large Cree band of people in the Subarctic forests of Canada. They moved to the Plains and took up buffalo hunting full time in the early nineteenth century and were subsequently referred to as "Plains" Cree. They allied with the **Assiniboine** and entered the Plains as traders before becoming nomadic hunters. Each band had a **military society**; the Cree had a **Sun Dance**, and individuals attempted vision quests. These politically autonomous bands settled on several reservations: in Alberta, Saskatchewan, Montana (Rocky Boy, particularly), and North Dakota. Their population was about 3,000 in 1809; 7,000 in 1871; 9,000 in 1929; and 43,761 in 1973. Their term for themselves means "speakers of the same language." "Cree" is from an Ojibwa term for a band that cannot be identified but that roamed in the James Bay region in the early seventeenth century. The French adopted this word and used it to refer to all the Cree (DeMallie, 650).

Plains Ojibwa   Like the Cree, the Ojibwa are speakers of an Algonkian language. They lived in the forested Subarctic. A few bands left the main group and moved out onto the Plains to embrace a buffalo-hunting way of life in the mid-nineteenth century. Actually, they absorbed many different peoples as "Ojibwa" and intermarried with Cree and Assiniboine. In the late eighteenth century they reportedly traded occasionally in Mandan villages. When the fur trade collapsed in the 1820s and 1830s they began moving southward onto the Plains. They reside on reservations in North Dakota (Turtle Mountain), Montana (Rocky Boy), Saskatchewan, and Manitoba. Some remained landless and unrecognized as "bands" or "tribes." Their term of self-designation was borrowed as "Ojibwa" or "Chippewa."

Pleistocene Era   This was the Ice Age, a geological period of about two million years in which ice masses advanced and retreated, affecting environments around the world. Sea levels were lowered from time to time, which resulted in land bridges between areas formerly separated by ocean. In the Northern Hemisphere the last glacial advance lasted 60,000 years and ended just over 10,000 years ago.

Plenty Coups   Born in the second half of the nineteenth century, Plenty Coups was a Mountain Crow descended from the chief Long Hair, who signed a peace treaty in 1825 with the United States. As a youth he had a vision that validated accommodation with the Americans; his vision gave supernatural sanction to a ranching economy. He had an outstanding career as a warrior. After reservation settlement, he ranched and owned a trading post where he used his resources to maintain a following. He went to Washington as a delegate to negotiate the 1880 cession, and as a chief he cultivated contacts with lobbyists, government officials, and church officials. He was so well known that in 1921 he represented all Indians at the dedication of the Tomb of the Unknown Soldier. He was a participant in both the Tobacco Society and the Catholic Church. Plenty Coups died in 1932.

polygyny   The custom of a man having more than one wife. In Plains communities, if a man took a second wife (or more), he often married his wife's sister or cousin. This reinforced his bond with his in-laws, and usually the women worked well together.

Ponca   The Ponca originally were one of the **Omaha** clans; they separated probably in the late seventeenth or early eighteenth century. Ponca were organized into **patrilineal clans** assigned to **moieties**. Individuals and clans were ranked; chieftainship was hereditary, and there were two principal chiefs. Shamans or men and women who had acquired great power from dreams and visions of spiritual representations of the life force Wakada (see **Wakonta**) formed societies; **military societies** also were important. Clan bundles represented the Ponca's relationship with Wakada, and certain responsibilities fell to the clans as a result of the bundle history. The Ponca also came together for the **Sun Dance**, probably acquired from contacts with nomadic groups on the Plains.

The Ponca were a small group with a council that represented all the bands or villages. Their population was about 800 in 1780; 730 in 1876; 1,258 in 1960; and 4,387 in 1998 (1,895 Northern Ponca and 2,492 Southern Ponca). "Ponca" was their term of self-designation, the meaning of which is obscure (DeMallie, 430–31).

Poundmaker   Poundmaker (1842–86) was born on the Saskatchewan River and raised by the Blackfeet chief Crowfoot. He adopted a policy of peaceful coexistence between his people, the Plains Cree and Ojibwa, and the Canadian settlers. He was chief of the Plains Cree in 1878 and he signed Treaty No. 6, agreeing to accept a reservation. When conditions on the reservation deteriorated and his people were desperately hungry, he joined with others in raiding settlements during the Riel (**Northwest**) **Rebellion** of 1885. One settler was killed and the Cree camp at Cut Knife Creek was attacked in retaliation. Poundmaker was arrested and sent to prison for three years. He obtained early release but died soon after.

powwows   The term refers to dances held from the post–World War II era to the present. They are attended by many different Plains peoples, and sometimes non-Indians as well. War and gourd dancing predominate, along with giveaways and other rituals.

Pueblo (Indians)   Native people who lived in stone or adobe houses in towns in the Southwest were referred to as "Pueblo" Indians by the Spaniards. The Pueblo people had markets and trade centers that attracted traders from distant regions. The Spanish participated in this trading tradition. The term "Pueblo" was used generally after the Spanish withdrew. Pueblo people farmed, growing corn and beans. The towns along the Rio Grande River (for example, San Juan and Taos) used irrigation ditches and had fairly centralized political organization based on moiety chiefs (see **moieties**). Religious ceremonies revolved around agricultural rituals. In the upland region to the west, the Hopi and Zuni peoples lived in towns on mesas, were organized into matrilineal clans, and had little centralization of political organization. Religious societies were responsible for directing much of the towns' activities.

Pueblo Revolt   On August 11, 1680, Popé, an Indian from San Juan pueblo, launched an attack on Spanish colonists. He had organized a pan-Pueblo revolt against the officials who imposed harsh labor requirements and the Catholic priests who used brutal punishments to force conversion to Christianity. Men from almost all the Pueblos participated in the eviction of colonists and officials, driving them away from the Pueblo towns and out of Santa Fe. At least 380 Spanish colonists were killed, 73 of them able-bodied men. In 1692 the Spanish reconquered the area.

Quanah (Parker)   In 1836 the Comanche captured a nine-year-old girl, Cynthia Parker, from a Texas settlement. She lived with the Comanche twenty-four years, married a Comanche man, and gave birth to Quanah about 1855. When he was in his twenties, he was a warrior and raider. After 1875 he rose to prominence as an intermediary chief, becoming an ally of American officials and parlaying that into benefits for his band. He favored leasing pasture to cattlemen and used the income and gifts of cattle to support followers. He was the most important Comanche leader of peyote ritual and served on the business committee. He died in 1911.

Quapaw   The Quapaw lived in the lower Mississippi valley east of the Plains (although some scholars classify them as Plains Indians, which points to the limitations of the "culture area" approach). They had a close historical relationship to the Omaha, who broke off from an ancestral population and moved to the Plains. In the late seventeenth century the Quapaw had hostile relations with their neighbors in the Southeast. They were on good terms with the culturally and linguistically similar Osage to the west. In the late eighteenth century they began to make hunting trips to the Arkansas River at the edge of the Plains but lived in eastern Arkansas. They also were extensively involved in the slave trade, raiding into the Plains. In 1804 they were in three villages on the Arkansas River and one village on the Mississippi, intermarrying with the Choctaw and living in bark longhouses. In 1826 they were moved to Caddo lands in Indian Territory and in 1834 they received a reservation in the eastern part of Indian Territory. In 1682 their population was about 6,000; in 1910, 231. In 1996 there were 2,510 enrolled Quapaw.

Quiscat   An important Wichita (Tawakoni) leader. He worked to maintain good relations with the Spanish in the 1770s.

Red Cloud   Red Cloud (1821–1909) was born near the fork of the Platte River. He was a skilled warrior who led the Sioux, Cheyenne, and Arapaho war over the Bozeman Trail. He fought so well that the United States agreed to withdraw the army forts in Montana. When he signed the Fort Laramie Treaty of 1868, he thought he was guaranteed a reservation in the Platte valley near Fort Laramie. He made several trips to Washington to secure a reservation in the White River area rather than on the Missouri River. He worked for peace between the Sioux and the United States, refusing to participate in the Black Hills war. Instead he became expert at influencing public opinion, criticizing government policy and attracting huge crowds when he toured in the East. He pressured Crazy Horse to surrender in order to try to restore peace. He also discouraged people from embracing the Ghost Dance. He gradually lost influence on the Pine Ridge reservation.

Red River Métis   Métis people are of mixed Indian and European descent and have a way of life that represents a blend of Indian and European traditions. For example, they went on buffalo hunts but transported supplies and robes in carts. They spoke Michif, a composite language of Cree and French. Some groups of Métis began leaving their settlements in the Red River Valley in Canada and moving out onto the Plains more or less permanently after they were excluded from economic opportunities in Canada in the mid-nineteenth century. Some Métis went to Saskatchewan and Alberta. Despite their significant contributions to the development of the Canadian economy and society, the government refused to recognize their rights in their homeland; this led to two rebellions, the last in 1885 (see **Northwest Rebellion**). They received no reservations but have political associations in Canada that pursue nationalistic goals. In 1991 the self-identified population was somewhere between 100,000 and 240,000.

Red River War   Before 1870 buffalo were hunted in the winter when the hair was thickest and the robes brought a good price. In 1870 a new tanning process was developed that allowed for the use of short-hair hides; as a result, the buffalo were hunted year round by American professional hunters who used high-powered Sharp rifles. These developments threatened the Indian economy. Led by Comanches, some Comanche, Southern Cheyenne, and Kiowa warriors attacked a group of professional hunters at Adobe Walls on the South Canadian River in 1874. Other hostilities followed until the army defeated them late in 1875.

Sacajawea   Sacajawea was a Shoshone woman from Idaho who was captured in 1800 at age twelve by Hidatsas and purchased by the trader and trapper Charbonneau. She joined his household, and when he was hired by Lewis and Clark as their interpreter on their expedition, she and her baby came with him. Her presence helped project an image of peaceful intent for the expedition, and she helped with the camp work. When the party reached the upper Missouri, she guided them and interpreted for them when they encountered her brother, then the leader of a band of Shoshone. By 1810 she and her husband had left the Missouri River society; there is no firm evidence about where or when she died.

Sand Creek Massacre   Colonel John Chivington, leader of the Colorado volunteers, and territorial governor John Evans instructed peaceful camps of Southern Cheyenne and Arapaho to locate near Fort Lyon, where they would be safe. Subsequently, Chivington ordered a surprise attack on the camp. Seven hundred men with howitzers killed almost 500 men, women, and children on November 29, 1864.

Santa Fe Trail   This trail went from Independence, Missouri across Kansas, Oklahoma, and New Mexico to Santa Fe. From 1821 to 1880, it was a busy commercial route with traffic moving both ways. It became obsolete when the railroad was built. The first successful commercial expedition was in 1821 by William Becknell, who took goods to Santa Fe on horseback and returned the next year transporting goods in wagons. He and other traders used Independence and Westport (Kansas City) as terminus points. The goods were then shipped from Santa Fe to the interior of Mexico and California. In the 1820s the trail was a target of Indian raiders. After the Mexican War the U.S. Army tried to protect commerce in the region.

"Santee"   See **"Sioux."**

Satanta   Satanta or White Bear (1830–78) was a Kiowa war leader in the 1860s and 1870s. He was born on the Northern Plains and raided deep into Texas and Mexico as well as on the **Santa Fe Trail**. In 1866 he was the most important war chief and one of three principal chiefs (the other two were Kicking Bird and Lone Wolf, both less hostile to Americans). He signed the **Medicine Lodge Creek Treaty** and tried to avoid trouble with the army in 1868 when Custer attacked **Black Kettle**'s village on the Washita River. He and Lone Wolf approached military leaders to assure them of their loyalty, but General Sheridan had them seized and held hostage. The Kiowa were told that these leaders would be killed if they did not surrender to the troops. Later, in 1871, as trespassing settlers undermined the Kiowa's ability to support themselves, Satanta participated in raids. For this he was arrested and sentenced to death. Eastern reformers protested, and instead he was imprisoned. Lone Wolf and Kicking Bear interceded and obtained his release in 1873. When some Kiowas were involved in attacks on professional buffalo hunters who were destroying the herds near them (see **Red River War**), the army arrested Satanta again (despite his lack of involvement) and sent him back to prison, where he committed suicide. In 1963 his grandson was able to get his remains and rebury them at Fort Sill near the Kiowa community.

Sarcee   The Sarcee were Beaver Indians who spoke an Athapaskan language and lived in the Subarctic. In the eighteenth century they moved south to hunt on the Plains in the summer and wintered north in the Subarctic woodlands. They allied with the Blackfeet Confederacy and became full-time buffalo hunters, becoming fluent in the Blackfoot language. They borrowed **military societies** and the **Sun Dance** from the Blackfeet. They have been on a reservation near Calgary since 1883. Their population was about 650 in the 1780s; 420 in 1870; 160 in 1924; and 1,264 in 1997. Their self-designation has an obscure meaning. The origin of the name "Sarcee" is unknown (DeMallie, 636–37).

Sauk   The Sauk lived in the **Eastern Woodlands**, farming and hunting. They were driven from Michigan to Wisconsin in the early seventeenth century by the Iroquois. In 1733 they took in refugees from the Fox tribe, angering the French, who were at odds with the Fox. Forced out of Wisconsin, they went to Iowa. In the nineteenth century the Americans wanted them to move west of the Mississippi. The last of the Sauk who were resisting were defeated in 1832 (see **Black Hawk War**). The Sauk were pressured to cede their land in Iowa and settled on a reservation in Kansas. In 1869 they resettled in Indian Territory (as the Sac and Fox Tribe).

Seminole   In the seventeenth century, Creek groups from Georgia and Alabama had helped the English eliminate the native peoples in Florida. Afterward, in the eighteenth century, Creek groups (actually made up of diverse peoples from different backgrounds and speaking different languages) settled the region, establishing farms and towns. In the nineteenth century, more Creeks and other refugees came to escape the fighting between Americans and native peoples in the Southeast. By the 1760s the native people in Florida were known as "Seminole" (or "pioneers" in the Muskogee language of the Creeks). The United States attempted to dislodge them and force them to remove to Indian Territory in the early nineteenth century. The Seminole fought three wars with the United States in an effort to remain in Florida. Some Seminoles relocated to Indian Territory and obtained land west of the Creek, but some groups remained in Florida and succeeded in obtaining reservations there.

Seven Years' War   Fighting started between several Indian groups loyal to France and Anglo-American settlers in 1754. In 1756 the quarrel developed into a war between the French and the English, with Indian allies on each side. The two countries were competing for trade in and control of North America. England won the war and expelled France from Canada, the Great Lakes area, and Louisiana. They concluded a peace in 1763, the Treaty of Paris. This war is also referred to as the French and Indian War.

Shawnee   The Shawnee, a confederacy of five divisions, lived in the Ohio valley in the late seventeenth century. They were attacked by the Iroquois and started dispersing. In the late eighteenth century, some had moved to Spanish territory and some stayed in Ohio until they had to cede their land after the Revolutionary War. From Ohio they were removed to Kansas, where they came into conflict with Plains groups, and then Oklahoma. Some Shawnee in Texas allied with the Caddo.

"Shoshone"   In the seventeenth century the Shoshone-speaking peoples lived throughout Oregon and Idaho and in the foothills east of the Rocky Mountains in Montana and Wyoming. On the Plains they hunted buffalo. They were on good terms with the Comanche and adopted the horse in the eighteenth century. They began to raid on the Northern Plains when they had many horses and groups like the Blackfeet had none. In the nineteenth century they traded with American trappers in southwestern Wyoming and with the Crow. From 1780 to 1825, the Blackfeet Confederacy, having acquired the horse and the gun, drove the Shoshone back into or west of the Rockies.

"Sioux"   The three main divisions of the Sioux (Santee, Yankton and Yanktonai, and Teton) share similar social organization, ceremonies, and cultural beliefs and values, and individuals in these divisions intermarried. The Santee were east and west (in the area of the Minnesota River) of the Mississippi River in the eighteenth century and were subdivided into four groups. The Yankton and Yanktonai each had two divisions and the Teton had seven divisions by the nineteenth century. Divisions were politically autonomous but sometimes more than one division camped together. The Santee lived in winter and summer camps and supported themselves by hunting buffalo and other game, fishing, collecting wild rice and other plants, and growing corn. At the time of contact with Europeans they lived in Minnesota; in 1863 they engaged in a major conflict with settlers and the United States, which resulted in their dispersal (see **Sioux Uprising**). Yankton and Yanktonai were west of the Santee as far as the Missouri River, supporting themselves by hunting buffalo and doing some farming, while the more westerly Teton were exclusively buffalo hunters and were organized into seven politically autonomous groups (Oglala, Brule, Minneconjou, Hunkpapa, Black-feet, Sans Arc, Two Kettles) organized into bands. Sioux lived in bands or groups of families, each led by a man who inspired his followers' confidence and re-spected the opinions of other prominent men in the band. Individuals viewed fa-ther's and mother's relatives in the same way; Sioux did not have clans (see **ma-trilineal clans, patrilineal clans**). The band leader and his council of prominent men appointed outstanding warriors to police the camp when necessary. The Teton had formally organized military societies that did this. Sioux bands came together for Sun Dances (for the Sioux, a prayer for health and well-being) in which they tried to attract supernatural help by prayer-sacrifice to the pervasive life force Wa Kan Tanka (see **Wakonta**). Individuals also undertook vision quests to obtain aid from a personal spirit helper for curing, warfare, and other activities and participated in various group rituals. Yankton and Yanktonai curers were or-ganized into societies. Among the Teton, a tribal medicine bundle was kept by one of the divisions and there were several militiary societies in each division who promoted bravery in addition to a group of warriors appointed by the council to police the camp. The Teton also had curing societies. After waging military ac-tion to protect their hunting grounds, by the late nineteenth century the Sioux settled on several reservations: the Santee on Fort Peck, Spirit Lake, Crow Creek, Santee, Sisseton (or Lake Traverse), small reservations in Minnesota, and in Canada; the Yankton on Yankton; the Yanktonai on Crow Creek, Standing Rock, Fort Peck, Spirit Lake, and in Canada. The Oglala Teton settled on Pine Ridge; the Brule Teton on Lower Brule and Rosebud; the Hunkpapa Teton on Fort Peck, Standing Rock, and in Canada; and the Blackfeet, Minneconjou, Sans Arc, and Two Kettle divisions of the Teton on Cheyenne River (and some Blackfeet Teton on Standing Rock).

In 1804 the total Sioux population was estimated to be 8,410. In 1990 the Santee numbered about 7,000; the Yankton and Yanktonai, about 7,000; and the Teton, about 89,000. The term "Sioux" is from an Ottawa word (meaning "foreign language speaker") borrowed by the French and shortened. Their self-designation means "allies" (*Dakota* in Santee, *Nakota* in Yankton and Yank-tonai, and *Lakota* in Teton). "Teton" comes from the term used by other Sioux for this division; it may mean "prairie village." "Yankton" is derived from the Sioux term meaning "village on the end," and "Yanktonai" means "little village on the end." "Santee" in Sioux means "to camp at Knife quarry," and the four divisions of the Santee are self-designated: Mdewakantan ("holy lake village"); Wahpekute ("leaf shooters"); Wahpeton ("leaf village"); Sisseton (possibly "swampy village") (DeMallie, 748–56, 830).

Sioux Uprising   The "**Santee**" had a long history of friendly, close interper-sonal relations with traders in their country and intermarriage was widespread.

As kinsmen, the traders adhered to Santee values of sharing, mutual aid, and respect. By the 1850s traders and their descendants were deviating from these standards to make larger profits. They helped manipulate the Santee into land cessions in 1851 and 1859, in which they lost most of their land in Minnesota and accepted two reservations on the Minnesota River, only to see the compensation go to the traders. The new settlers refused to enter into respectful relations with the Santee. The Indians became dependent on credit from traders and supplies from the government. They blamed the threat of famine on the traders and settlers, which led Santee warrior societies to the conclusion that the traders and settlers were enemies and that by driving them away they might revitalize Santee traditions. In the fighting that followed, more than 500 settlers were killed, despite the heroic actions of many Santees who saved and protected settlers. Peace eventually was restored and the Santee were expelled from Minnesota (although some later were resettled).

Sits in the Middle of the Land   A Mountain Crow, he was born about 1798. Sits in the Middle of the Land was a war leader in intertribal conflicts and represented the Crow in the 1868 treaty council where they ceded some of their territory and retained a large portion of it in the Bighorn River valley, which became the basis for their reservation.

Sitting Bull (Arapaho)   Sitting Bull (1855–1934) embraced the Ghost Dance while living in Wyoming with the Northern Arapaho in 1889. He moved to Indian Territory to join his brothers there and settled among the Southern Arapaho, selecting an allotment along the North Canadian River near his brothers. He began to hold large intertribal Ghost Dances where he chose other Ghost Dance leaders and mentored Ghost Dance devotees.

Sitting Bull (Hunkpapa Sioux)   Sitting Bull (1831–90) was born in South Dakota. He fought the U.S. Army in the 1870s to protect the buffalo range on the Northern Plains. He surrendered in 1881 and was held under guard for two years. He then settled on Standing Rock reservation, where he was a successful farmer and stockman. In 1885 he traveled with Buffalo Bill's Wild West Show. He took up the political cause of the Sioux again during the breakup of the Great Sioux Reservation, trying to prevent the allotment of reservation land. He was an apostle of the Ghost Dance, which attracted reprisals from the Indian agent. Indian police were sent to arrest him in 1890, and he was killed in a scuffle.

slavery   Before Europeans arrived in North America, Plains people took captives when they had the opportunity in conflicts with enemies. Children usually were adopted and integrated into the captor's community. Some Plains groups might torture an adult captive for revenge purposes. Women might become wives of men in the community and others might be attached to households to do menial tasks, but not tasks that people in the household would not do. The slave trade fostered by Europeans introduced an economic motive in warfare. Plains groups (some more than others, depending on where the markets were) began raiding other groups for captives to sell to Europeans, or they traded for captives to resell to Europeans. Slavery in this sense caused population depletion and dislocation and created an atmosphere of terror in some regions. The peak period for slave raiding on the Plains was the eighteenth century. Captivity and slavery also contributed to the multilingual nature of Plains societies and to the exchange of technology and ideas.

Spiro   Spiro is a fifty-acre Mississippian archaeological site in eastern Oklahoma on the Arkansas River. It probably was occupied by Caddoan speakers from 700 to 1450; its peak was between 1200 and 1400. This was the ceremonial center of a vast polity. It had satellite towns and small farms. There was a small resident population at Spiro, but it held an important place in regional trade, apparently controlling trade between the West (the Plains and Southwest) and east of the Mississippi. The people associated with Spiro hunted small game, gathered plants, and fished, but were organized into ranked or stratified social groups. This is most obvious in the burials; some were for elites and have an elaborate structure and grave goods, but commoners were buried in cemeteries. There are two large pyramidal mounds that were platforms for public buildings and six low mounds that served as platforms for funerary structures.

Spotted Tail   Spotted Tail (1823–81) tried to help his people adjust to domination by the United States by working for compromise and accommodation. His father was a Northern Sioux and his mother a Brule. He was an accomplished warrior by the age of thirty and was involved in the fighting after the **Grattan Massacre**. He was wounded in 1855 during the retaliatory campaign of General **William Harney**. Harney took captives to hold as hostages, including Spotted Tail's wife and baby. Spotted Tail then surrendered and was sent to Forts Leavenworth and Kearny for confinement for one year. He participated in the Indian War of 1864–65 but advised peace during the war over the Bozeman Trail in 1866–68. Spotted Tail signed the 1868 Fort Laramie Treaty, agreeing to settle on a reservation. He and his people went to an agency on the Missouri River, but he successfully campaigned to move the agency west to the White River area. In 1881, a rival, Crow Dog (1835–1910), shot and killed Spotted Tail. This act resulted in a Supreme Court case in which the court decided that the federal government could not prosecute Indian crimes on Indian land; the Brule settled the matter in a traditional manner, with Crow Dog's family paying compensation to Spotted Tail's.

Standing Bear   Standing Bear (1829–1908) was one of the main Ponca chiefs in 1877 when the Ponca were forced to move to Indian Territory. In 1879 he decided to move back to Nebraska, in part because he wanted to bury the body of his recently deceased son where his other relatives were buried. A small group traveled north and were arrested by the commander of the army in the Nebraska region, General George Crook. With help from a local journalist, Thomas H. Tibbles, the plight of Standing Bear's group was publicized. Two attorneys volunteered to defend him against arrest and confinement. They applied for a writ of habeas corpus on his behalf. The federal government denied relief on the grounds that an Indian was not a person under the terms of the Constitution. Eventually the Supreme Court ruled in Standing Bear's favor. He buried his son, and with the help of reformers, was allowed to stay in Nebraska. He went on tour with Tibbles and **Francis** and **Susette La Flesche** to shape public opinion about Indian affairs.

"Stoney"   The Stoney are closely related to the "**Assiniboine**," but by the end of the eighteenth century they had a separate political identity. The Stoney lived in two politically autonomous divisions (north and south). In the north they hunted forest animals and fished. In the south they often allied with the "**Cree**" against the **Blackfeet confederacy**. Those closest to the Plains were nomadic buffalo hunters. Some large bands had military societies. Bands were led by men who could attract a following. Individuals tried to acquire access to the pervasive life force (see **Wakonta**) through vision quests (see **medicine bundle**) and participated in a **Sun Dance**.

They now live on several reservations in Alberta. Their population was about 556 in 1877 and 6,000 in 1997. Their self-designation was "*Nakota*" (meaning "allies"). The Plains Cree term for both the Stoney and the Assiniboine was "Assiniboine" or "stone Sioux" (DeMallie, 602–3).

Sun Dance   This ceremony was used by nomadic Plains tribes as a vehicle for prayer-sacrifice. "Sun Dance" was the English term, but Plains peoples all had native terms for the ceremony (for example, the Arapaho term would translate to "offerings lodge"). In some versions of the ceremony (the Arapaho and Cheyenne rituals, for example) the participants dramatized events in creation. In some tribes, an individual had to make a vow (as a prayer-sacrifice) to sponsor the Sun Dance; then others participated. For some peoples, it was primarily a vehicle to acquire supernatural help in war. Sacrifice demonstrated sincerity and attracted favorable response from supernatural sources of power;

sacrifice was made in the form of food and property donated to others and as body sacrifice, usually through fasting or piercing the skin and breaking it free from the center pole of the ceremonial lodge. Pieces of skin also might be cut off and offered by men or women in the lodge.

Ten Bears   Ten Bears (1792–1872) was a warrior and leader from the Yamparika band of Comanches. He went to Washington on a delegation to negotiate on behalf of the Comanche and represented Comanches at the Treaty of Little Arkansas in 1865 and at the **Treaty of Medicine Lodge Creek** in 1867. He also was on the 1872 delegation to Washington and opposed the warriors who participated in the **Red River War**.

"Teton"   See "**Sioux**."

Tinhiouen   Tinhiouen was the most important Caddo *caddi* in the 1760s, 1770s, and 1780s. He was from the Kadohadacho division of the Caddo. The Spanish medaled him, and he helped them negotiate with the Wichita and Comanche. He died in 1789.

Tiratwahat   The Pawnee term for the power of creation. This power was diffused throughout the universe and was hierarchically represented in the spirit world. Humans gained assistance by showing respect through various kinds of rituals.

Tonti, Henri   Tonti was a soldier in French service before he joined La Salle in **Illinois** country in the 1680s. The French were trading along the Illinois River. He traveled with La Salle down the Mississippi and they, with other French Canadians, built Arkansas Post at the mouth of the Arkansas River in 1686. As commander of the French establishments in the Illinois country, Tonti visited the Caddo in 1690 on a search for La Salle, who had not returned from an expedition. His behavior offended the Caddo, and this situation helped reinforce their positive relationship with the Spanish. Tonti wrote about his observations.

travois   The travois was a wood and rawhide platform used by Indians to transport items. Before the introduction of the horse, it was drawn by dogs; a larger version was built for horses. Two poles were tied to a horse and a loading platform of sticks made at the base, at the other ends of the poles. Women made and owned travoises, which wore out after about a year. The travois was used into the twentieth century because it held up better than the wagon in rough terrain.

Treaty of Prairie du Chien   In 1830 William Clark (see **Lewis and Clark expedition**) negotiated a treaty on behalf of the federal government with the Santee, Omaha, Iowa, Otoe-Missouria, and Yankton, as well as the **Sauk** and their Fox allies. The tribes ceded land, and the government agreed to pay them annuities (see **annuity payments**). This was a large treaty council involving many delegates. Clark used threats of army attacks to gain the tribes' consent. The Omaha and Otoe-Missouria retained hunting rights in the ceded area. Clark also deceived the tribes by assuring them that the ceded area would not be settled. Treaty negotiations such as the council at Prairie du Chien, Michigan were common in the early nineteenth century, as the United States expanded west.

"Ute"   The Ute peoples lived in northern New Mexico, western Colorado, and Utah; they got horses and traded with the Spanish in the seventeenth and early eighteenth centuries. They moved from a mountainous region to the Plains, where they harassed the Pueblos and hunted buffalo. They sold captives they took from other Indian groups in Utah. They allied with the Comanche to strengthen their position, but their relations soured and the Comanche drove them back west.

voyageurs   At the close of the seventeenth century many individuals traveled by canoe through the interior of Canada to trade for furs, which they sold to merchants in Montreal. These men were referred to as *voyageurs*. This term later was applied to selected *coureurs de bois* hired by merchants (*bourgeois*) in Montreal to arrange trading alliances with individuals and villages.

Wakonta   *Wakonta* or *Wa Kan Tanka* is the Sioux term for the power of creation. This power was diffused throughout the universe and could be used by humans who established a respectful relationship with its representatives in the spirit world.

War of 1812   The conflict lasted from 1811 to 1815 in America. The British enlisted the aid of many Indian groups, the most effective of which was the large coalition of warriors under the leadership of Tecumseh, a Shawnee. Tecumseh was killed in 1813 and, in the end, Britain's Indian allies could not help her cause. The fighting centered around the Great Lakes area, particularly Detroit and Mackinac and the trade there. At the Treaty of Ghent in 1815, Britain and the United States made peace and the United States promised that Indians would have the same territory and status as in 1811. Shortly thereafter, the promises were broken.

warfare   Before the arrival of Europeans, warfare on the Plains was largely a matter of revenge expeditions. The goal was to avoid loss of life in the revenge party. On the Northern Plains, two large groups might face each other behind large shields and try to inflict damage. Occasionally a surprise attack might result in the taking of a few captives. The acquisition of the horse changed the way Plains men (and occasionally women who opted for the warrior's life) fought and added an economic motive for war. The shield was made smaller so it could be easily carried on horseback, and it covered the vital organs. Horses were rigged out in rawhide armor. The goal of a raiding party was to steal horses and return safely. The gun was adapted for use by a mounted rider. Both the horse and the gun also made possible the territorial dispossession of groups that lacked one or both. Fighting was more face to face and war parties went out frequently; this resulted in a higher casualty rate. Successful warriors received great prestige, and Plains societies developed a system of ranked exploits, called coups. Certain brave acts counted for more prestige than others and certain acts were required for particular kinds of leadership positions (see "**Crow**"). Men were socialized, then, to be aggressive and vigilant in a dangerous world.

White Plume   White Plume was a Kaw chief in the early nineteenth century. Louis Gonville, a French interpreter and trader, married his daughter, and they had three daughters who married sons of prominent St. Louis merchants. White Plume signed a cession treaty between the Kaw and the United States in 1833 in which he got grants of land for himself and his intermarried family members. This alienated other chiefs, and White Plume called on Indian agents to provide him with support to counter his opposition. After he signed the treaty, he gradually lost influence as his fortunes declined; his alliance with the United States did not result in prosperity for his village. His village in the Mission Creek region was some distance from the other three Kaw villages and was the most welcoming to missionaries; this estrangement created lasting fissures among the Kaw.

"Wichita"   The Wichita had politically autonomous divisions but were treated as one "tribe" by the United States. The Wichita villages farmed and hunted buffalo. Descent probably once was matrilineal but, by the eighteenth century, individuals equated siblings and cousins, which created a larger group of kinsmen who cooperated in hunting. The Wichita had a council of warriors who selected a village chief, who had considerable authority. Wichita believed in an all-pervasive life force that was manifested in celestial beings as well as other beings in nature. There were societies of people with the power to cure and bring prosperity, which they acquired in dreams in which they made contact with the life force. The societies had **medicine bundles**.

The population of all these groups was possibly 20,000 in 1601 and 6,000 in 1719, although the information is somewhat speculative. In 1960 there were 700 "Wichita" and in 1984, 1,170; in 1998, the enrolled population was 1,912. "Wichita" was the name of one village, and it was adopted by the French. The self-designation for the Wichita was derived from another band name and meant "tattooed around the eyes." Other major divisions were Taovaya (a self-designation of obscure meaning), Tawakoni (of obscure meaning), and Iscani (a self-designation of "Wako," of obscure meaning) (DeMallie, 563–64).

Winnebago   The Winnebago spoke a Siouan language. They lived in Wisconsin in the seventeenth century and traded with the French. They were at odds with the groups speaking Algonkian languages. The Americans pressured them to cede their lands in Wisconsin in the 1820s and 1830s. They were removed to Iowa, Minnesota, the Crow Creek reservation in South Dakota, and finally their own reservation (purchased from the Omaha) in Nebraska in 1865. This removal put pressure on the Plains tribes who were being crowded by the Eastern immigrant tribes.

Wovoka   Wovoka ("Cutter") was the Paiute name of the Ghost Dance prophet. His English name was Jack Wilson. Born in 1860, he had revelations about a new religion that would help Indians deal with their reservation life. He was a curer and shaman and had been exposed to Christianity. The new religion was a blend of elements from Paiute religious tradition and Christianity, and it stressed that humans should work together in harmony. He died in 1932.

"Yankton"   See "**Sioux.**"

"Yanktonai"   See "**Sioux.**"

Yellowtail, Robert   He was born in the mid-1880s and became an important Crow leader in the twentieth century. A Mountain Crow, Yellowtail went to Riverside boarding school in California and became an interpreter and helper for Crow chiefs, including **Plenty Coups**, in dealings with the federal government. He served on the business committee and also ran unsuccessfully for state office. In 1934 he became the superintendent of the Crow reservation during John Collier's tenure as director of the **Bureau of Indian Affairs**. Yellowtail was a successful rancher as well.

yuwipi   "Yuwipi" means "they wrap him up" in the language of the Teton Sioux. It is a curing ceremony in which a ritual specialist or curer with access to supernatural forces performs a ceremony to cure a patient. The yuwipi specialist is tied up in a darkened room or lodge and calls on spirits to appear and cure the patient. The spirits arrive and untie the specialist, often touching or communicating with the patient. When the room is again lit, the yuwipi curer has been untied. The patient's relatives attend and pray for him during the ceremony. This ritual is widely practiced among Siouan-speaking and Algonkian-speaking peoples in the Eastern Woodlands and Northern Plains.

Part III

Chronology

12,000–16,000 B.P.
Humans enter the Great Plains.

11,500 B.P.
Clovis technology used by big game hunters in the Plains region.

11,000 B.P.
Folsom technology used by big game hunters in the Plains region.

7,600–2,000 B.P.
Archaic or foraging tradition spreads throughout the Plains in response to climatic conditions.

6,500–4,500 B.P.
Modern species of bison evolves.

2,250–1,000 B.P.
Plains Woodland tradition develops in some regions, influenced by Eastern Woodlands developments, including some domestication of plants, pottery, and mound-building.

900 A.D.
Plains Village tradition of sedentary farming villages appears along streams; includes the introduction of domesticated corn and beans.

950
Arrival of Middle Missouri villagers in the Missouri River valley and beginning of development of Southern Plains Village traditions.

1000
Beginning of development of Plains Village traditions on the Central Plains.

1400
Great Bend tradition of Southern Plains farming villages of Caddoan speakers develops in Arkansas River valley.

1492
Christopher Columbus lands in the West Indies.

ca. 1450–1500
The Apache begin to enter the Southern Plains.

1500
Caddoan speakers settle in Middle Missouri area near Siouan speakers.

1535
Jacques Cartier claims eastern Canada for France.

1541–42
Hernando De Soto's expedition reaches Caddo country in the Red River valley.

1542
Coronado travels from the Southwest across the Southern Plains to Wichita villages.

1550–1600
People from the Oneota tradition (ancestors of Osage and other Siouan speakers) begin to enter the lower Missouri River region.

1598
Juan de Oñate establishes a Spanish colony in New Mexico, introducing a market for slaves and making horses available to native peoples.

1602

Horses are acquired by the Wichita.

1608

The French establish Quebec colony.

1668

The British form the Hudson's Bay Company and begin selling guns to North-east Indians in contact with Plains peoples.

1670

The British establish Carolina colony.

1675

The Dismal River tradition (associated with the Apache) of farming villages is well established on the Southern Plains.

1680

The Pueblo Revolt results in more horses being introduced onto the Plains.

1684

La Salle comes down the Illinois River to the Gulf of Mexico and founds a French colony in Louisiana (near Galveston, Texas), which lasts three years, and French traders begin regular transactions with Indians in the lower Missouri River region.

The French build Lake Nipigon Post in Assiniboine country in Canada.

1686

Arkansas Post is established at the mouth of the Arkansas River by Henri de Tonti and other French traders from Canada, and the gun trade expands.

1699

The French establish Cahokia trading post in the lower Missouri region.

1700

Well-armed Chickasaws begin intensive attacks and slave raids on Caddos.

The Cheyenne enter the northeastern periphery of the Plains.

The French and Spanish agree on a border between their territories in eastern Texas.

1706

The Comanche enter the Southern Plains.

1710
Teton Sioux bands begin moving toward the Missouri River.

1713
The French establish Natchitoches Post.

1718
The French establish New Orleans, which becomes a major market for slaves.

1719
Bénard de La Harpe visits Wichita villages and establishes direct trade relations
for France.

1721
The Spanish establish Los Adaes in Texas.

ca. 1735
The Comanche displace the Apache from the Southern Plains.

1738
La Vérendrye visits Mandan villages from his posts in Canada.

1739
Fort Cavagnolle is built on the Missouri River by French traders to trade directly with Indians on the lower Missouri.

1741
The Mandan have horses.

1746
The Wichita and the Comanche form an alliance.

1751
A smallpox epidemic spreads throughout the Southern Plains.

1754–63
The French and Indian or Seven Years' War affects trade on the Plains as
Britain expels France from Canada and the French cede Louisiana west
of the Mississippi River to Spain.

ca. 1758
The Wichita are pushed south of the Arkansas River by attacks from the Osage and others.

1764
St. Louis is established by Spanish interests.

1770s
Osage attacks force the Wichita south into Texas.

1774
The Hudson's Bay Company begins to expand into Saskatchewan River country, building Cumberland House, a major trading center.

1776–83
The Revolutionary War establishes the independence of the United States.

1777
The new government of the United States assumes authority over Indian affairs.

1780–81
A smallpox epidemic spreads throughout the Plains.

1780
Mandan and Hidatsa villages combine on the Knife River.
The Cheyenne affiliate with the Arikara on the Grand River.

1780s
The Blackfeet Confederacy displaces the Shoshone from northern Montana.

1787
The U.S. Constitution is adopted and Congress assumes the power to regulate commerce with Indian tribes.

1790s
Emigrant Indians from east of the Missouri River begin entering the southeastern region of the Plains.

1793
The Hudson's Bay Company builds Brandon trading house on the Assiniboine River among Assiniboines.

1795

Fort Carondelet is built by Auguste Chouteau among the Osage.

1796

The factory system of government trading houses is established for trade with Indians (it is abolished in 1822).

1800

Spain retrocedes Louisiana to France.
The Comanche and the Kiowa form an alliance.
The Teton Sioux largely control trade on the Missouri River.

1801–02

A smallpox epidemic decimates native peoples in the Missouri River region.

1803

The United States purchases Louisiana from France.

1804–06

The Lewis and Clark expedition explores the upper Missouri River.

1808

The Osage cede part of their territory in Missouri and Arkansas.

1810

The Cherokee begin to migrate into Arkansas.

1812

The United States goes to war against Great Britain.
Louisiana becomes a state.

1815

The Treaty of Portage des Sioux is signed between the United States and several Sioux tribes, which accept the protection of the United States and agree to peace.

1816

Smallpox sweeps throughout the Southern Plains.

1817

Fort Teton trading post is built at the mouth of the Bad or Teton River.

1818

Congress authorizes the appointment of federal agents to deal with Indian tribes.
The Osage cede more land in Missouri and Arkansas.
The United States signs a treaty of friendship and peace with the Pawnee.

1821

Mexico wins its independence from Spain.
Missouri becomes a state.

1824

The Bureau of Indian Affairs is created within the War Department.

1825

The Treaty of Prairie du Chien is signed between the United States and several
    tribes in the Great Lakes area, including former enemies, the Sioux and
    Ojibwa; it establishes peace and U.S. protection of the Indians and a
    boundary between them. Trespassing settlers soon make these agreements
    moot.

1826

The American Fur Company secures a monopoly over the fur trade.

1829

The American Fur Company establishes Fort Union trading post at the mouth
    of the Yellowstone River.

1830

The Indian Removal Act authorizes the removal of Indians from east of the
    Mississippi.
A treaty is signed at Prairie du Chien in which land cessions are made by the
    Sioux, Otoe and Missouria, Iowa, and Omaha.

1831

The buffalo robe trade supersedes the trade in beaver pelts.

1833

The Pawnee cede land in Kansas and Nebraska.

1834

Fort Laramie trading post is built by the American Fur Company on the Platte
    River in order to trade for robes on the Central and Southern Plains.

1835

The Camp Holmes peace treaty is signed between the United States and the Wichita, Comanche, and Kiowa.

The Caddo cede land in Louisiana, and most move to Indian Territory or join other Caddo in Texas.

1836

Texas wins its independence from Mexico.

A cholera epidemic sweeps the Southern Plains.

1837–39

Smallpox sweeps through the Southern Plains and up the Missouri River.

1839

The Osage still living off the reservation settle with the main body of the tribe on their reservation in Kansas.

1840

The Cheyenne and Arapaho make peace with the Comanche, Kiowa, and Plains Apache.

1840s

The traffic along the Oregon (Overland) Trail and Santa Fe Trail begins to disrupt bison hunting.

1845

The United States annexes Texas.

The Hidatsa and Mandan move north and found Like-a-Fishhook village.

1846–48

The United States and Mexico fight a war, at the close of which Texas, New Mexico, and California are transferred to the United States.

1846

The Pawnee and the Kaw cede more land in Nebraska and Kansas.

1849

The Bureau of Indian Affairs is transferred from the War Department to the Department of the Interior.

Fort Laramie is purchased by the United States and made into a military fort.

Cholera sweeps the Southern Plains.

1851

The United States signs the Fort Laramie peace treaty with the Arapaho, Cheyenne, Sioux, Mandan, Hidatsa, Arikara, and Assiniboine, and territorial boundaries are defined.

The Santee agree to a reservation.

1853

A peace council is held at Fort Atkinson between the United States and the Comanche, Kiowa, and Plains Apache.

The Otoe agree to cede most of their reservation on the Kansas–Missouri line.

1854–56

The Grattan Massacre in 1854 precipitates General Harney's expedition against the Teton in the Platte River country.

1854

The United States signs treaties with the Otoe-Missouria, Omaha, and Iowa in which they cede most of their land and agree to settle on reservations in Nebraska.

The Kansas–Nebraska Act organizes the area as a territory and opens it to settlement.

The Wichita and Caddo settle on the Brazos reservation in Texas.

1855

The United States signs a peace treaty with the Blackfeet Confederacy on the Judith River and territorial boundaries are assigned.

1857

The Pawnee cede most of their land and accept a small reservation in Nebraska.

1858

The Ponca and Yankton Sioux cede most of their land and accept small reservations in Nebraska.

1859

The Wichita and Caddo are settled on a reservation in Indian Territory.

The Pawnee settle on their reservation on the Loup River.

Gold is discovered in Colorado.

The Kaw sell some of their reservation land in Kansas.

1861–65

The Civil War is fought; some Plains Indians support one side or the other, although few are involved in heavy fighting.

1862

The Arikara leave their village and move north to join the Mandan and Hidatsa at Like-a-Fishhook village.

1862–63

The Sioux Uprising in Minnesota results in attacks by the Santee on settlers and retaliation from the U.S. Army.

1864

The Sand Creek Massacre, an attack by Colorado militia on a peaceful camp of Southern Cheyenne and Arapaho, leads to the Indian War of 1864–65.

1865

The Osage cede part of their Kansas reservation.

1865–67

Teton Sioux under the leadership of Red Cloud fight U.S. troops over the opening of forts along the Bozeman Trail to facilitate settlement.

1867

The Treaty of Medicine Lodge Creek is signed between the United States and the Southern Cheyenne, Southern Arapaho, Kiowa, Comanche, and Plains Apache; it assigns reservations to the Cheyenne and Arapaho and the Kiowa, Comanche, and Plains Apache in Indian Territory.
The Dominion of Canada is established.

1868

The Fort Laramie Treaty is signed between the United States and the Teton Sioux, Northern Arapaho, and Northern Cheyenne; it assigns the tribes to reservations.
The United States signs a treaty with the Crow in which they cede land in return for a large reservation in Montana.

1869

President Grant creates the Board of Indian Commissioners to oversee the management of Indian reservations; this is part of Grant's Peace Policy.
The Cheyenne and Arapaho reservation in Indian Territory is established by executive order.

The United States attends a peace council at Fort Buford, Montana, with the Yanktonai and Santee.

1870
The Osage cede more of their reservation in Kansas.

1871
Congress ends formal treaty making with Indian tribes.

1871–77
Canada signs treaties with the Plains Cree, Assiniboine, and Blackfeet and establishes reservations.

1872
The Osage settle in Indian Territory on their reservation.
The Kaw agree to sell their Kansas reservation and move to Indian Territory.
Reservations are established for the Oglala and Brule Sioux in the White River country.

1873
The Kaw arrive in Indian Territory.
Fort Peck is established as an agency in Montana for several tribes, including the Yanktonai.
The president establishes a reduced reservation in Montana for the Blackfeet and Gros Ventre.

1873–75
The Pawnee move to Indian Territory.

1876
Custer's forces are annihilated at the Little Bighorn River in Montana.
The Teton, Northern Cheyenne, and Northern Arapaho sign an agreement under protest to settle on reservations. Whether the Black Hills are ceded is in dispute.

1876–77
The Ponca are forced to move to Indian Territory.

1878
The Northern Cheyenne are moved to Indian Territory and subsequently flee north.
The Northern Arapaho are settled on the Shoshone reservation in Wyoming.

1879

Standing Bear, a Ponca leader, leaves Indian Territory and returns to Nebraska. After he is arrested amid great public outcry, the U.S. Circuit Court in the District of Nebraska orders him released, declaring that as a "person" he should decide his own residency (*Standing Bear v. Crook*).

1880

The Northern Ponca settle on a small reservation in Nebraska.

1880–81

The Otoe-Missouria move to Indian Territory.

1881

Sitting Bull, Hunkpapa leader, surrenders to the army.

1882

The Omaha reservation in Nebraska is allotted.

1883

The Iowa get a reservation in Indian Territory.

1884

Elk v. Wilkins is decided by the Supreme Court; John Elk, living apart from his Indian community, is denied the right to vote in Omaha and the court upholds this, declaring that he is not a citizen.

1885

The Major Crimes Act gives the federal government jurisdiction over seven crimes on Indian reservations and reverses an earlier court decision (*Ex Parte Crow Dog*) that Indian tribes had jurisdiction in criminal matters involving their members.

1887

Congress passes the General Allotment Act (the Dawes Act) providing for allotment of Indian lands in severalty.

1888

The Blackfeet–Gros Ventre reservation is reduced and broken into three reservations.

1889

The Ghost Dance is introduced on Plains reservations.

The Great Sioux reservation is reduced and subdivided into six smaller reservations.

1890
The Wounded Knee Massacre occurs at Wounded Knee, South Dakota; Sioux Ghost Dance followers are killed in an attack by troops.

1891
Congress amends the Dawes Act to allow leasing of Indian land.
The Jerome Commission begins negotiating with the tribes in Indian Territory to allot reservation lands and sell the surplus.

1903
Lone Wolf v. Hitchcock is decided by the Supreme Court, which rules that Congress has plenary authority and can abrogate treaties. Lone Wolf, a Kiowa, brought suit to stop allotment, which was a violation of the Treaty of Medicine Lodge Creek.

1906
Congress passes the Burke Act, which amends the Dawes Act, allowing the Secretary of the Interior to issue patents in fee to allottees.

1907
Oklahoma becomes a state.

1908
Winters v. United States is decided by the Supreme Court, which decrees that on reservations Indians are entitled to water necessary for the development of the reservation. The case involves the Fort Belknap reservation.

1924
Congress passes the Indian Citizenship Act, which declares Indians citizens of the United States.

1928
The Meriam Report, "The Problem of Indian Administration," is published.

1934
The Johnson–O'Malley Act is passed, authorizing contracts with states for educational and other services to Indians.
Congress passes the Indian Reorganization Act.

1935

Congress establishes the Indian Arts and Crafts Board.

1936

Congress passes the Oklahoma Indian Welfare Act.

1944

The National Congress of American Indians is organized.

1946

Congress passes the Indian Claims Commission Act.

1953

Congress passes House Concurrent Resolution 108, which states the intention
to withdraw federal protection from Indian tribes.

1954

Indian hospitals and health care are transferred from the BIA to the Public
Health Service of the Department of Health, Education and Welfare.

1964

The Economic Opportunity Act passes, permitting tribal governments to participate in War on Poverty programs.

1968

The American Indian Civil Rights Act passes, guaranteeing the application of
the Bill of Rights to Indians in relation to tribal governments, providing a
model code for Courts of Indian Offenses, and requiring states to obtain
Indian consent before assuming jurisdiction on Indian land.
The American Indian Movement is organized.

1970

President Richard Nixon expresses the policy of "self-determination without
termination" in a special address to Congress.

1972

The Indian Education Act provides funding for special education programs for
Indians and establishes an Office of Indian Education at the BIA.
The Trail of Broken Treaties caravan reaches Washington, D.C. and occupies
the BIA building.

1973

Wounded Knee, South Dakota, is occupied by AIM members and supporters.

The Comprehensive Employment and Training Act provides training and employment opportunities for Indians and emphasizes Indian participation in managing programs.

1975

The Indian Self-Determination and Education Assistance Act (Public Law 638) passes, authorizing the contracting of programs by tribal governments.

1976

The Indian Health Care Improvement Act passes, authorizing increased incremental funding for health services to improve health care for Indians.

1977

Assistant Secretary for Indian Affairs, a new post in the Department of the Interior with more power than the director of the BIA, is established.

1978

The Tribally Controlled Community College Assistance Act passes, providing funds for colleges operated by tribal communities.

The Indian Child Welfare Act passes, giving tribal courts jurisdiction over children of tribe members.

Congress passes the American Indian Religious Freedom Act, which recognizes Indians' right to practice native religion.

1979

The Supreme Court awards the Teton Sioux $122.5 million for the illegal seizure of the Black Hills but the Sioux insist on the return of land rather than monetary compensation.

1988

The Indian Gaming Regulatory Act provides the statutory basis for the operation of gaming establishments and provides for the negotiation of compacts between states and tribes.

1990

Congress passes the Native American Graves Protection and Repatriation Act.

Part IV

Resources

1. RESEARCH: METHODS AND HISTORY

Research on Plains culture and history has largely been the province of anthropologists and historians, who have tried to improve their theories and methods over time. That effort is sketched in the following paragraphs. Both anthropology and history rely on documentary sources written by participants in the events being studied (primary sources); they include letters, diaries and journals, reports, transcripts, and maps. The essence of scholarly tradition in these fields is the *critical* use of these sources. Information is evaluated in terms of the basis of the author's expertise and potential for bias and the history of the document (including its authenticity and authorship). The accuracy of translation is another concern, although ideally the document should be studied in the form closest to the original. Historians pioneered the critical evaluation of documentary sources. Anthropologists have shown resourcefulness in identifying European and Euro-American bias and in identifying nontraditional kinds of sources (such as native texts and descriptions of museum collections). Anthropologists who study living communities are referred to as cultural or social or sociocultural anthropologists, to distinguish them from archaeologists. These scholars are known for their participant-observation method; this is the approach used in field study, which means "going into the field," that is, living in the community about which he or she wants to learn. The anthropologist usually resides one, two, or more years in the community, living with a family and learning the local etiquette, the language (if necessary), how people in the community are related, and how they define "family," "friend," "leader," "religion," and so on. He or she learns appropriate ways of observing activity within the family or community and appropriate ways of conversing with people. With the permission of people in the community, these observations are recorded in notebooks or on a tape recorder. The anthropologist begins to try to develop a "theory" of how the society is organized and how its members understand the world around them. Later, he or she spends months, even years, continuing to analyze these records. The result is a published ethnography, a description of the community or of some facet of life there. The study of native language, once an important part of the anthropological tradition, is now academically autonomous. The work of linguists is particularly relevant in the effort to establish historical relationships between languages that reflect contacts or genetic relationships and in addressing the challenge of folk etymologies (the attribution of meaning to native terms, particularly names of peoples) that misidentify groups and distort the historical record. Archaeologists, or archaeological anthropologists, have continued to build on the work of William Duncan Strong and his students on the village sites and have worked more extensively throughout the Plains. Recently, Native American scholars have tried to introduce their own perspective either in the context of anthropological or historiographical training or from an interdisciplinary approach. Let's look first at the history of the anthropology of Native North America.[1]

The study of the indigenous peoples of the United States first was undertaken by the National Museum (now the Smithsonian Institution), which employed scholars to gather information. There was no formal training in the social science of anthropology at this time, but these museum employees organized their studies around the idea of cultural evolution—that all societies move from primitive to civilized stages. American Indians were viewed as being "stuck" at a more primitive stage than Euro-Americans. Scholars wanted to accumulate information and artifacts and arrange them in evolutionary sequence, physically in museum cases as well as in a grand theory of human history. For policy makers in the United States, this view justified the removal of Indians as obstacles to progress and the imposition of assimilation policy to speed up the "evolution" of Indian society. Museum collections exhibit the heritage of this early work. However, the Bureau of American Ethnology, a division of the museum that was charged with obtaining information about native peoples, also employed individuals who did not conform to institutional policy. Two made major contributions to our understanding of Plains Indians (and American Indian communities generally) in the late nineteenth century. James

Owen Dorsey began his studies for the museum when he was a missionary, but instead of merely collecting the information he was instructed to record among the Omaha (and other Plains peoples), he lived with the people and made a record of actual, everyday behavior, of disagreements over Omaha custom, and of the plight of the Omaha during the assimilation program. He recorded narratives of the Omaha in their language in order to try to understand the insider's view. Dorsey trained and hired native people, such as James Murie and Francis La Flesche, to do research in their own communities. James Mooney was a journalist by profession whose Irish background made him sympathetic to the plight of Native Americans and unwilling to accept the notion that Indians merely were obstacles to progress. He was sent to study the Ghost Dance movement to evaluate how dangerous it was. He lived in Indian camps and made a record of Indian personalities, viewpoints, and strategies — in short, the human condition of people he encountered. He compared the Ghost Dance to other new religions, such as Christianity. Later, Mooney did additional work among the Kiowa, whose own record of their history, in the form of pictographs or winter counts, he took seriously, thus incorporating the "insider's view" in his study. Mooney became an advocate for the Plains people, even testifying on their behalf against the prohibition of peyote.[2]

One critic of the Bureau of American Ethnology was Franz Boas. Boas rejected the cultural evolution model, arguing that native peoples must be understood on their own terms. Adaptation to diverse environments and particular historical circumstances was what shaped the lifeways of native peoples, not their progression on an evolutionary ladder. Boas also challenged the prevailing notion of "race" as a determinant of human achievement. He argued that the indigenous adaptations native people made to different environments and the beauty of their philosophical and artistic traditions were worthy of respect. Boas started a graduate program in anthropological training at Columbia University in 1898 and taught several of the anthropologists who spent their professional lives studying Plains peoples. Boas's students accumulated a body of knowledge about Plains peoples that has greatly enhanced our understanding of these ways of life. But Boas believed that native societies were doomed to extinction and that a record should be made before the Euro-American way of life overwhelmed Indian lifeways. Thus, his students set out to interview elderly Indians and reconstruct a nineteenth-century version of the Plains experience, not to record present-day culture and ongoing changes. Robert Lowie made trips to several Plains communities but is probably most known for his work with the Crow. He worked during the first decade of the twentieth century putting together a detailed record of Crow recollections of firsthand experiences and of their stories about earlier times. He was there at the time peyote was introduced to the Crow but carefully omitted this from his published account. Lowie constructed an "as if" picture of Crow life—that is, he tried to record a culture unaffected by American contact and was not particularly concerned with how and why it had changed over time. This style of reporting is often referred to as the "ethnographic present." Alfred Kroeber was another of Boas's students. He did not spend as much time as Lowie studying in the field (that is, living in a community) on the Plains. At the turn of the century, he visited the Arapaho and the Gros Ventre, selected interpreters, and interviewed a few elderly people about the topics that concerned him, specifically ceremonies and the decorative arts. Despite the limitations of the Boasian approach, subsequent scholars have been able to make good use of the record left by these anthropologists.[3]

By the 1930s, anthropologists realized that native peoples had not disappeared as distinct communities. The population had actually increased since the late nineteenth century. A new paradigm developed to try to account for the persistence of native communities, and a minority, counter-reaction to this approach also took shape. The dominant view between World Wars I and II was the acculturation model. Originally, this perspective was intended to examine mutual change when peoples came into contact. But in the United States, anthropologists tended to approach the study of social and cultural change in terms of the progressive loss of a distinct Indian way of life. In other words, a list of "traditional" elements or traits derived from the earlier reconstructions was compared with contemporary Indian ways of life. The degree to which traditional elements were replaced was viewed as the degree of assimilation into mainstream American society. Individuals within an Indian community were thought to exhibit degrees of assimilation as well. Thus, anthropologists began describing "culture loss" and cultural disorganization and characterizing individuals as "marginal" or psychologically maladjusted. Boas's student Margaret Mead applied this perspective to her 1930 study of the Omaha, whose way of life she described as an "odd collection of traditions, once integrated, now merely coexistent." She characterized variant viewpoints and social change among the Omaha as "disequilibrium." Her study focused on women and the extent to which the disintegrating way of life produced "delinquency" among the maladjusted individuals. This approach influenced many anthropologists during the next three decades.[4]

Alexander Lesser offered an alternative vision. Lesser was influenced by the archaeologist William Duncan Strong, who excavated village sites and tried to correlate archaeological information with documentary accounts and maps of explorers and traders to make as full a description as possible. Strong showed that Plains villages had adjusted and changed dramatically before their contact with Europeans. Lesser studied the interconnections among economy, politics, family, and religious customs diachronically. That is, he rejected the acculturation model and argued for the necessity of a historical approach as a way of understanding change. Lesser saw change among the Pawnee at the time the Ghost Dance Hand Game was developing as a positive affirmation of Pawnee values and as a means to cope with their dire circumstances. Innovations, then, were not simply products of exchange between two peoples that reflected disorganization; they were products of the political domination and economic expansion of Western interests. Strong and Lesser influenced graduate students in anthropology at Columbia University in the 1930s. Their dissertations (published in the 1950s), based on documentary sources for the most part, represent what Joan Vincent calls the Lesser-Strong paradigm and take the position that economic changes in the prereservation era drove changes in other areas. Joseph Jablow studied how the Cheyenne middleman role in trade relations transformed their political organization. Preston Holder examined why the village and nomadic peoples fared so differently during the fur trade era. Oscar Lewis focused on the effect of the fur trade on Blackfeet gender roles and leadership. Frank Secoy examined how the incorporation of the horse and the gun on the Plains affected military activity. And Bernard Mishkin studied how Kiowa social relations and warfare were transformed by adoption of the horse. For example, warfare had an economic dimension. As a point of contrast, Lowie's description of Plains warfare stressed that it was not a fight for territory but an attempt to "execute a 'stunt,' to play a game according to whimsical rules." These pioneer studies have shaped our current understanding of Plains history, but probably more influential with the general public was E. Adamson's textbook, which presented a primitivist, ethnographic present picture of Plains lifeways.[5]

In the 1950s, A. R. Radcliffe-Brown came from England to the University of Chicago and introduced an approach prevalent in Britain, the analysis of the way parts of a society work together to maintain its stability. This approach influenced the work of Fred Eggan and his students in studies of Plains social organization, especially kinship. Eggan himself was influential in introducing studies that stressed how ecological factors played a role in changing Plains lifeways. For example, he concluded that the kinship system of the Cheyenne (and, he argued, probably less successfully, the Arapaho) changed from unilineal descent to a more flexible, expansive system when they moved onto the Plains to follow the buffalo herds year-round. The unpredictable nature of a hunting way of life made a flexible, bilateral kinship system adaptive; for example, individuals and families could leave a group where food was scarce and join one where they had relatives (people they considered close relatives, whether or not there was a close biological relationship) who were more prosperous. Still, the acculturation model continued to be applied in the 1960s. For example, George and Louise Spindler identified differential "acculturation" among Blackfeet individuals in a study of personality disorganization. Edward Bruner's article on the Mandan was part of a larger comparative project on how particular kinds of contact between peoples had changed different Native American groups over time. This study, drawing on documentary sources, was far more sophisticated than acculturation studies like the Spindlers' that basically compared lists of traits. But the emphasis remained on how "traditional" ways were or were not perpetuated.[6]

To turn now to the work of historians, the understanding of the history of the American West and the Indian's place in it was greatly influenced by books like those of Francis Parkman. In this view Indians were an obstacle, but otherwise not a significant factor in the history of the American West. The studies of the fur trade, like that of Din and Nasatir, were not unsympathetic to Indians and good accounts of the dynamics of trade, but they focused on the traders and largely ignored the internal affairs of Indian communities. Much of the writing of historians who studied "Indian history" delved into the development of federal Indian policy rather than the effects of that policy in particular communities and described the Indian wars in terms of the "winning of the West." The work of Robert Utley, for example, thoroughly researched the organization of an army on the frontier and its tactics in the battles with Indian groups, but did not explore the same issues from the perspective of the Indian opposition. Scholars edited "captivity narratives" and wrote biographies of famous warriors, such as Sitting Bull. The acculturation paradigm dovetailed with studies by historians in that both treated Indians as vestiges of the past. In a sense, then, both the acculturationists and the historians documented culture loss. Professional historians' emphasis on Anglo-American initiatives in "frontier" studies still characterized much historical writing after the 1960s. Historical studies of the twentieth century, with the exception of works on twentieth-century federal Indian policy (for example, those by Alison Bernstein, Donald Fixico, and Michael Lawson) are generally lacking.[7]

The 1960s marked a major turning point in both anthropology and history, which led to changes in the way scholars wrote about native peoples on the Plains and elsewhere. Anthropologists turned their attention to the origins and ramifications of rebellions against colonization and efforts to form new nations. Work in native North America was slighted for research abroad or in urban areas, where the civil rights movement had given visibility to minorities. Three developments—the process approach, symbolic anthropology, and political economy theory—transformed the field of anthropology, and the few anthropologists still studying native North Americans felt those influences. The process approach was a reaction against studies that emphasized stability and focused on describing social groups ahistorically; thus, African peoples under the yoke of colonial rule were described as if their customs bore no relation to events in the colonial past or to ongoing conflicts. In the process approach, social events and individuals' strategies and ambitions in social contexts are the object of study. This method was used to study how people competed for power in newly emerging nations and in Native American communities, for example. In symbolic anthropology, "culture" refers to more or less shared ideas. The ideas people have about their world change in response to external social events. In interpreting what is going on around them, communities make change meaningful in ways that support their group identity and their values.

Loretta Fowler synthesized the process approach and symbolic anthropology in a 1982 study of political change among the Northern Arapaho. From the viewpoint of Arapaho leaders, they had to find a way to deal with and reassure dominant, hostile federal officials while not alienating their own people, who lived by different values. These leaders became expert in devising strategies that allowed them to use actions, words, and objects that meant one thing to officials (for example, a commitment to "civilization") and something else to their constituents, namely generosity, loyalty to Arapaho goals, and reverence for religious tradition. Social innovations were interpreted in such a way that they expressed traditional values; old customs were reinterpreted so that they took on new meanings and helped Arapaho people adapt to their changing circumstances. This understanding of "culture" (which is equally applicable to European or Euro-American communities) became the key to understanding social change for many anthropologists in the 1980s and 1990s. Efforts to refine the concept of culture included attention to the fact that in native communities (as in all communities) there are divergent views about cultural meanings and social goals. One basis for disagreement is the different life experiences of people in a community, for example, elders and youths. This topic is explored in Fowler's 1987 study of the Fort Belknap reservation. The community was in a process of ritual revitalization and the elder generation and younger people had different views of the meaning of "traditional" and "Indian" identity. This study was a processual account of how these groups influenced each other and, in so doing, transformed their community in the 1980s. While also based on field studies in the late 1960s and 1970s, both of Fowler's books draw on the historical method to explain how and why these peoples changed in the ways that they did.[8]

One of the main proponents of political economy theory was Eric Wolf, who was a student of Lesser and drew on the Lesser-Strong paradigm as well as work done by other scholars in Latin America and elsewhere. From the political economy perspective, at the heart of social change are the transformations brought by the spread of capitalism and the political dominance of allies of the capitalist sector. Native people were stripped of their resources and exploited in their labor; in this way, they became absorbed into the poorest sector of American society. Transformations in family and religious life followed from these economic changes. Joseph Jorgensen was influenced by this approach; he referred to the plight of Indians as "internal colonialism" and influenced scholars before Wolf's work was published. John Moore's study of the Cheyenne, drawing on oral history and documentary research, shows how Cheyenne polity was reorganized in response to the emergence of a new Colorado economy and the destruction of the robe trade through which the Cheyenne had prospered. Trade was reoriented to the emigrant trains and in response military societies reoriented Cheyenne life to raiding. They reorganized the kinship and political institutions in the process. Moore argues that, in fact, they formed a "new nation." Moore's work on the powwow in the Cheyenne community stresses the economic role of this ritual in helping people cope with poverty. Thomas Biolsi's study of the implementation of the Indian Reorganization Act by the tribal governments at Rosebud and Pine Ridge emphasizes how the powerlessness of the Sioux in the process of reorganization led to an inability to challenge the source of their deprivation, namely federal/corporate dominance.[9] In the context of the social movements of the 1970s, Patricia Albers and Beatrice Medicine edited a collection of essays on gender issues. Here, the negative stereotypes about Plains women and Plains peoples in general are addressed and challenged.[10]

By the late 1980s and 1990s, anthropologists were exploring ways to integrate these three approaches; that is, to present the interplay of power and meaning in historical context. Biolsi argues that on Pine Ridge and Rosebud reservations, state adminstrative practices such as property ownership, determination of "competence," and registration of "blood" quantum constructed "new kinds" of individuals whose self-interests were manipulated by the state. These processes of subjugation determined how Sioux thought about themselves and how they perceived their self-interest. Fowler has studied the social and symbolic components of dominance among the Southern Cheyenne and Arapaho. Physical and economic sanctions compelled and constrained them and influenced choices and strategies. Negative Indian imagery, in which they were portrayed as morally deficient, was used by officials and settlers in western Oklahoma to rationalize federal intervention into the lives of the Cheyenne and Arapaho. The focus of this study is on the patterns of resistance to social and symbolic dominance in the context of tribal politics: how resistance developed and why some of the Indian imagery was internalized and some rejected. Fowler argues that both accommodation and resistance to dominance are central to an understanding of this community's transformation over time and to an understanding of contemporary tribal politics.[11]

While the imposition of Western representations of Plains Indians is critiqued in studies like Albers and Medicine's, and Fowler's, the work of anthropologists themselves has been criticized along these lines. Museum exhibits and collections are examined as artifacts of domination and as ways that Euro-Americans control the representations of Plains Indians. This critique has had an impact on the way that anthropologists do fieldwork and write ethnography. In Luke Lassiter's study of Kiowa song makers, he interjects himself into the description so that the ongoing conversations and analysis are represented as dialogues between himself and his consultants. Kiowa commentary stands on its own rather than being summarized or organized by the anthropologist. In his book describing the repatriation of Omaha ritual objects, Robin Ridington also includes his own personal reactions to the work of Fletcher and La Flesche on Omaha religion and his personal involvement in the recovery of the Omaha's sacred pole from the Peabody Museum.[12]

Historians were as affected as anthropologists by the national and global changes of the 1960s and 1970s. A critical reappraisal of U.S. Indian policy began to take center stage. Robert Berkhofer has surveyed the antecedents of that policy and evaluated the federal government's key Indian legislation and its implementation. A major contribution of this work is Berkhofer's demonstration of the link between Indian imagery and federal policy and, in addition, the link between that imagery and the popular arts and media representation of Indians. Plains Indians, generally stereotyped and used as symbolic of Indians in general, figure in Berkhofer's critique. Frederick Hoxie reexamines U.S. Indian policy, situating it in the context of a racist ideology that was applied to immigrant as well as minority experiences. New kinds of work were published: studies of women (for example, that of Riley) and biographies of individuals who were not warriors (such as Wilson's work on Charles Eastman). Although still rare, works were attempted that did not merely mention Indians as objects of a wider narrative on the conquest but that examined Indians' own social systems and belief systems in the context of their dealings with federal officials. Two examples are Hoxie's work on the Crow and Price's on the Oglala at Pine Ridge.[13]

Native American historians and scholars from an interdisciplinary tradition, including literary studies, have begun to bring a new focus to Plains history and culture. Native writers such as Delphine Red Shirt incorporate their own life experiences into their work. In anthropology, Beatrice Medicine has recently written about her personal experiences. Potential for a better understanding of Plains peoples rests on an improved understanding of the contributions of the various academic disciplines: historians learning more about anthropological theory and method, anthropologists learning more about historiography and regional history, and serious dialogue between academic scholarship and native reflection. In general, Plains studies lag behind scholarship in other regions where there are comparative history, regional synthesis and analysis, and multiple studies of the same events and conditions.[14]

NOTES

1. Douglas R. Parks, "The Importance of Language Study for the Writing of Plains Indian History," in Colin G. Calloway, ed., *New Directions in American Indian History* (Norman: University of Oklahoma Press, 1988), 153–97; Raymond J. DeMallie, "'These Have No Ears': Narrative and the Ethnohistorical Method," *Ethnohistory* 40 (4) (1993): 515–38. See also the sections on Published Primary Sources and Archaeology under "Resources" below.

2. Curtis M. Hinsley, *Savages and Scientists: The Smithsonian Institution and the Development of American Anthropology, 1846–1910* (Washington, DC: Smithsonian Institution Press, 1981); James Owen Dorsey, *Omaha Sociology* (New York: Johnson Reprint, 1970 [1884]); James Mooney, *The Ghost-dance Religion and the Sioux Outbreak of 1890*. Fourteenth Annual Report of the Bureau of American Ethnology, 1892–93 (Washington, DC: Smithsonian Institution Press, 1896).

3. Robert H. Lowie, *The Crow Indians* (New York: Farrar and Rinehart, 1935); Alfred L. Kroeber, *The Arapaho* (Lincoln: University of Nebraska Press, 1983 [1902–07]); Alfred L. Kroeber, *Ethnology of the Gros Ventre* (New York: AMS Press, 1978 [1908]).

4. Margaret Mead, *The Changing Culture of an Indian Tribe* (New York: Columbia University Press, 1932), 3–15, 186, 222.

5. Alexander Lesser, *The Pawnee Ghost Dance Hand Game: Ghost Dance Revival and Ethnic Identity* (Madison: University of Wisconsin Press, 1978 [1933]); Preston Holder, *The Hoe and the Horse on the Plains: A Study of Cultural Development Among North American Indians* (Lincoln: University of Nebraska Press, 1970); Joseph Jablow, *The Cheyenne in Plains Indian Trade Relations, 1795–1840* (Seattle: University of Washington Press, 1966 [1951]); Frank Secoy, *Changing Military Patterns on the Plains* (Seattle: University of Washington Press, 1966 [1953]); Oscar Lewis, *The Effects of White Contact Upon Blackfoot Culture* (Seattle: University of Washington Press, 1973 [1942]); Bernard Mishkin, *Rank and Warfare Among the Plains Indians* (Lincoln: University of Nebraska Press, 1992 [1940]); Lowie, 219; E. Adamson Hoebel, *The Cheyennes: Indians of the Great Plains* (New York: Holt, Rinehart, Winston, 1960). And see Joan Vincent, *Anthropology and Politics: Visions, Traditions, and Trends* (Tucson: University of Arizona Press, 1990), 232–34.

6. Fred Eggan, *Social Anthropology of North American Tribes* (Chicago: University of Chicago Press, 1955 [1937]); Fred Eggan, "The Cheyenne and Arapaho in the Perspective of the Plains: Ecology and Society," in *The American Indian: Perspectives for the Study of Social Change* (Chicago: Aldine, 1966), 45–77. And see Raymond J. DeMallie, "Fred Eggan and American Indian Anthropology," in *North American Indian Anthropology: Essays on Society and Culture*, ed. Raymond J. DeMallie and Alfonso Ortiz (Norman: University of Oklahoma Press, 1994), 3–22; George Spindler and Louise Spindler, "The Instrumental Activities Inventory: A Technique for the Study of the Psychology of Acculturation," *Southwestern Journal of Anthropology* 21 (1965): 1–23; Edward M. Bruner, "Mandan," in *Perspectives in American Indian Culture Change*, ed. Edward H. Spicer (Chicago: University of Chicago Press, 1961), 187–277.

7. Francis Parkman, *France and England in North America*, 2 vols., ed. David Levin (New York: Viking, 1983); Gilbert C. Din and Abraham P. Nasitir, *The Imperial Osages: Spanish-Indian Diplomacy in the Mississippi Valley* (Norman: University of Oklahoma Press, 1983); Robert M. Utley, *Frontiersmen in Blue: The United States Army and the Indian, 1848–1865* (New York: Macmillan, 1967); Robert M. Utley, *The Lance and the Shield: The Life and Times of Sitting Bull* (New York: Henry Holt, 1993); Alison R. Bernstein, *American Indians and World War II: Toward a New Era in Indian Affairs* (Norman: University of Oklahoma Press, 1991); Donald L. Fixico, *Termination and Relocation: Federal Indian Policy, 1945–1960* (Albuquerque: University of New Mexico Press, 1986); Michael L. Lawson, *Damned Indians: The Pick-Sloan Plan and the Missouri River Sioux, 1944–80* (Norman: University of Oklahoma Press, 1982). And see Frederick E. Hoxie, "The Problems of Indian History," *The Social Science Journal* 25 (4) (1988): 389–99 and Willard Rollings, "In Search of Multisided Frontiers: Recent Writing on the History of the Southern Plains," in Calloway, 79–96.
8. Loretta Fowler, *Arapahoe Politics, 1851–1978: Symbols in Crises of Authority* (Lincoln: University of Nebraska Press, 1982) and *Shared Symbols, Contested Meanings: Gros Ventre Culture and History, 1778–1984* (Ithaca: Cornell University Press, 1987). Thomas W. Kavanagh also applied the process approach in his study of Comanche political change (*Comanche Political History: An Ethnohistorical Perspective, 1706–1875* [Lincoln: University of Nebraska Press, 1996]).
9. Eric R. Wolf, *Europe and the People Without History* (Berkeley: University of California Press, 1982); Joseph G. Jorgensen, "Indians and the Metropolis," in *The American Indian in Urban Society*, ed. Jack O. Waddell and O. Michael Watson (Boston: Little, Brown, 1971) and *The Sun Dance Religion: Power for the Powerless* (Chicago: University of Chicago Press, 1972); John H. Moore, *The Cheyenne Nation: A Social and Demographic History* (Lincoln: University of Nebraska Press, 1987) and "How Pow-Wows and Giveaways Redistribute the Means of Subsistence," in *The Political Economy of North American Indians* (Norman: University of Oklahoma Press, 1993), 240–69; Thomas Biolsi, *Organizing the Lakota: The Political Economy of the New Deal on the Pine Ridge and Rosebud Reservations* (Tucson: University of Arizona Press, 1992).
10. Patricia C. Albers and Beatrice Medicine, eds., *The Hidden Half: Studies of Plains Indian Women* (Washington, DC: University Press of America, 1983).
11. Thomas Biolsi, "The Birth of the Reservation: Making the Modern Individual Among the Lakota," *American Ethnologist* 22 (1995): 28–53; Loretta Fowler, *Tribal Sovereignty and the Historical Imagination: Cheyenne-Arapaho Politics* (Lincoln: University of Nebraska Press, 2002).
12. Luke E. Lassiter, *The Power of Kiowa Song: A Collaborative Ethnography* (Tucson: University of Arizona Press, 1998); Robin Ridington and Dennis Hastings, *Blessing for a Long Time: The Sacred Pole of the Omaha Tribe* (Lincoln: University of Nebraska Press, 1997).
13. Robert E. Berkhofer, *The White Man's Indian: Images of the American Indian from Columbus to the Present* (New York: Knopf, 1978); Frederick E. Hoxie, *A Final Promise: The Campaign to Assimilate the Indians, 1880–1920* (Lincoln: University of Nebraska Press, 1984); Glenda Riley, *Women and Indians on the Frontier, 1825–1915* (Albuquerque: University of New Mexico Press, 1984); Raymond Wilson, *Ohiyesa: Charles Eastman, Santee Sioux* (Urbana: University of Illinois Press, 1983); Frederick E. Hoxie, *Parading Through History: The Making of the Crow Nation in America, 1805–1935* (Cambridge: Cambridge University Press, 1995); Catherine Price, *The Oglala People, 1841–1879* (Lincoln and London: University of Nebraska Press, 1996).

14. Delphine Red Shirt, *Turtle Lung Woman's Grandmother* (Lincoln: University of Nebraska Press, 2002); Beatrice Medicine, *Learning to Be an Anthropologist and Remaining "Native": Selected Writings*, ed. Sue-Ellen Jacobs (Urbana: University of Illinois Press, 2001).

2. BIBLIOGRAPHIES AND RESEARCH AIDS

Blaine, Martha Royce. *The Pawnees: A Critical Bibliography*. Bloomington: Indiana University Press, 1980.

Danky, James P. and Mureen E. Hady, eds. *Native American Periodicals and Newspapers, 1828–1982: Bibliography, Publishing Record, and Holdings*. Westport, CT: Greenwood Press, 1984.

De Witt, Donald L. *American Indian Resource Materials in the Western History Collections, University of Oklahoma*. Norman: University of Oklahoma Press, 1990.

Dobyns, Henry F. *Native American Historical Demography: A Critical Bibliography*. Bloomington: Indiana University Press, 1976.

Hill, Edward E., comp. *Guide to Records in the National Archives of the United States Relating to American Indians*. Washington, DC: National Archives and Records Service, 1981.

Hoebel, E. Adamson. *The Plains Indians: A Critical Bibliography*. Bloomington: Indiana University Press, 1977.

Hoover, Herbert T. *The Sioux: A Critical Bibliography*. Bloomington: Indiana University Press for The Newberry Library, 1979.

Johnson, Steven L. *Guide to American Indian Documents in the Congressional Serial Set: 1817–1899*. New York: Clearwater Publishing, 1977.

Miller, Jay, Colin G. Calloway, and Richard A. Sattler, comps. *Writings in Indian History, 1985–1990*. Norman: University of Oklahoma Press, 1995.

Murdock, George P. and Timothy J. O'Leary. *Ethnographic Bibliography of North America*, 5 vols. 4th ed. New Haven: Human Relations Area Files, 1975.

Powell, Peter J. *The Cheyennes, Maheoo's People: A Critical Bibliography*. Bloomington: Indiana University Press for The Newberry Library, 1980.

Prucha, Francis Paul. *A Bibliographical Guide to the History of Indian-White Relations in the United States*. Chicago: University of Chicago Press, 1977.

——. *Indian-White Relations in the United States: A Bibliography of Works Published, 1975–1980*. Lincoln: University of Nebraska Press, 1982.

Ruoff, A. LaVonne Brown. *American Indian Literatures: An Introduction, Bibliographic Review, and Selected Bibliography*. New York: Modern Language Association of America, 1990.

Swagerty, William R., ed. *Scholars and the Indian Experience: Critical Reviews of Recent Writing in the Social Sciences.* Bloomington: Indiana University Press for The Newberry Library, 1984.

3. ARCHAEOLOGY

Bell, Robert E., ed. *Prehistory of Oklahoma.* Orlando, FL: Academic Press, 1984.
A series of essays written for specialists.

Fagan, Brian M. *Ancient North America: The Archaeology of a Continent.* London: Thames and Hudson, 2000.
Excellent chapters on the prairie plains and upland plains, written for the nonspecialist. The best source for an overview of Plains archaeology.

Jennings, Jesse D., ed. *Ancient North Americans.* San Francisco: W. H. Freeman, 1983.
The essays in the book are well written and accessible to the nonspecialist. Articles pertinent to the Plains concern the earliest occupation, an overview of the Plains region and its settlement prior to the arrival of Europeans, and a discussion of the domestication of plants in North America.

Schlesier, Karl H., ed. *Plains Indians,* A.D. *500–1500: The Archaeological Past of Historic Groups.* Norman: University of Oklahoma Press, 1994.
A collection of essays written for specialists in Plains archaeology. The articles summarize what is known about various regions. The editor's conclusions are highly speculative.

Wedel, Waldo R. *Prehistoric Man on the Great Plains.* Norman: University of Oklahoma Press, 1961.
This is a clearly written, detailed overview of Plains archaeology. The book is updated in:

———. "The Prehistoric Plains," in *Ancient North America,* ed. Jesse D. Jennings. San Francisco: W. H. Freeman, 1983, 203–41.

Wood, W. Raymond, ed. *Archaeology on the Great Plains.* Lawrence: University Press of Kansas, 1998.
A collection of articles on the Paleo-Indian, Archaic, Woodland, and Villager traditions written for specialists. The book includes a chapter on historical archaeology (for example, fur trade posts, military posts, battlefields).

4. PUBLISHED PRIMARY SOURCES

Boller, Henry A. *Among the Indians: Eight Years in the Far West, 1858–1866*. Ed.
Milo Milton Quaife. Cheyenne, WY: R. R. Donnelley, 1959.

Boller was born in 1836 into a prosperous family and went west in a spirit of
adventure to work in the fur trade. He clerked for competitors of the American
Fur Company and spent 1858 to 1862 in the Mandan and Hidatsa villages; he
also worked at Fort Union, where he was in contact with Blackfeet and others.
He writes about the smallpox epidemic, Sioux raids, and trading customs,
among other activities.

Catlin, George. *Letters and Notes on the Manners, Customs and Conditions of
the North American Indians*. New York: Dover, 1973 [1841].

Catlin set out to document in his paintings the way of life of Plains Indians in
the 1830s. He visited with the Teton at Fort Pierre and with the Mandan in their
villages. Moving in fur trade society, he came in contact with many well-known
Indians of the time and recorded his observations of Blackfeet, Crow, Assiniboine, Cree, Hidatsa, Iowa, Kaw, Pawnee, Otoe, Omaha, Comanche, Osage,
Kiowa, and Wichita.

Chardon, Francois A. *Chardon's Journal at Fort Clark, 1834–39*. Ed. Annie
Heloise Abel. Pierre, SD: South Dakota State Department of History, 1932.

Chardon was the trader at Fort Clark and recorded observations of Mandan,
Hidatsa, and Arikara and others.

Coues, Elliott, ed. *New Light on the Early History of the Greater Northwest: The
Manuscript Journals of Alexander Henry and of David Thompson,
1799–1814*. 3 vols. New York: Francis P. Harper, 1897.

Henry was a fur trader with the North West Company and served at a post
on the Red River, where he made observations about the conflict between the
Ojibwa and the Sioux. On the Saskatchewan River he served at several posts
among the Blackfeet, Gros Ventre, Assiniboine, and Cree. He also visited the
Mandan villages. The Thompson journals cover his service on the upper
Saskatchewan River from 1808 to 1811.

Denig, Edwin Thompson. *Five Indian Tribes of the Upper Missouri: Sioux,
Arickaras, Assiniboines, Crees, Crows*. Norman: University of Oklahoma
Press, 1961.

Denig was born in 1812 and worked for the American Fur Company beginning in 1833. For twenty-three years he was a fur trader on the upper Missouri

River. In 1855–56 he wrote these brief descriptions of five tribes with whom he had a long acquaintance.

Fowler, Jacob. *The Journal of Jacob Fowler.* Ed. Elliott Coues. New York: Francis
    P. Harper, 1898.
    Fowler was born in 1765 and worked as a surveyor and explorer on the Southern Plains. He kept a journal of a trading and exploring expedition in 1821–22 in the Arkansas and Canadian River area. He traveled to Taos, meeting on the way Arapahos, Comanches, Kiowas, and others.

Garrard, Lewis H. *Wah-to-yah and the Taos Trail.* Cincinnati: H. W. Derby, 1850.
    In 1846 Garrard joined Ceran St. Vrain at Bent's Fort. He was a youth who visited Cheyenne camps and observed the life of traders on the Southern Plains. The book was first published in 1850.

Gates, Charles M., ed. *Five Fur Traders of the Northwest: Being the Narrative of
    Peter Pond and the Diaries of John Macdonell, Archibald N. McLeod, Hugh
    Faries, and Thomas Connor.* St. Paul: Minnesota Historical Society, 1965.
    Pond, trader and explorer, wrote an ethnographic description in 1774 of the Yankton, Yanktonai, and Santee and of trade on the northeastern Plains.

Glass, Anthony. *Journal of an Indian Trader: Anthony Glass and the Texas Trad-
    ing Frontier, 1790–1810.* Ed. Dan L. Flores. College Station: Texas A & M
    Press, 1986.
    Glass's journal contains information about Wichita life in 1808–09, tribal locations and settlement patterns, Indian politics, and other aspects of life on the frontier.

James, Edwin. *James's Account of S. H. Long's Expedition of 1819–1820.* Vols.
    15–17 in *Early Western Travels,* ed. Reuben Gold Thwaites. New York:
    Arthur Clark, 1905 [1823].
    The Secretary of War ordered Major S. H. Long to explore the American West. The trip was recorded in journals that contain observations about Kaw, Pawnee, Otoe, Missouria, Iowa, Sioux, Omaha, Kiowa, Arapaho, Comanche, Cheyenne, and Osage.

La Harpe, Bénard de. "Exploration of the Arkansas River, 1721–22." Trans.
    Ralph A. Smith. *The Arkansas Historical Quarterly* 10 (4) (1951): 339–63.
    La Harpe provides the first detailed description of life in Wichita villages. Much of his writing has not been translated and published; this article represents a portion of it.

Leonard, Zenas A. *Narrative of the Adventures of Zenas Leonard*. Lincoln: University of Nebraska Press, 1978 [1934].
Leonard was a trapper who lived with the Crow in the 1830s.

Marquis, Thomas B. *Memories of a White Crow Indian* [Thomas Le Forge]. Lincoln: University of Nebraska Press, 1974 [1928].
Le Forge lived with the Crow in the 1860s.

Maximilian, Alexander Philip Prinz zu Wied. *Travels in the Interior of North America, 1832–34* [1843].Trans. H. Evans Lloyd. Vols. 22–24 in *Early Western Travels, 1748–1846*, ed. Reuben Gold Thwaites. Cleveland: Arthur H. Clark, 1904–07.
Maximilian, accompanied by the gifted painter Karl Bodmer, traveled up the Missouri spending time in the Mandan and Hidatsa villages and continuing up into Montana. Maximilian recorded his observations about the Indians he met, and Bodmer painted portraits of many of these individuals.

Moulton, Gary E., ed. *The Journals of the Lewis and Clark Expedition*. 12 vols. Lincoln: University of Nebraska Press, 1983.
Lewis and Clark traveled to the Mandan villages and wintered there from 1804 to 1805, obtaining much information about Indians from the traders. In the spring they continued traveling up the Missouri River to Montana, where they got horses from Shoshones and continued west. In the spring of 1806 they returned, getting into a skirmish with the Blackfeet and stopping again at the Mandan and Hidatsa villages before arriving in St. Louis.

Parker, John, ed. *The Journals of Jonathan Carver and Related Documents, 1766–1770*. St. Paul: Minnesota Historical Society, 1976.
Carver, an explorer, wrote an ethnographic description of the Santee Sioux in 1766–67.

Parkman, Francis. *The Oregon Trail: Sketches of Prairie and Rocky Mountain Life*. 2 vols. Boston: Little, Brown, 1898 [1872].
Parkman was a youthful adventurer when he traveled west on the Oregon Trail in 1846. He wrote about his observations of encounters with Indians (particularly the Teton Sioux), life at Bent's Fort, and the geography of the region. Parkman wrote with a bias, in that he had a negative view of Indians and their occupation of the frontier.

Tabeau, Pierre-Antoine. *Tabeau's Narrative of Loisel's Expedition to the Upper Missouri*. Ed. Annie Heloise Abel. Norman: University of Oklahoma Press, 1939.

Tabeau, a French-Canadian ex-schoolteacher, went on trading expeditions in 1794, 1795, and 1802 up the Missouri River. In 1804 he spent months living in the Arikara villages, where he obtained much information about the tribes who came in contact with the Arikara. Much of this information was passed on to Lewis and Clark. Tabeau kept journals from 1803 to 1805 and used these in writing his narrative years later.

Thompson, David. *David Thompson's Narrative, 1784–1812*. Ed. Richard Glover. Toronto: Champlain Society, 1962.

Thompson was born in 1770 and worked for the North West Company. In 1785 he traveled up the Saskatchewan River in the company of Crees and on the Saskatchewan River he visited the Blackfeet. He also visited in the Mandan villages. He wrote this account from journals and recollections in 1844.

Tixier, Victor. *Tixier's Travels on the Osage Prairies*. Ed. John Francis McDermott. Trans. Albert J. Salvan. Norman: University of Oklahoma Press, 1940 [1844].

Tixier was born in France in 1815. He came to America in 1839 on an adventure and stayed one year. From a base in St. Louis, he spent much time with the Osage and met members of other tribes. He also made drawings of his trip.

Truteau, Jean Baptiste. "Journal of Jean Baptiste Truteau Among the Arikara Indians." Trans. H. T. Beauregard. *Missouri Historical Society Collections* 4 (1912): 9–48.

Truteau spent the winter of 1795–96 with the Arikara and in 1794 wintered near the Omaha. His journal has information about life in the villages and also information he recorded about other tribes.

Wood, W. Raymond and Thomas D. Thiessen. *Early Fur Trade on the Northern Plains: Canadian Traders Among the Mandan and Hidatsa Indians, 1738–1818*. Norman: University of Oklahoma Press, 1985.

The authors provide an overview of trade in the Mandan villages and edit narratives of several traders: John MacDonell, David Thompson, Francois-Antoine Larocque, and Charles McKenzie.

5. GENERAL AND COMPARATIVE STUDIES

Anderson, Gary Clayton. *The Indian Southwest, 1580-1830: Ethnogenesis and Reinvention*. Norman: University of Oklahoma Press, 1999.

Based on primary sources, this is a history of social change in the greater Southwest, focusing on the ways native societies reorganized over time, developing new social institutions and understandings. The book discusses Apache, Caddo, Wichita, and Comanche peoples.

Bernstein, Alison R. *American Indians and World War II: Toward a New Era in Indian Affairs*. Norman and London: University of Oklahoma Press, 1991.
An overview of Indian experiences during World War II and the impact of the war on Indian policy and in Indian communities. This history focuses on 1941–47 and relates the war era to subsequent termination and self-determination policies.

Carlson, Paul H. *The Plains Indians*. College Station: Texas A & M University Press, 1998.
An overview of Indian-white history.

Castile, George Pierre. *To Show Heart: Native American Self-Determination and Federal Indian Policy, 1960–1975*. Tucson: University of Arizona Press, 1998.
Castile, an anthropologist, worked for the War on Poverty programs in Washington. He offers a good behind-the-scenes perspective on the origin and development of self-determination policy in the context of the civil rights movement in the 1960s and 1970s.

Clark, Blue. *Lone Wolf vs. Hitchcock: Treaty Rights and Indian Law at the End of the Nineteenth Century*. Lincoln: University of Nebraska Press, 1994.
A clearly written account of the Lone Wolf case, including the impact of allotment on the Kiowa and the repercussions of the Lone Wolf court decision on the lives of American Indians everywhere.

Clark, William Philo. *The Indian Sign Language*. Philadelphia: L. R. Hammersly, 1885.
Clark served in the army where he kept company with Indian scouts and had the opportunity to interview Plains Indians. The book describes the signs for a basic vocabulary and provides detailed information about this vocabulary.

Cowger, Thomas W. *The National Congress of American Indians: The Founding Years*. Lincoln: University of Nebraska Press, 1999.
A history of the NCAI over a twenty-year period, using NCAI records and interviews with members.

Curtis, Edward S. *The North American Indian*, 20 vols. Ed. Frederick Webb Hodge. 1907–30; reprint, New York: Johnson Reprint, 1970.

Curtis traveled to most of the Plains tribes and recorded information while photographing people and activities, most designed to illustrate life in the nineteenth century.

DeMallie, Raymond J., ed. *Handbook of North American Indians: Plains*, vol. 13, 2 parts. General ed. William C. Sturtevant. Washington, DC: Smithsonian Institution Press, 2001.
Brief summaries of the culture, social organization, and history of all the peoples of the Plains, including contemporary communities, and essays on the general history and the archaeology of the region. Good sections on sources.

Dickason, Olive Patricia. *Canada's First Nations: A History of Founding Peoples from Earliest Times*. Norman: University of Oklahoma Press, 1992.
An overview of Canadian history from prior to the arrival of Europeans to the 1990s. The work takes full account of the history of the native peoples there, including their relations with European settlers.

Dunlay, Thomas W. *Wolves for the Blue Soldiers: Indian Scouts and Auxiliaries with the United States Army, 1860–90*. Lincoln: University of Nebraska Press, 1982.
Excellent history of the incorporation of American Indians into the American military from prior to the Civil War to the 1890s. A particularly good discussion of scouting.

Ewers, John C. *The Horse in Blackfoot Indian Culture with Comparative Material from Other Western Tribes*. Washington, DC: Smithsonian Institution Press, 1980 [1955].
Excellent study based on primary sources of the diffusion of the horse and the way its introduction changed Plains Indian societies. Discusses horse care, breeding, training, gear, and trading.

———. *Plains Indian History and Culture: Essays on Continuity and Change*. Norman: University of Oklahoma Press, 1997.
A collection of some of Ewers's finest work, including essays on the influence of the fur trade on Plains Indians, the influence of epidemics on Plains peoples, symbols of chiefly authority in Spanish Louisiana, the history of women's clothing on the Southern Plains, the making and use of maps by Plains Indians, and women's roles in Plains warfare.

Fixico, Donald L. *Termination and Relocation: Federal Indian Policy, 1945–1960*. Albuquerque: University of New Mexico Press, 1986.

Gives an overview of the history and effects of termination policies during the eras of Truman and Eisenhower. Includes an evaluation of the relocation program.

Gibson, Arrell M. *The American Indian: Prehistory to the Present.* Lexington, MA: D. C. Heath, 1980.
Overview of the important place of Indians in American history. Covers Indian life from prior to European arrival to the 1970s.

Gilmore, Melvin R. *Uses of Plants by the Indians of the Missouri River Region.* Lincoln: University of Nebraska Press, 1991 [1919].
Gilmore describes the collection, uses (for food, clothing, medicine, and ornamentation), and culture surrounding wild plants.

Green, Jerome A., ed. *Lakota and Cheyenne: Indian Views of the Great Sioux War, 1876–1877.* Norman: University of Oklahoma Press, 1994.
A good counterperspective to studies of Indian wars based on the perspective of the U.S. military.

Holder, Preston. *The Hoe and the Horse on the Plains: A Study of Cultural Development Among North American Indians.* Lincoln: University of Nebraska Press, 1970.
Based on primary documents, an excellent study of the impact of European entry onto the Plains on the lives of villagers and nomadic groups. Holder focuses on the Pawnee and Arikara and accounts for their decline and the concomitant prosperity and dominance of the Sioux.

Horr, David Agee, ed. *American Indian Ethnohistory: Plains Indians,* 23 vols. New York: Garland, 1974.
A multivolume series consisting of reports on the history, migrations, and territories of Plains peoples, prepared for the Indian Claims Commission hearings.

Hoxie, Frederick E. *A Final Promise: The Campaign to Assimilate the Indians, 1880–1920.* Lincoln: University of Nebraska Press, 1984.
An account of Indian policy from the 1880s to the 1920s, focusing on assimilation. Hoxie argues that federal policy was reflective of changes in the ideas and events in American society at large.

Iverson, Peter, ed. *The Plains Indians of the Twentieth Century.* Norman and London: University of Oklahoma Press, 1985.

A collection of essays on allotment, water rights, the New Deal, World War II, the federal water projects, and Indian leadership.

John, Elizabeth. *Storms Brewed in Other Men's Worlds*. Norman: University of Oklahoma Press, 1996.
A comprehensive history of interactions between Europeans and native peoples in the Southwest and Southern Plains based on primary sources.

Kappler, Charles J. *Indian Affairs, Laws and Treaties*. 5 vols. Vol. 2 Treaties. New York: Interland, 1972.
A compilation of the texts of all the treaties made between the United States and the Plains tribes.

Kehoe, Alice B. *The Ghost Dance: Ethnohistory and Revitalization*. New York: Holt, Rinehart and Winston, 1989.
Clearly written account for a general audience of the Ghost Dance religion and its spread through American Indian communities. Also discusses anthropological approaches to the study of religion.

Lowie, Robert H. *Indians of the Plains*. Lincoln: University of Nebraska Press, 1982 [1954].
A comparative overview of Plains peoples, their food, dwellings, dress, marriage and family, political organization, warfare, hunting, trade, art, recreation, and religion.

Lux, Maureen K. *Medicine That Walks: Disease, Medicine, and Canadian Plains Native People, 1880–1940*. Toronto: University of Toronto Press, 2001.
This is an important study of the effects of malnutrition and hunger on Indian health and on policy makers' views of Indians as racially inferior. Lux argues that racism in the Euro-Canadian health care system justified policies that resulted in poor living conditions and poor health among Northern Plains peoples (Blackfeet, Assiniboine, Cree). Lux also discusses native healing practices.

Means, Russell. *Where White Men Fear to Tread: The Autobiography of Russell Means*. With Marvin J. Wolf. New York: St. Martin's Press, 1995.
Means was a prominent leader in the American Indian Movement.

Milner, Clyde A. *With Good Intentions: Quaker Work Among the Pawnees, Otos, and Omahas in the 1870s*. Lincoln: University of Nebraska Press, 1982.
An evaluation of Grant's Peace Policy and its implementation on Nebraska reservations.

Mooney, James. *The Ghost-dance Religion and the Sioux Outbreak of 1890.* Fourteenth Annual Report of the Bureau of American Ethnology for 1892–93. Washington, DC: Smithsonian Institution Press, 1896.
Pioneering anthropological study of the spread of a religious movement, based on firsthand observation and situated in the context of new religious movements everywhere. Includes sketches of the Arapaho, Cheyenne, Sioux, Caddo, and Kiowa.

Morris, John W., Charles R. Goins, and Edwin C. McReynolds. *Historical Atlas of Oklahoma.* 3rd ed. Norman: University of Oklahoma Press, 1986.
Contains maps and information about the native peoples who settled in Indian Territory.

Nasatir, A. P. *Before Lewis and Clark: Documents Illustrating the History of the Missouri.* 2 vols. St. Louis: St. Louis Historical Documents Foundation, 1952.
An overview of French exploration and trade on the lower Missouri River from 1673 to 1806; includes documents of the period.

Otis, D. S. *The Dawes Act and the Allotment of Indian Lands.* Ed. Francis Paul Prucha. Norman: University of Oklahoma Press, 1973.
A history of the development of allotment policy, the Indian response, and the effects of allotment up to 1900.

Philp, Kenneth L. *John Collier's Crusade for Indian Reform, 1920–1954.* Tucson: University of Arizona Press, 1980.
Philp discusses Collier's background, philosophy, and programs and the opposition to the New Deal. Collier was Commissioner of Indian Affairs from 1933-1945.

——. *Termination Revisited: American Indians on the Trail to Self-Determination, 1933–1953.* Lincoln: University of Nebraska Press, 1999.
A reassessment of federal termination policy and the diverse reactions of native peoples to it.

Powers, William K. *War Dance: Plains Indian Musical Performance.* Tucson: University of Arizona Press, 1990.
Good overview of the history of the powwow, including Plains Indian music and dance and a comparison of Northern and Southern Plains traditions.

Prucha, Francis Paul. *The Great Father: The United States Government and the American Indians*, 2 vols. Lincoln: University of Nebraska Press, 1984.
Standard work on U.S. policy toward American Indians.

Ray, Arthur J. *Indians in the Fur Trade: Their Role as Trappers, Hunters and Middlemen in the Lands Southwest of Hudson Bay, 1660–1870*. Toronto: University of Toronto Press, 1974.
Good overview of the fur trade, its effect on Cree and Assiniboine middlemen, intertribal relations, ecology of western Canada, and demographic patterns.

Royce, Charles C., comp. *Indian Land Cessions in the United States*. Eighteenth Annual Report of the Bureau of American Ethnology. Washington, DC: Government Printing Office, 1899.
Contains maps of all the land cessions made by Indian peoples; an excellent resource.

Secoy, Frank Raymond. *Changing Military Patterns of the Great Plains Indians*. Lincoln: University of Nebraska Press, 1992 [1953].
An excellent study, based on primary sources, of changes in warfare patterns after the introduction of the horse and the gun. The book compares these changes on the Southern and Northern Plains and makes generalizations about the impact of trade on political organization, power relations, and population movements.

St. Germain, Jill. *Indian Treaty-Making Policy in the United States and Canada, 1867–1877*. Lincoln: University of Nebraska Press, 2001.
A comparative study of treaty negotiation with Sioux, Cheyenne, Kiowa, and Comanche in the United States and Blackfeet, Cree, and Ojibwa in Canada.

Stewart, Omer C. *The Peyote Religion: A History*. Norman: University of Oklahoma Press, 1987.
Very thorough study of the earliest use of peyote to its dissemination and use in the United States from 1885 to the late twentieth century. Includes a discussion of efforts to suppress peyote ritual.

Sutton, Imre. *Indian Land Tenure: Bibliographical Essays and a Guide to the Literature*. New York: Clearwater Publishing, 1975.
A discussion of aboriginal occupancy and territoriality, land cession, land administration, land policy and management, and land claims. Includes an extensive bibliography, including studies of tribes.

Sutton, Imre, ed. *Irredeemable America: The Indians' Estate and Land Claims*. Albuquerque: University of New Mexico Press, 1985.
Essays on land claims, the Indian Claims Commission, and anthropologists as expert witnesses in land claim cases. The book also includes a case study of Pawnee land claims.

Taylor, Graham D. *The New Deal and American Indian Tribalism*. Lincoln: University of Nebraska Press, 1980.
Study of the design and implementation of the IRA; includes the diverse reaction of tribes to the new policy and the effects of the IRA on tribal government and economy. Useful for comparative analysis, although it suffers from an oversimplified view of Indian identity and its relationship to "blood."

Townsend, Kenneth William. *World War II and the American Indian*. Albuquerque: University of New Mexico Press, 2000.
A history of Indian entry and participation in World War II and the war's effects on the Indian communities. Some information that complements Bernstein's work.

Utley, Robert M. *Frontier Regulars: The United States Army and the Indian, 1866–1890*. New York: Macmillan, 1973.
The standard work on the Indian wars of the 1860s and 1870s; describes military tactics, battles, the army as a social institution, military technology, and military lifestyle. Includes the war over the Bozeman Trail, the Red River War on the Southern Plains, the war with Sitting Bull on the Northern Plains, Custer's fight at the Little Bighorn, and the Ghost Dance conflict.

——. *Frontiersmen in Blue: The United States Army and the Indian, 1848–1865*. New York: Macmillan, 1967.
Comprehensive military history of the period between the Mexican War and the close of the Civil War and the standard work on the Indian wars. Includes the organization of the frontier army, garrison life, skirmishes between troops and the Sioux in the 1850s, and the Indian War of 1864–65.

Will, George F. and George E. Hyde. *Corn Among the Indians of the Upper Missouri*. Lincoln: University of Nebraska Press, 2002 [1917].
This is a comprehensive work covering planting and cultivation, harvesting, methods of preparation of food, corn as an article of trade, the sacred significance of corn, and ceremonies relevant to the cultivation of corn. The book also discusses varieties of corn grown by villagers on the Plains and in the Eastern Woodlands and the Southwest.

Wishart, David J. *An Unspeakable Sadness: The Dispossession of the Nebraska Indians.* Lincoln: University of Nebraska Press, 1994.
Very good comparative history of the Pawnee, Omaha, Otoe, Missouria, and Ponca from 1800 to 1885.

——. *The Fur Trade of the American West, 1807–1840: A Geographical Synthesis.* Lincoln: University of Nebraska Press, 1979.
Good overview of the development of the fur trade, including the Rocky Mountain trapping system and the upper Missouri trade utilizing water transportation. Discusses the role of the Indian as hunter and trader.

Wright, Muriel H. *A Guide to the Indian Tribes of Oklahoma.* Norman: University of Oklahoma Press, 1951.
Basic information on all the tribes in Oklahoma, but not always reliable and not very informative about culture and social organization.

6. TRIBAL STUDIES

Arapaho

Anderson, Jeffrey D. *The Four Hills of Life: Northern Arapaho Knowledge and Life Movement.* Lincoln: University of Nebraska Press, 2001.
An overview and analysis of turn-of-the-century ethnography and collections of myths. The book also describes events from the 1980s to the present.

Fowler, Loretta. *The Arapaho.* New York: Chelsea House, 1990.
Written for a general audience, the book compares Northern and Southern Arapaho history, culture, and social organization.

——. *Arapahoe Politics, 1851–1978: Symbols in Crises of Authority.* Lincoln: University of Nebraska Press, 1982.
Combines research based on primary documents and ethnography to examine changes in Northern Arapaho leadership from the prereservation era through the reservation period, including the late 1960s and early 1970s.

——. *Tribal Sovereignty and the Historical Imagination: Cheyenne-Arapaho Politics.* Lincoln: University of Nebraska Press, 2002.
A study of social and cultural change among the Southern Cheyenne and Arapaho from 1869 to 1999, this work focuses on the forms of social and ideological dominance experienced by these peoples and the ways that they coped

with the inequalities inherent in their relations with federal representatives and settlers in Oklahoma.

Kroeber, Alfred L. *The Arapaho*. Lincoln and London: University of Nebraska Press, 1983 [1902, 1904, 1907].
  Ethnographic description of religious and ceremonial organization and decorative arts.

Trenholm, Virginia Cole. *The Arapahoes, Our People*. Norman: University of Oklahoma Press, 1970.
  Historical account of the Northern and Southern Arapaho from the early nineteenth century to the beginning of reservation life.

Arikara

Cash, Joseph H. See **Mandan.**

Dorsey, George A. *Traditions of the Arikara*. Carnegie Institution of Washington Publication no. 17, 1904.
  A collection of creation stories and trickster tales.

Holder, Preston. "Social Stratification Among the Arikara," *Ethnohistory* 5 (3) (1958): 210–18.
  A reconstruction of nineteenth-century social structure; the article discusses the hereditary ranking of families and the economic underpinnings of rank differentials.

Libby, O. G., ed. *The Arikara Narrative of the Campaign Against the Hostile Dakotas, June 1876*. North Dakota Historical Collections 6 (1920).

Meyer, Roy W. See **Mandan**.

Parks, Douglas R. *Myths and Traditions of the Arikara Indians*. Lincoln and London: University of Nebraska Press, 1996.
  This work contains an extensive overview of Arikara lifeways and history and a collection of oral traditions about creation, historical events, and Coyote (the trickster) tales.

Assiniboine

Denig, Edwin Thompson. *The Assiniboine*. Ed. J. N. B. Hewitt. Norman: University of Oklahoma Press, 2000.

Denig, a trader among the Assiniboine, wrote an ethnographic description in 1854 in answer to queries from the Bureau of American Ethnology. He describes hunting, habitat, technology, medicine, government, trade, warfare, law, religion, family life, death, and ceremonial life. The work was first published in 1930. This edition includes a useful introduction by David R. Miller.

Farnell, Brenda. *Wiyuta Assiniboine Story Telling with Signs.* (Computer laser optical disk.) Austin: University of Texas Press, 1995.
This CD-ROM shows how Plains Indian sign talk is still an integral part of the storytelling tradition. The disk includes a videotape performance of a storyteller and English translation of the native text. The CD is a companion to Farnell's book on the subject, written for specialists.

Long, James Larpenteur. *Land of the Nakoda.* Helena, MT: Writers' Program, Montana, State Publishing Co., 1942.
Long (born in 1888 and named First Boy) was an Assiniboine from Fort Peck reservation who based this manuscript on oral history sources and wrote it under the auspices of the Works Progress Administration's Writers Project. Long's father was a BIA employee and his mother was the daughter of a trader and an Assiniboine woman. He was raised by his Assiniboine grandmother and was bilingual.

Lowie, Robert H. *The Assiniboine.* American Museum of Natural History Anthropological Papers 4 (1) (1909).
In 1907 Lowie spent seven weeks among the Stoney in Canada and, in 1908, one month among the Assiniboine at Fort Belknap reservation. The monograph covers hunting, food, dwellings, dress, recreation, art, war, family and marriage, religion, and leadership.

Blackfeet

Dempsey, Hugh A. *Crowfoot, Chief of the Blackfeet.* Norman: University of Oklahoma Press, 1989.
Crowfoot (1830–90) was a Blood who became a chief of the Blackfoot in Canada and led the tribe for twenty years. This biography does a good job of presenting the struggle over available choices during reservation times.

——. *Red Crow, Warrior Chief.* Lincoln and London: University of Nebraska Press, 1980.
This is a biography of Red Crow (1830–1900), head chief of the Blood from 1870 to 1900 and a leader in early reservation times.

Ewers, John C. *The Blackfeet: Raiders on the Northwestern Plains*. Norman: University of Oklahoma Press, 1958.
    Written for the nonspecialist, this is a historical ethnography of the Black-feet from prior to the introduction of the horse in the 1740s to the early reservation years.

Farr, William E. *The Reservation Blackfeet, 1882–1945: A Photographic History of Cultural Survival*. Seattle and London: University of Washington Press, 1984.
    An excellent selection of photographs with brief commentary on Blackfeet history.

Hanks, Lucien M. and Jane Richardson Hanks. *Tribe Under Trust: A Study of the Blackfoot Reservation of Alberta*. Toronto: University of Toronto Press, 1950.
    The Hankses did a field study on the reservation in 1938, 1939, and 1941. They reconstructed Blackfoot lifeways by interviewing elders and recorded observations about contemporary social organization, property concepts, subsistence, family life, religion, and leadership. They believed that the Blackfoot were experiencing "cultural breakdown."

McFee, Malcolm. *Modern Blackfeet: Montanans on a Reservation*. New York: Holt, Rinehart and Winston, 1972.
    The only anthropological account of the twentieth-century Blackfeet; the book's focus is on intertribal diversity. McFee began his research on the reservation in 1959 and concluded it in 1970.

Rosier, Paul C. *Rebirth of the Blackfeet Nation, 1912–1954*. Lincoln: University of Nebraska Press, 2001.
    A detailed history of the business council and Blackfeet leadership and their effort to influence Bureau of Indian Affairs policy. Rosier focuses on relations between "full-" and "mixed-blood" Blackfeet.

Samek, Hana. *The Blackfoot Confederacy, 1880–1920: A Comparative Study of Canadian and United States Indian Policy*. Albuquerque: University of New Mexico Press, 1987.
    Comparison of the administration of Blackfeet reservations in Canada and the United States: reservation economy, land policy, missionization, social control.

Wessel, Thomas R. "Political Assimilation on the Blackfoot Indian Reservation, 1887–1934: A Study in Survival." In *Plains Indian Studies: A Collection of Essays in Honor of John C. Ewers and Waldo R. Wedel*, ed. Douglas H.

Ubelaker and Herman J. Viola. Smithsonian Contributions to Anthro-
pology 30. Washington, D.C., 1982, 59–72.
A biographical sketch of the political career of the Montana Blackfeet leader
Robert Hamilton.

Wissler, Clark. *A Blackfoot Source Book: Papers by Clark Wissler.* New York:
Garland, 1986.
A collection of Wissler's studies of Blackfeet lifeways in the nineteenth
century.

Caddo

Carter, Cecile. *Caddo Indians: Where We Come From.* Norman: University of
Oklahoma Press, 1995.
A history of the Caddo peoples from contact to 1859 based on primary
sources and written from the perspective of a Caddo scholar. Draws attention
to the cultural and historical differences between different Caddo communities
and interweaves accounts of contemporary Caddoans into the historical record.

Dorsey, George A. *Traditions of the Caddo.* Lincoln and London: University of
Nebraska Press, 1997 [1905].
Contains creation and migration narratives and Coyote (trickster) stories.
Has a good introduction.

La Vere, David. *The Caddo Chiefdoms: Caddo Economics and Politics, 700–1835.*
Lincoln: University of Nebraska Press, 1998.
Discussion of Caddo history from the perspective of leadership and chang-
ing leadership institutions.

Newkumet, Vynola Beaver and Howard L. Meredith. *Hasinai: A Traditional
History of the Caddo Confederacy.* College Station: Texas A & M University Press, 1988.
Coauthored by a tribe member, this work explains how the turkey dance
symbolizes key events in Caddo history and describes all the important dances
in Caddo ceremonial life.

Smith, F. Todd. *The Caddo Indians: Tribes at the Convergence of Empires,
1542–1854.* College Station: Texas A & M Press, 1995.
A history based on primary sources of the Caddo confederacy from the time
of contact with Europeans to the time of their removal from Texas. Covers
three Caddo confederacies.

―――. *The Caddo, the Wichita and the United States, 1846–1901.* College Station: Texas A & M Press, 1996.

The only history of agency life during the Brazos reserve period (1854–59), the Civil War era, the establishment of Wichita Agency, and life on the Wichita reservation from 1879 to 1901.

Cheyenne

Berthrong, Donald J. *The Cheyenne and Arapaho Ordeal: Reservation and Agency Life in the Indian Territory, 1875–1907.* Norman: University of Oklahoma Press, 1976.

A detailed historical study of the Cheyenne and Arapaho agency. Includes the escape of Dull Knife and Little Wolf from the agency, the allotment process, and the problems between settlers and the Cheyenne and Arapaho.

―――. "Legacies of the Dawes Act: Bureaucrats and Land Thieves at the Cheyenne-Arapaho Agencies of Oklahoma." In *The Plains Indians of the Twentieth Century,* ed. Peter Iverson. Norman and London: University of Oklahoma Press, 1985, 31–53.

Excellent historical study of the means by which settlers and government officials colluded to strip the Cheyenne and Arapaho of their land and property in the early twentieth century.

―――. *The Southern Cheyenne.* Norman: University of Oklahoma Press, 1963.

History of the Southern Cheyenne from the late seventeenth century to 1875.

Fowler, Loretta. See **Arapaho**.

Grinnell, George Bird. *The Cheyenne Indians: History and Society.* 2 vols. New Haven: Yale University Press, 1923.

Grinnell recorded extensive information about nineteenth-century Cheyenne life. Although he was an amateur ethnologist, Grinnell's work is the best general source of information.

Hyde, George E. *The Life of George Bent, Written from his Letters.* Ed. Savoie Lottinville. Norman: University of Oklahoma Press, 1968.

Bent was the son of the trader William Bent and his Cheyenne wife. His letters contain firsthand accounts of many of the events and people in Cheyenne history.

Little Coyote, Bertha and Virginia Giglio. *Leaving Everything Behind: The Songs and Memories of a Cheyenne Woman.* Norman: University of Oklahoma Press, 1997.

Bertha Little Coyote is a Southern Cheyenne.

Llewellyn, Karl N. and E. Adamson Hoebel. *The Cheyenne Way: Conflict and Case Law in Primitive Jurisprudence*. Norman: University of Oklahoma Press, 1941.
This is a study of dispute settlement in the late nineteenth century based largely on interviews.

Mann, Henrietta. *Cheyenne-Arapaho Education, 1871–1982*. Boulder: University Press of Colorado, 1997.
Mann is a Southern Cheyenne. This work is based on her dissertation.

Moore, John H. *The Cheyenne*. Cambridge, MA: Blackwell, 1996.
An overview of Cheyenne history, social organization, and culture written for the general reader. It is particularly good for an explanation of cosmology and ceremony.

Petersen, Karen Daniels. *Plains Indian Art from Fort Marion*. Norman: University of Oklahoma Press, 1971.
This is a study of the prisoners (Cheyenne, Arapaho, Kiowa) at Fort Marion and the paintings they completed while in captivity.

Powell, Peter John. *People of the Sacred Mountain: A History of the Northern Cheyenne Chiefs and Warrior Societies, 1830–1879*. San Francisco: Harper and Row, 1981.
Detailed history of the Northern and Southern Cheyenne, including the perspective of Cheyenne oral history.

Stands in Timber, John and Margo Pringle Liberty. *Cheyenne Memories*. New Haven: Yale University Press, 1967.
These are recollections and stories from Stands in Timber about Northern Cheyenne history.

Svingen, Orlan J. *The Northern Cheyenne Indian Reservation, 1877–1900*. Niwot, CO: University Press of Colorado, 1993.
Based on records of the agency and focusing on administrative history, the book highlights the Cheyenne struggle to obtain and keep a reservation in Montana.

Comanche

Hagan, William T. *Quanah Parker, Comanche Chief*. Norman: University of Oklahoma Press, 1993.

————. *United States–Comanche Relations: The Reservation Years*. New Haven: Yale University Press, 1976.

Good history of Comanche relations with the United States from the Treaty of Medicine Lodge Creek through the early reservation days when cattle leasing influenced reservation politics. It also discusses the Jerome Agreement and the allotment process and provides much material on Quanah Parker.

Harris, LaDonna. *A Comanche Life*. Ed. H. Henrietta Stockel. Lincoln: University of Nebraska Press, 2000.

The life story of Harris, founder of Oklahomans for Indian Opportunity and an advocate for Native Americans on the national scene.

Hoebel, E. Adamson. *Political Organization and Law-ways of the Comanche Indians*. Memoirs of the American Anthropological Association 54 (1940).

A study of Comanche dispute settlement based on field interviews in 1933.

Jones, David E. *Sanapia: Comanche Medicine Woman*. Prospect Heights, IL: Waveland Press, 1984 [1972].

The life story of a Comanche healer, this work has information on the lives of women and reservation experiences.

Kavanagh, Thomas W. *Comanche Political History: An Ethnohistorical Perspective, 1706–1875*. Lincoln: University of Nebraska Press, 1996.

Very detailed ethnohistory of Comanche relations with the Spanish, Mexicans, and Americans, with emphasis on the changing political organization, including the formation of bands and divisions.

Meadows, William C. See **Kiowa.**

Noyes, Stanley. *Los Comanches: The Horse People, 1751–1845*. Albuquerque: University of New Mexico Press, 1993.

Readable, general account of Comanche life and relations with other peoples on the Southern Plains.

Nye, Wilbur S. *Carbine and Lance: The Story of Old Fort Sill*. Norman: University of Oklahoma Press, 1969 [1937].

Based on personal experiences and interviews with Comanche, Kiowa, Cheyenne and Arapaho, Wichita, and Caddo participants, Nye describes events in the Fort Sill area and the Southern Plains generally in the 1860s and 1870s. His focus is on the Indian wars and army maneuvers.

Rollings, Willard H. *The Comanche*. New York: Chelsea House, 1989.
    Written for a general audience, the book covers Comanche history from the eighteenth century to the 1980s.

Wallace, Ernest and E. Adamson Hoebel. *The Comanche: Lords of the Plains*. Norman: University of Oklahoma Press, 1988 [1952].
    Wallace did archival work and interviewed Comanches in 1945, and Hoebel did fieldwork in 1933. The book covers Comanche economy, life cycle, religion, politics and dispute settlement, and warfare. There is a chapter on reservation life up to the allotment process.

Crow

Fitzgerald, Michael O. *Yellowtail, Crow Medicine Man and Sun Dance Chief: An Autobiography*. Norman: University of Oklahoma Press, 1991.

Frey, Rodney. *The World of the Crow Indians: As Driftwood Lodges*. Norman: University of Oklahoma Press, 1987.
    A study of contemporary Crow life, focusing on cultural organization.

Hoxie, Frederick E. *The Crow*. New York: Chelsea House, 1989.
    Written for a general audience, the book covers the Crow from the early nineteenth century to the 1980s.

——. *Parading Through History: The Making of the Crow Nation in America, 1805–1935*. Cambridge: Cambridge University Press, 1995.
    A comprehensive history of the Crow people to the early 1930s. A significant contribution of the book is its discussion of how Crow social organization affected the actions of tribe members in their dealings with the United States.

Linderman, Frank B. *Plenty-coups: Chief of the Crows*. Lincoln: University of Nebraska Press, 2002 [1930].
    The life of a prominent Crow warrior and leader who lived in the nineteenth and early twentieth century and had a major influence on the reorganization of Crow society.

——. *Pretty-shield: Medicine Woman of the Crows*. Lincoln: University of Nebraska Press, 1973 [1932].
    An excellent perspective on women's lives. Pretty Shield was a contemporary of Plenty Coups.

Lowie, Robert H. *The Crow Indians*. New York: Farrar and Rinehart, 1935.
Detailed ethnography based on Lowie's interviews and observations on the Crow reservation in 1907, 1910–16, and 1931. He describes largely pre-reservation kinship, political organization, life cycle, work, oral literature, war, and religion. Very readable by nonspecialists.

McGinnis, Dale K. *The Crow People*. Phoenix: Indian Tribal Series, 1972.
Written for a general audience, the book covers Crow history from the nineteenth century to the 1960s.

Nabokov, Peter, ed. *Two Leggings: The Making of a Crow Warrior*. Lincoln: University of Nebraska Press, 1982 [1967].
An autobiography of a nineteenth-century warrior, with much material on his efforts to build a military career.

Voget, Fred W. *The Shoshoni-Crow Sun Dance*. Norman: University of Oklahoma Press, 1984.
Very detailed anthropological study of an important religious innovation: how a Crow visionary obtained a ceremony from the Wind River Shoshone and introduced it to the Crow community, where it became incorporated into Crow tradition. Excellent insights into Crow culture and history.

———. *They Call Me Agnes: A Crow Narrative Based on the Life of Agnes Yellowtail Deernose*. Norman: University of Oklahoma Press, 1995.
An excellent account of Crow life from about 1910 to the present. Agnes Deernose was born in 1908, and this account is based on her life and that of her husband.

Wildschut, William and John C. Ewers. *Crow Indian Beadwork: A Descriptive and Historical Study*. Contributions from the Museum of the American Indian, Heye Foundation, v. 16, 1959.
A description of the characteristics and history of beadwork, including men's dress clothing, women's dress clothing, robes and blankets, moccasins, riding gear, and containers.

Gros Ventre

Cooper, John M. *The Gros Ventres of Montana, Part 2, Religion and Ritual*. Ed. Regina Flannery. Washington, DC: Catholic University of America Press, 1957.

Detailed reconstruction of nineteenth-century life.

Flannery, Regina. *The Gros Ventres of Montana, Part 1. Social Life*. Washington, DC: Catholic University of America Press, 1953.
An overview of Gros Ventre history and a reconstruction of nineteenth-century social life.

Fowler, Loretta. *Shared Symbols, Contested Meanings: Gros Ventre Culture and History, 1778–1984*. Ithaca: Cornell University Press, 1987.
Combines the analysis of primary documents and ethnography to provide an overview of Gros Ventre history from Gros Ventre perspectives. An examination of how the different perspectives of old and young Gros Ventres shaped political and ritual revivalism in the 1970s and 1980s. Also includes a discussion of relations between the Gros Ventre and Assiniboine on the Fort Belknap reservation, including how each group has influenced the other.

Hidatsa

Bowers, Alfred W. *Hidatsa Social and Ceremonial Organization*. Lincoln: University of Nebraska Press, 1992 [1963].
Comprehensive ethnographic study of the nineteenth-century Hidatsa. Bowers came to Fort Berthold reservation in 1932 and did ethnographic work there for more than twelve years. He recorded long narratives about leadership, kinship, men's and women's societies, warfare, mythology, and ceremonies.

Cash, Joseph H. See **Mandan**.

Gilman, Carolyn and Mary Jane Schneider. *The Way to Independence: Memories of a Hidatsa Indian Family, 1840–1920*. St. Paul: Minnesota Historical Society Press, 1987.
This is an excellent catalog of an exhibit on the Hidatsa, which incorporates material on Waheenee, her brother Wolf Chief, and her son Goodbird. Wolf Chief was born in 1849 and lived into the 1930s; Waheenee or Buffalo Bird Woman was born in 1839 and lived into the late 1920s. Goodbird was born in 1869. Tools, clothing, food preparation, ceremonies, and other activities are shown through objects, photos, and the recollections of this family. There are essays by specialists on the natural environment, religion, archaeology, and museum collections. The exhibit was based on the work of Gilbert Wilson, who studied the Hidatsa between 1906 and 1918. The emphasis of this work is on the adaptations and strategies family members used to adjust to their new circumstances yet retain their Hidatsa identity.

Goodbird, Edward. *Goodbird the Indian: His Story*. New York: Fleming H. Revell, 1914.
The autobiography of Goodbird, focusing on his life on the reservation.

Meyer, Roy W. See **Mandan**.

Schneider, Mary Jane. *The Hidatsa*. New York: Chelsea House, 1989.
For a general audience, a sketch of the Hidatsa from before contact to the present.

Wilson, Gilbert. *Waheenee: An Indian Girl's Story*. Lincoln: University of Nebraska Press, 1981 [1921].
The autobiography of Waheenee, focusing on prereservation times.

Iowa

Blaine, Martha Royce. *The Ioway Indians*. Norman: University of Oklahoma Press, 1979.
A history from the earliest contacts with Europeans to the allotment era.

Kaw

Unrau, William E. *The Kansa Indians: A History of the Wind People, 1673–1873*. Norman: University of Oklahoma Press, 1971.
A history from the Kaw's earliest contact with Europeans through their participation in the fur trade, their reservation life in Kansas, and their removal to Indian Territory.

———. *The Kaw People*. Phoenix: Indian Tribal Series, 1975.
Written for a general audience, a brief history of the Kaw from early contact with Europeans to the 1970s.

Kiowa

Boyd, Maurice. *Kiowa Voices*. 2 vols. Fort Worth: Christian University Press, 1981–83.
Kiowa oral history, including creation stories and stories about historical events.

Kracht, Benjamin R. "The Kiowa Ghost Dance, 1894–1916: An Unheralded Revitalization Movement." *Ethnohistory* 39 (4) (1992): 452–77.

A study of the introduction, suppression, and revival of the Ghost Dance. The focus of the article is on cultural persistence.

Lassiter, Luke E. *The Power of Kiowa Song: A Collaborative Ethnography*. Tucson: University of Arizona Press, 1998.
An anthropological study of Kiowa singing, written as a dialogue between the anthropologist and the singers.

Lassiter, Luke Eric, Clyde Ellis, and Ralph Kotay. *The Jesus Road: Kiowas, Christianity, and Indian Hymns*. Lincoln: University of Nebraska Press, 2002.
An interesting study of Christianity and its indigenization among the Kiowa. The work is based on the collaboration of an anthropologist, a historian, and a native singer.

Marriott, Alice. *The Ten Grandmothers*. Norman: University of Oklahoma Press, 1989 [1945].
A reconstruction of life in the nineteenth century and early twentieth century based on oral history. Marriott did fieldwork from 1935 to 1944.

Meadows, William C. *Kiowa, Apache, and Comanche Military Societies: Enduring Veterans, 1800 to the Present*. Austin: University of Texas Press, 1999.
Detailed, comparative study of the history of military societies and their transformations in social form and meaning from the early nineteenth century to the 1990s.

Mooney, James. *Calendar History of the Kiowa Indians*. Washington, DC: Smithsonian Institution Press, 1979 [1898].
Mooney did fieldwork in the 1890s. The book is a sketch of Kiowa history, a reconstruction of nineteenth-century social organization and religion, and a detailed description of Kiowa "calendars" dating from 1832 to 1892. Plains Indians (including Sioux, Kiowa, and Blackfeet) had "winter counts," which were pictographic calendars that recorded important events in tribal history.

Richardson, Jane Hanks. *Law and Status of the Kiowa Indians*. New York: Monographs of the American Ethnological Society, 1940.
A reconstruction of Kiowa life in the nineteenth century based on fieldwork in 1935. The book is innovative for its time because of its focus on the manipulations of individuals, shown in a series of case histories that focus on how leaders competed for followers, how people tried to improve their positions in the social ranking system, and how individuals' statuses affected the outcome of dispute settlement.

Tsa To Ke, Monroe. *The Peyote Ritual: Visions and Dreams*. San Francisco: Grabhorn, 1957.
A personal account from a tribe member.

Wunder, John R. *The Kiowa*. New York: Chelsea House, 1989.
Written for a general audience; an overview of Kiowa history.

Mandan

Bowers, Alfred W. *Mandan Social and Ceremonial Organization*. Moscow, Idaho: University of Idaho Press, 1950.
Most complete ethnography of the nineteenth-century Mandan. Bowers studied the Mandan in the 1930s and 1940s, focusing on the household, kinship, life cycle, leadership, and ceremonies.

Bruner, Edward M. "Mandan." In *Perspectives in American Indian Cultural Change*. Ed. Edward H. Spicer. Chicago: University of Chicago Press, 1961, 187–277.
An anthropological overview of how Mandan society changed in response to different kinds of contact with Europeans and Americans. Discusses small village life from 1250 to 1500, pre-horse village life from 1500 to 1750, the fur trade era from 1750 to 1762, the agency period from 1862 to 1883, and reservation life from 1883 to 1953.

Cash, Joseph H. and Gerald W. Wolff. *The Three Affiliated Tribes*. Phoenix: Indian Tribal Series, 1974.
Written for a general audience, this is a history of Fort Berthold peoples from fur trade times to the 1970s.

Meyer, Roy W. *The Village Indians of the Upper Missouri: The Mandans, Hidatsas, and Arikaras*. Lincoln: University of Nebraska Press, 1977.
This is the only detailed history of the three tribes. It covers the fur trade era, the settlement on Fort Berthold reservation, the allotment process, life during the Depression, World War II participation, and reservation life in the 1960s.

Omaha

Boughter, Judith A. *Betraying the Omaha Nation, 1790–1916*. Norman: University of Oklahoma Press, 1998.
Written by a tribe member, this history focuses on the Omaha during the fur trade, the treaty-making era, the early reservation years in Nebraska, allotment and its aftermath, and land sales after the turn of the century.

Dorsey, James Owen. *Omaha Sociology*. Third Annual Report of the Bureau of American Ethnology, 1881–82. New York: Johnson Reprint, 1990.

Dorsey lived in the Omaha village, learned the language, and recorded much information about the lives of the Omaha before their economic decline.

Fletcher, Alice C. and Francis La Flesche. *The Omaha Tribe*. 2 vols. Lincoln: University of Nebraska Press, 1992 [1911].

Fletcher was associated with the Omaha for twenty-nine years and worked closely with La Flesche for twenty-five years. This work is a well-illustrated reconstruction of the Omaha life cycle, clans, chieftainship, sacred pole and bundle ceremony, subsistence, family and marriage, music, warfare, secular and sacred societies, medicine, and religion. It contains a brief history of the Omaha, including their relationships to other Siouan-speaking tribes. La Flesche obtained much information in the native language and observed Omaha life as he grew up in the village.

La Flesche, Francis. *The Middle Five: Indian Schoolboys of the Omaha Tribe*. Lincoln and London: University of Nebraska Press, 1963 [1900].

Born in 1857, La Flesche was the son of Joseph La Flesche, who was the son of a French trader and an Omaha woman. Raised among the Omaha, he attended the Presbyterian mission boarding school on the Omaha reservation. This is his firsthand account of his experiences there. Later, La Flesche worked for the Indian Office, received his degree in law, and worked for anthropologists at the Bureau of American Ethnology on the ethnography of the Omaha and Osage.

Osage

Bailey, Garrick A. "Changes in Osage Social Organization, 1673–1906." *University of Oregon Anthropological Papers* 5 (1973).

An interesting anthropological study of Osage life from early contact to the early twentieth century, emphasizing the changes in social organization and the reasons for those changes.

Baird, W. David. *The Osage*. Phoenix: Indian Tribal Series, 1972.

Written for a general audience, the book covers the fur trade period through the 1960s.

Din, Gilbert C. and A. P. Nasatir. *The Imperial Osage: Spanish-Indian Diplomacy in the Mississippi Valley*. Norman: University of Oklahoma Press, 1983.

A general history of trade on the lower Missouri River.

La Flesche, Francis. *The Osage and the Invisible World: From the Works of Francis La Flesche*. Ed. Garrick A. Bailey. Norman: University of Oklahoma Press, 1995.

La Flesche did fieldwork among the Osage, where his Omaha language and the Osage language were mutually intelligible. His intent was to explain Osage beliefs so that their intellectual tradition would be revealed to be as sophisticated as that of Old World peoples and to demonstrate the continuity in Osage ideas over time. Bailey provides an excellent introduction to the life of La Flesche and, based on La Flesche's work, to Osage cosmology, religious organization and symbols, ritual structure, the clan system, and political structure. The book focuses on the texts of two rituals, which were prayers as well as instruction for the Osage in origin stories and the history and validity of political organization. Bailey argues that the Siouan-speaking peoples shared an idea system that originated in the Southeast ceremonial centers.

Mathews, John Joseph. *The Osages: Children of the Middle Waters*. Norman: University of Oklahoma Press, 1961.

An account of the Osage from before the arrival of Europeans to the early 1920s. Lacking in scholarly documentation, the book expresses Mathews's point of view as an Osage. Mathews was a student at the University of Oklahoma and Oxford University, and a professional writer.

Rollings, Willard H. *The Osage: An Ethnohistorical Study of Hegemony on the Prairie-Plains*. Columbia: University of Missouri Press, 1992.

This work focuses on the Osage's domination of the Southern Plains based on their position in the fur trade.

Wilson, Terry P. *The Osage*. New York: Chelsea House, 1988.

Written for a general audience, the book covers Osage history from the late seventeenth century to the 1980s.

——. *The Underground Reservation: Osage Oil*. Lincoln: University of Nebraska Press, 1985.

A good history of the Osage, including their internal organization, from after their removal to Indian Territory to the 1980s. The work focuses on the effect of oil income on the tribe.

Otoe-Missouria

Chapman, Berlin B. *The Otoes and Missourias: A Study of Indian Removal and the Legal Aftermath*. Oklahoma City: Times Journal Publishers, 1965.

Based on Chapman's work on the Otoe-Missouria claim, the book covers relations with the United States in the early nineteenth century, land transactions, removal to Oklahoma, boarding school education, and the claim settlement.

Edmunds, R. David. *The Otoe-Missouria People*. Phoenix: Indian Tribal Series, 1976.
A general audience, this work covers the fur trade era to the 1970s.

Whitman, William. *The Oto*. New York: Columbia University Press, 1937.
This work is based on an anthropological field study done in 1935 by one of Franz Boas's students. Whitman reconstructs social organization, subsistence, warfare, social control, religion, and ritual based on interviews. He views the Otoe as experiencing "cultural breakdown."

Pawnee

Blaine, Martha Royce. *Some Things Are Not Forgotten: A Pawnee Family Remembers*. Lincoln: University of Nebraska Press, 1997.
A history of reservation life based on the recollections of the Blaine family. Martha Blaine is a historian who was married to a member of the Blaine family. Includes allotment, the Ghost Dance, land loss, ceremonies, school.

Fletcher, Alice C. *The Hako: Song, Pipe, and Unity in a Pawnee Calumet Ceremony*. Lincoln and London: University of Nebraska Press, 1996 [1904].
For specialists, this is a detailed description of the calumet ceremony.

Grinnell, George Bird. *Two Great Scouts and their Pawnee Battalion: The Experiences of Frank J. North and Luther H. North, Pioneers in the Great West, 1856–1882*. Cleveland, OH: Arthur H. Clark, 1928.
An account of Pawnee scouting experiences.

Lesser, Alexander. *The Pawnee Ghost Dance Hand Game: Ghost Dance Revival and Ethnic Identity*. Madison: University of Wisconsin Press, 1978 [1933].
This is a pioneering book based on ethnohistorical study and interviews of elderly Pawnees in the 1930s. The focus is on the process of change in Pawnee society during the 1890s. The discussion of ritual process is very detailed, as is the account of the transfer of the Ghost Dance and the Hand Game to the Pawnee and the form these rituals took as they revitalized Pawnee traditions.

Murie, James R. *Ceremonies of the Pawnee*. 2 vols. Ed. Douglas R. Parks. Smith-
    sonian Contributions to Anthropology 27. Washington, DC: Smithsonian
    Institution Press, 1981.
    James Murie (1862–1921) was a Pawnee educated at Hampton Institute and
Haskell. He worked with anthropologists in the 1890s and developed a career as
an ethnographer. In this work he recorded information on the Skiri and South
Band ceremonies. The monograph is quite detailed and most useful to specialists.

Tyson, Carl N. *The Pawnee People*. Phoenix: Indian Tribal Series, 1976.
    Written for a general audience, the book covers the fur trade era to the 1970s.

Weltfish, Gene. *The Lost Universe: Pawnee Life and Culture*. Lincoln: Univer-
    sity of Nebraska Press, 1977 [1965].
    An excellent description of life in a Pawnee village from an anthropologist's
reconstruction based on fieldwork in the 1930s among the Pawnee.

Plains Apache

Brant, Charles S., ed. *Jim Whitewolf: The Life of a Kiowa Apache Indian*. New
    York: Dover, 1991.
    This life history was recorded in 1948–49 and the names of individuals have
been changed. "Jim Whitewolf"'s nephew interpreted for Brant, and Whitewolf spoke English as well. The book is valuable for its extended introduction
on Plains Apache lifeways and history.

Meadows, William C. See **Kiowa.**

Plains Cree

Dempsey, Hugh A. *Big Bear: The End of Freedom*. Lincoln: University of Ne-
    braska Press, 1984.
    This is a biography of Big Bear, who was born in 1825 and became an im-
portant leader. He tried to negotiate with the Canadian government for good
terms and tried to pressure the government to keep promises made at treaty
councils. He was viewed as a troublemaker by Canadian officials; during the
Riel (Northwest) Rebellion in 1885, when some of his followers killed Canadians, he was arrested despite his efforts to stop the violence. He was sent to prison
and died in 1888. He has descendants at Rocky Boy reservation in Montana.

Mandelbaum, David G. *The Plains Cree*. New York: AMS Press, 1979 [1940].
    The best source on the Plains Cree.

Miller, J. R., ed. *Sweet Promises: A Reader on Indian–White Relations in Cana-da*. Toronto: University of Toronto Press, 1991.
Articles on Plains Cree and Métis relations with Canada.

Milloy, John S. *The Plains Cree: Trade, Diplomacy and War, 1790 to 1870*. Win-nipeg: University of Manitoba Press, 1988.
This is a history of trade and intertribal relations, and a description of social and political organization.

Ponca

Cash, Joseph H. and Gerald W. Wolff. *The Ponca People*. Phoenix: Indian Trib-al Series, 1975.
Written for a general audience.

Dorsey, George A. *The Ponca Sun Dance*. Field Columbian Museum, Anthro-pological Series 7 (2) (1905).
For the specialist, a description of the Sun Dance ceremony.

Howard, James H. *The Ponca Tribe*. Lincoln and London: University of Ne-braska Press, 1995 [1965].
This monograph gives a brief history of the Ponca and a description of econ-omy, art, social organization, warfare, and religion. Howard also discusses the different histories of the Northern and Southern Ponca and how these shaped modern life.

Jablow, Joseph H. *Ponca Indians. American Indian Ethnohistory: Plains*. Ed. David Agee Horr. New York: Garland, 1974.
A history of the Ponca, focusing on territory and population movements and relations with other tribes and the United States and largely dealing with the eighteenth and nineteenth centuries.

Whitman, William. "Xube, a Ponca Autobiography." *Journal of American Folk-lore* 52 (204) (1939): 180–93.

Sioux

Anderson, Gary Clayton. *Kinsmen of Another Kind: Dakota–White Relations in the Upper Mississippi Valley, 1650–1862*. Lincoln: University of Nebraska Press, 1984.
Focuses on the reasons for the Sioux Uprising.

Biolsi, Thomas. *Organizing the Lakota: The Political Economy of the New Deal on the Pine Ridge and Rosebud Reservations*. Tucson: University of Arizona Press, 1992.
A good study of the implementation and effect of the IRA programs on Pine Ridge and Rosebud reservations from 1933 to 1945. Biolsi's argument is that the IRA worked to disempower the Sioux.

Bonvillain, Nancy. *The Teton Sioux*. New York: Chelsea Press, 1994.
Written for a general audience, this book covers the history of the Teton from the seventeenth century to the 1980s.

DeMallie, Raymond J. "The Lakota Ghost Dance: An Ethnohistorical Account." *Pacific Historical Review* 51 (4) (1982): 385–405.
A consideration of the Ghost Dance among the Teton Sioux from the perspective of Teton cultural assumptions and values.

——. "The Sioux in Montana and Dakota Territories: Cultural and Historical Background of the Ogden B. Read Collection." In *Vestiges of a Proud Nation: The Ogden B. Read Northern Plains Indian Collection*. Burlington, VT: Robert Hull Fleming Museum, 1986.
A good discussion of the movements, actions, and viewpoints of the Teton, Yanktonai, and Assiniboine on the Northern Plains from 1805 to 1890.

DeMallie, Raymond J., ed. *The Sixth Grandfather: Black Elk's Teachings Given to John G. Neihardt*. Lincoln: University of Nebraska Press, 1984.
This work includes the narratives of Black Elk about his life in prereservation and reservation days. DeMallie provides commentary and discusses the way the narratives were changed in Neihardt's work *Black Elk Speaks*.

DeMallie, Raymond J. and Douglas R. Parks, eds. *Sioux Indian Religion: Traditions and Innovations*. Norman: University of Oklahoma Press, 1987.
Essays on the belief system in the nineteenth century, mythology, the Sun Dance, the establishment of Christianity, contemporary religion (including the yuwipi, peyote, and innovations in the Sun Dance).

Ewers, John C. *Teton Dakota: Ethnology and History*. Berkeley, CA: U.S. Department of the Interior, 1937.
Well-written overview accessible to the general reader. Covers food and clothing, hunting, war, art, games, political organization, the life cycle, medicine, and religion, and provides a brief history of relations with the United States.

Feraca, Stephen E. *Wakinyan: Lakota Religion in the Twentieth Century*. Lincoln: University of Nebraska Press, 1998.

An overview of religious thought and practice, this work describes contemporary rituals, including the Sun Dance, sweat lodge, vision quest, yuwipi ceremony, and peyote ceremony.

Grobsmith, Elizabeth S. *Lakota of the Rosebud: A Contemporary Ethnography*. New York: Holt, Rinehart, and Winston, 1981.

Grobsmith did her field study during the conflict between AIM and the Sioux people on Rosebud reservation. The book provides a firsthand account of life on the reservation during this period with emphasis on discussion of variant lifestyles of the Sioux people. Discusses tribal government and relations with the federal government, the powwow and giveaways, religion, language, and education.

Hoover, Herbert T. *The Yankton Sioux*. New York: Chelsea House, 1988.

Written for a general audience, the book covers Yankton history from the seventeenth century to the 1970s.

Hyde, George E. *Spotted Tail's Folk: A History of the Brule Sioux*. Norman: University of Oklahoma Press, 1961.

A history of the Brule division of the Teton that focuses on their leader Spotted Tail. Discusses Spotted Tail's efforts to establish the Brule on Rosebud in a way that would enable economic survival and the perpetuation of the Sioux way of life. Spotted Tail's role is contrasted with Red Cloud's in the 1860s.

Meyer, Roy W. *History of the Santee Sioux: United States Indian Policy on Trial*. Lincoln: University of Nebraska Press, 1967.

Covers the fur trade era, treaties, the 1862 uprising, and reservation life up to the 1940s.

Olson, James C. *Red Cloud and the Sioux Problem*. Lincoln: University of Nebraska Press, 1965.

A history that focuses on Red Cloud's role in the Sioux resistance movement in the 1860s and his efforts to secure a reservation in an area acceptable to the Sioux.

Pickering, Kathleen Ann. *Lakota Culture, World Economy*. Lincoln: University of Nebraska Press, 2000.

Based on research on Pine Ridge and Rosebud reservations, this is a study of the modern reservation economy and its marginalization within the national economy.

Powers, Mala N. *Oglala Women: Myth, Ritual, and Reality*. Chicago: University of Chicago Press, 1980.
    Mala Power's fieldwork was primarily in 1980. This anthropological study focuses on gender roles and ideology from prereservation to contemporary times. It is organized in terms of the life cycle.

Powers, William R. *Oglala Religion*. Lincoln: University of Nebraska Press, 1977.
    Powers did his fieldwork in the 1960s and 1970s. This book studies how religion is a focus for Oglala identity. There is a good discussion of the Sioux belief system, the use of the pipe, the sweat lodge, the vision quest, funeral rites, and the Sun Dance.

———. *Yuwipi: Vision and Experience in Oglala Ritual*. Lincoln: University of Nebraska Press, 1982.
    This is a very readable account of a yuwipi ceremony on Pine Ridge, the motives and activities of the participants, and the historical context in which the modern yuwipi ceremony developed.

Red Shirt, Delphine. *Bead on an Anthill: A Lakota Childhood*. Lincoln: University of Nebraska Press, 1997.
    Memoir about growing up in modern times on Rosebud reservation and in South Dakota generally.

Riney, Scott. *The Rapid City Indian School, 1898–1933*. Norman: University of Oklahoma Press, 1999.
    Comprehensive study of the school's living conditions, curriculum, daily schedule, discipline, and employees, as well as the relations between Sioux people and the school.

Schusky, Ernest L. *The Forgotten Sioux: An Ethnohistory of the Lower Brule Reservation*. Chicago: Nelson-Hall, 1975.
    Schusky's fieldwork was from 1958 to 1960. This history of the Brule covers prereservation times, the reservation years, and the 1950s.

Wagoner, Paula L. *"They Treated Us Just Like Indians": The Worlds of Bennett County, South Dakota*. Lincoln: University of Nebraska Press, 2002.
    Very readable account of Bennett County, situated between Pine Ridge and Rosebud reservations, where Sioux live interspersed among non-Indians. The book focuses on cultural identity and race relations.

Walker, James R. *Lakota Society*. Eds. Raymond J. DeMallie and Elaine A. Jahner. Lincoln: University of Nebraska Press, 1982.

Walker lived on the Pine Ridge reservation eighteen years (1896–1914) and recorded much of what he observed about Oglala life. Wissler's studies are largely based on Walker's notes. Walker and some literate Oglala also wrote portions of Wissler's manuscripts. Walker recorded observations on the organization of bands and camps, the system of government, family life, the buffalo hunt, warfare, sexuality, and winter counts. In describing daily life, he notes how disparate views are accommodated, and in accounts of history he notes that there is disagreement among the Sioux. Included in the Walker material is an eyewitness account of the Wounded Knee Massacre.

White, Richard. "The Winning of the West: The Expansion of the Western
    Sioux in the Eighteenth and Nineteenth Centuries." *Journal of American
    History* 65 (1978): 319–43.
A good article summarizing the Sioux expansion west of the Missouri River and their relations with other tribes and traders.

Wichita

Dorsey, George A. *Mythology of the Wichita*. Norman: University of Oklahoma
    Press, 1995 [1904].
A collection of creation stories, trickster tales, and stories about historical events.

Harper [John], Elizabeth Ann. "Taovayas in Frontier Trade and Diplomacy,
    1719–1768." *Chronicles of Oklahoma* 31 (1953): 268–89; "Taovayas in Fron-
    tier Trade and Diplomacy, 1769–1779." *Southwestern Historical Quarter-
    ly* 57 (1953): 181–201; "Taovayas in Frontier Trade and Diplomacy,
    1779–1835." *Panhandle-Plains Historical Review* 26 (1953): 41–72.
Historical study that focuses on the Taovaya division of the Wichita, published in three articles.

Newcomb, William W. *The People Called Wichita*. Phoenix: Indian Tribal Se-
    ries, 1976.
Written for the general audience, this is an overview of Wichita history through recent times.

Schmitt, Karl and Iva O. Schmitt. *Wichita Kinship, Past and Present*. Norman:
    University Book Exchange, 1952.
Written for the specialist, this is an interesting study of the changes in Wichita kinship terminology and behavior, including discussion of cultural persistence. The Schmitts' fieldwork was done between 1947 and 1950.

Smith, F. Todd. See **Caddo**.

———. *The Wichita Indians: Traders of Texas and the Southern Plains, 1540–1845*. College Station: Texas A & M Press, 2000.
  History of the Wichita peoples and the Kitsai from the time of contact with Europeans to the time of their removal from Texas to Indian Territory.

Wedel, Mildred Mott. "The Wichita Indians in the Arkansas River Basin." In *Plains Indian Studies: A Collection of Essays in Honor of John C. Ewers and Waldo R. Wedel*, ed. Douglas H. Ubelaker and Herman J. Viola. Washington, DC: Smithsonian Contributions to Anthropology 30, 1982, 118–34.
  Based on the account of La Harpe, a detailed look at the Wichita and the ways they changed after contact with Europeans.

7. SELECTED LITERARY WORKS

Bonnin, Gertrude (Sioux). *American Indian Stories*. Lincoln: University of Nebraska Press, 1986 [1921].

Chief Eagle, Dallas (Sioux). *Winter Count*. Denver: Golden Bell, 1968.

Cook-Lynn, Elizabeth (Sioux). *The Badger Said That* (poetry). New York: Vantage, 1977.

Deloria, Ella C. (Sioux). *Waterlily*. Lincoln: University of Nebraska Press, 1988 [1944].

Eastman, Charles A. (Sioux). *Indian Boyhood*. New York: Dover, 1971 [1902].

Henson, Lance (Cheyenne). *Naming the Dark* (poetry). Norman, OK: Point Riders, 1976.

Least Heat Moon, William (Osage). *Blue Highways: A Journey Into America*. Boston: Little, Brown, 1982.

Mathews, John Joseph (Osage). *Sundown*. Norman: University of Oklahoma Press, 1988.

Medicine Crow, Joseph (Crow). *From the Heart of the Crow Country: The Crow Indians' Own Stories*. Lincoln: University of Nebraska Press, 2000.

Momaday, N. Scott (Kiowa). *The Way to Rainy Mountain*. Albuquerque: University of New Mexico, 1969.

———. *The Names: A Memoir*. Tucson: University of Arizona Press, 1987 [1976].

Red Corn, Charles H. (Osage). *A Pipe for February: A Novel*. Norman: University of Oklahoma Press, 2002.

Standing Bear, Luther (Sioux). *Stories of the Sioux*. Lincoln: University of Nebraska Press, 1988.

Walters, Anna Lee (Otoe/Pawnee). *Ghost Singer*. Flagstaff, AZ: Northland, 1988.
Welch, James (Blackfeet/Gros Ventre). *Fools Crow*. New York: Viking, 1986.
——. *Winter in the Blood*. New York: Penguin, 1986 [1974].

8. VIDEO AND FILM

The American as Artist—Portrait of Bob Benn. 1976. 29 minutes. Produced by
     South Dakota ETV.
     The art of Sioux painter and sculptor Bob Benn.

Amiotte. 1976. 29 minutes. Producer: Bruce Baird (KUSD-TV), Director:
     Richard Muller.
     The art of Arthur Amiotte, Pine Ridge Sioux painter.

The Art of Being Indian—Filmed Aspects of the Culture of the Sioux. 1976. 29:15
     minutes. Produced by South Dakota ETV.
     Cultural heritage of the Sioux, focusing on the nineteenth century; illus-
trated with the works of painters George Catlin, Karl Bodmer, photographer
Edward Curtis, and others.

Children of the Long-Beaked Bird. 1976. 29 minutes. By Peter Davis. Producer:
     Swedish Television/Bullfrog Films.
     Documentary on the Crow of Montana produced for children. Shows
preparations for the Crow fair and powwow and a competitive "sing."

Contrary Warriors: A Story of the Crow Tribe. 1985. 58 minutes. Producers: Con-
     nie Poten and Pamela Roberts.
     Excellent, award-winning documentary on the Crow people, as told by
members of the tribe. Focuses on Robert Yellowtail and the struggle against allotment. Also, tribal members discuss economic problems, relocation, and the
role of women.

Dancing to Give Thanks. 1988. 29:37 minutes. Produced by Nebraska ETV.
     Highlights of the Omaha annual celebration; discusses the role of dancing
in Omaha cultural identity.

The Dawn Riders: Native American Artists. 1969. 27 minutes. By Robert and
     Dona DeWeese.
     Documentary of Indian painting, including pictographs, hide painting,
nineteenth-century drawing, and contemporary art. Highlights the Kiowa Five,
Blackbear Bosin (Kiowa-Comanche), and Dick West (Southern Cheyenne).

The Drum Is the Heart. 1982. 29 minutes. Producer: Randy Croce (MIGIZI
   Communications, Minneapolis).
   Focuses on Blackfeet powwows in Alberta and Montana, including discussion by tribal historians.

Giveaway at Ring Thunder. 1982. 15 minutes. Producer: Jan Wahl (Nebraska
   Educational Television).
   Combines archival photographs of Lakota (Teton) Sioux life, including
the giveaway, and a giveaway ceremony on Rosebud reservation when children are named. Defines the giveaway as a way to strengthen social bonds in
the community.

Good Medicine. 1979. 59 minutes. Producer: Chris Gaul (WQED-Pittsburgh).
   A documentary on Native American medicine; focuses on its holistic nature.
The video shows Rosebud reservation medicine men who describe their work;
the remainder concerns Navajo medicine men.

Health Care Crisis at Rosebud. 1973. 20:30 minutes. Produced by South Dakota Educational TV.
   Discusses health care problems resulting from a shortage of physicians on
Rosebud reservation.

Herman Red Elk—A Sioux Indian Artist. 1975. 29 minutes. By David Allen Silvian. Produced by South Dakota Educational TV.
   A Yankton Sioux artist from Fort Peck, Montana known for his hide paintings; describes the painting of a winter count.

Keep Your Heart Strong. 1986. 58:09 minutes. Produced by Deb Wallwork,
   Prairie Public Television.
   An inside view of the powwow and the values it expresses; footage from Fort
Berthold reservation.

Lakota Quillwork. 1985. 27 minutes. Producer/director: H. June Nauman.
   Excellent presentation of oral traditions related to Lakota (Teton) quillwork
and contemporary quillwork tradition. Two quillworkers on Pine Ridge reservation demonstrate the art, including the porcupine hunt, cleaning and sorting
quills, dyeing them, and making jewelry and dance regalia. In Lakota with
English translation.

Live and Remember. 1986. 28:54 minutes. Produced by Henry Smith, Solaris/Lakota Project.

Documentary based on oral tradition of Lakota (Teton) elders; subjects include the role of women in Indian society, animals, and the pipe.

Ni'bthaska of the Umonhon. 1987. 90 minutes. Produced by Chet Kincaid, Nebraska Educational TV and Native American Public Broadcasting Consortium.
A three-part series (three half hours) produced for children, about a thirteen-year-old Omaha boy going on his first vision quest and a buffalo hunt.

Oscar Howe—The Sioux Painter. 1973. 29 minutes. Produced by KUSD-TV.
The art of Oscar Howe, a Sioux from South Dakota.

Our Sacred Land. 1984. 28 minutes. Producer/director: Chris Spotted Eagle.
By native American independent filmmaker Chris Spotted Eagle; focuses on the struggle of the Sioux to regain the Black Hills. Includes discussions of religious freedom.

Rosebud to Dallas. 1977. 60 minutes. By Jed Riffe and Robert Rouse.
Follows five families who participate in the relocation program, moving from Rosebud reservation to Dallas. Includes interviews and conversations with family members, most of whom returned to the reservation.

The Spirit of Crazy Horse. 1990. 58 minutes. Producers: Michel Dubois and Kevin McKiernan; director: James Locker. (*Frontline* series, PBS Video).
An excellent video about the Wounded Knee takeover by the American Indian Movement and the repercussions on Pine Ridge reservation. Discusses the post–Wounded Knee nationalism that developed on the reservation that appealed to "full-" and "mixed-bloods" alike.

The Treaty of 1868. 1987. 60 minutes. Produced by Nebraska Educational Television.
This two-part series addresses "who really owns the Black Hills." Historic photos interwoven with opinions from contemporary Sioux, non-Indian residents of South Dakota, attorneys, and historians. Part 1 ("The Treaty of 1868") focuses on the viewpoints of the Sioux and the U.S. commissioners who signed the treaty. Part 2 ("The Black Hills Claim") highlights the political and legal battle over the legitimacy of the 1876 cession of the Black Hills.

The Trial of Standing Bear. 1988. 120 minutes. Produced by Nebraska Educational TV.
Dramatization of the 1877 forced removal of the Ponca from Nebraska to Indian Territory, the flight and arrest of Standing Bear on his journey back to

Nebraska, and the 1879 legal case in which Standing Bear won the right to remain in Nebraska.

War Paint and Wigs. 1980. 30 minutes. Producers: Robert Hagopian and Phil
    Lucas for KCTS/9 Seattle.
    The fifth program in a series, "Images of Indians," this examines how movie images of the "noble" and the "savage" Indian have affected Native American self-image and American stereotypes about Indian people. Much of the footage used is based on images of Plains Indians.

We Are One. 1986. Produced by Chet Kincaid, Nebraska Educational TV and
    Native American Public Broadcasting Consortium.
    An eight-part series of twenty-minute programs produced for children. The series describes childhood among the Omaha, focusing on two children. Included is family life, technology, storytelling, hunting, and gathering plants.

White Man's Way. 1986. 30 minutes. Producer: Christine Lesiak, Nebraska Educational TV.
    Focusing on Genoa School (in Pawnee country), this documentary examines the government boarding school.

9. INTERNET SOURCES

Tribal Web Pages

The content varies, but generally there is information about the tribal government and sometimes about the history and lifeways of the tribe, including recommended reading. URLs are up to date as of January 31, 2003.

Blackfeet Nation. http://www.blackfeetnation.com/

Cheyenne River Sioux. http://www.sioux.org/

Chippewa/Cree (Plains Cree and Ojibwa; Rocky Boy reservation). http://
    tlc.wtp.net/chippewa.htm

Crow. http://tlc.wtp.net/crow.htm

Ft. Peck (Assiniboine/Sioux). http://tlc.wtp.net/fortpeck.htm

Iowa. http://www.iowanation.org

Little Shell Chippewa (headquarters in Great Falls, MT; not federally recognized). http://tlc.wtp.net/little.htm

Northern Arapaho. http://tlc.wtp.net/arapaho.htm

Northern Cheyenne. http://tlc.wtp.net/northern.htm

Osage. http://www.osagetribe.com/

Pawnee. http://www.pawneenation.org/
Pine Ridge Sioux. http://www.lakotamall.com/ (see also http://www.lakotaoy-
ate.com/)
Rosebud Sioux. http://www.rosebudsiouxtribe.org/
Santee Sioux (Nebraska). http://ci.santee.ne.us/index.html-ssi
Standing Rock Sioux. http://www.standingrock.org/
Wichita. http://www.wichita.nsn.us/
Yankton Sioux. http://www.yanktonsiouxtribe.org/index.html

Museum and Historical Society Web Pages

American Museum of Natural History, New York. http://www.amnh.org/
Field Museum of Chicago. http://www.fmnh.org/
Historical Society of North Dakota. http://www.state.nd.us/hist/
Kansas State Historical Society. http://www.kshs.org/
Montana Historical Society. http://www.his.state.mt.us/
National Anthropological Archives. http://www.nmnh.si.edu/naa/
National Museum of the American Indian, Washington, DC. http://www.nmai.
si.edu/
Nebraska State Historical Society. http://www.nebraskahistory.org/
Oklahoma Historical Society. http://www.ok-history.mus.ok.us/
South Dakota Historical Society. http://www.sdhistory.org/
Wyoming State Historical Society. http://wyshs.org/

Other Useful Sites

Arizona State University (h-amindian) (Contains book reviews, recommended reading, discussion topics, links). http://www.asu.edu/clas/history/
h-amindian/
Black Elk's World (The text of *Black Elk Speaks* with links to additional information: biographies, historic and contemporary photographs, maps.
There is also a glossary for the Lakota language and a bibliography).
http://www.blackelkspeaks.unl.edu
National Congress of American Indians. http://www.ncai.org/
Native Web (reviews, books and museums, community news). http://www.na-
tiveweb.org

INDEX

A locator in **boldface** indicates an entry for the topic in part II (People, Places, and Events). Locators for subgroups (Teton Sioux, Northern Arapaho) are double-posted under the name of the broader group.